WOMAN'S WEEKLY

Colourful Cookery

WOMAN'S WEEKLY

Colourful Cookery

Compiled by
Janet Warren

Hamlyn
London . New York . Sydney . Toronto

Published by
The Hamlyn Publishing Group Limited
London · New York · Sydney · Toronto
Astronaut House, Feltham, Middlesex, England

ISBN 0 600 39421 2

Phototypeset by Keyspools Limited, Golborne, Lancashire
Printed in Spain
by Printer industria gráfica sa
Sant Vicenç del Horts Barcelona 1979
Depósito legal B. 27567-1979

Contents

Useful Facts and Figures

Notes on metrication

In this book quantities are given in Imperial and metric measures.

Exact conversion from Imperial to metric measures does not usually give very convenient working quantities and so the metric measures have been rounded off into units of 25 grams. This method of conversion gives good results in nearly all cases although in certain pastry and cake recipes a more accurate conversion is necessary to produce a balanced recipe. The table below shows the recommended equivalents.

Ounces	Approx g to nearest whole figure	Recommended conversion to nearest unit of 25
1	28	25
2	57	50
3	85	75
4	113	100
5	142	150
6	170	175
7	198	200
8	227	225
9	255	250
10	283	275
11	312	300
12	340	350
13	368	375
14	396	400
15	425	425
16 (1 lb)	454	450

Note As a general guide, 1 kg (1000 g) equals 2·2 lb or about 2lb 3oz.

Liquid measures The millilitre has been used in this book and the following table gives a few examples.

Imperial	Approx ml to nearest whole figure	Recommended ml
¼ pint	142	150 ml
½ pint	283	300 ml
¾ pint	425	450 ml
1 pint	567	600 ml
1½ pints	851	900 ml
1¾ pints	992	1000 ml (litre)

Spoon measures All spoon measures given in this book are level unless otherwise stated.

Can sizes At present, cans are marked with the exact (usually to the nearest whole number) metric equivalent of the Imperial weight of the contents, so we have followed this practice when giving can sizes.

Oven temperatures

The table below gives recommended equivalents.

	°C	°F	Gas Mark
Very cool	110	225	¼
	120	250	½
Cool	140	275	1
	150	300	2
Moderately cool	160	325	3
Moderate	180	350	4
Moderately hot	190	375	5
Fairly hot	200	400	6
Hot	220	425	7
Very hot	230	450	8
	240	475	9

Notes for American and Australian users

In America the 8-oz measuring cup is used. In Australia metric measures are now used in conjunction with the standard 250-ml measuring cup. The Imperial pint, used in Britain and Australia, is 20 fl oz, while the American pint is 16 fl oz. It is important to remember that the Australian tablespoon differs from both the British and American tablespoons; the table below gives a comparison. The British standard tablespoon, which has been used throughout this book, holds 17·7 ml, the American 14·2 ml, and the Australian 20 ml. A teaspoon holds approximately 5 ml in all three countries.

British	American	Australian
1 teaspoon	1 teaspoon	1 teaspoon
1 tablespoon	1 tablespoon	1 tablespoon
2 tablespoons	3 tablespoons	2 tablespoons
3½ tablespoons	4 tablespoons	3 tablespoons
4 tablespoons	5 tablespoons	3½ tablespoons

An Imperial/American guide to solid and liquid measures

Solid measures

IMPERIAL	AMERICAN
1 lb butter or margarine	2 cups
1 lb flour	4 cups
1 lb granulated or caster sugar	2 cups
1 lb icing sugar	3 cups
8 oz rice	1 cup

Liquid measures

IMPERIAL	AMERICAN
¼ pint liquid	⅔ cup liquid
½ pint	1¼ cups
¾ pint	2 cups
1 pint	2½ cups
1½ pints	3¾ cups
2 pints	5 cups (2½ pints)

NOTE When making any of the recipes in this book, only follow one set of measures as they are not interchangeable.

American terms

The list below gives some American equivalents or substitutes for terms and ingredients used in this book.

Equipment and terms
BRITISH/AMERICAN
baking tray/baking sheet
cake board/cake plate
deep cake tin/spring form pan
double saucepan/double boiler
dough or mixture/batter
flan tin/pie pan
frying pan/skillet
greaseproof paper/wax paper
grill/broil
gut fish/clean fish
hard-boil eggs/hard-cook eggs
loaf tin/loaf pan
minced/ground
muslin/cheesecloth
pastry or biscuit cutter/cookie cutter
patty or bun tins/muffiin pans or cups
piping bag/pastry bag
polythene/plastic
prove dough/rise dough
pudding basin/ovenproof bowl or pudding mold
roasting tin/roasting pan
sandwich tin/layer cake pan
stoned/pitted
Swiss roll tin/jelly roll pan
top and tail fruit/stem fruit
whisk eggs/beat eggs

Ingredients
BRITISH/AMERICAN
apple, cooking/ apple, baking
aubergine/eggplant
bacon rashers/bacon slices
beef suet, shredded/beef suet, chopped
bicarbonate of soda/baking soda
biscuits/crackers or cookies
biscuit mixture/cookie dough
black cherries/bing cherries
black grapes/purple grapes
black treacle/molasses
chipolata sausages/link sausages
chocolate, plain/chocolate, semi-sweet
cochineal/red food coloring
cocoa powder/unsweetened cocoa
coconut, desiccated/coconut, shredded
cornflour/cornstarch
courgettes/zucchini
cream, single/cream, light
cream, double/cream, heavy
demerara sugar/light brown sugar
essence/extract
flour, plain/flour, all-purpose
flour, self-raising/flour, all-purpose sifted with baking powder
glacé cherries/candied cherries
golden syrup/corn syrup
icing/frosting
head celery/bunch celery
lard/shortening
marrow/summer squash
ox tongue/beef tongue
shortcrust pastry/basic pie dough
scones/biscuits
sponge finger biscuits/ladyfingers
spring onion/scallion
stock cube/bouillon cube
sugar, icing/sugar, confectioners'
sultanas/seedless white raisins
tomato purée/tomato paste
yeast, fresh (1 oz/25 g)/yeast, compressed (1 cake)

Introduction

With nearly 70 years of *Woman's Weekly* magazine issues to choose from I have had a difficult but, I hasten to add, most enjoyable task selecting the recipes for this first ever all colour *Woman's Weekly* cookery book.

I must confess that some of the recipes are my particular favourites – but many are ones which, through your continuing correspondence, I know you, your family and friends find particularly useful and delicious. All the recipes have at some time appeared in the magazine and no doubt many of them you will recognise and enjoy trying again. But perhaps others were overlooked at the time of publishing, or some you didn't keep and will be pleased to rediscover.

As I hope that this book will be used in the kitchen for many years to come, the recipes are written for both metric and Imperial measures. Don't let this worry you – the only important point to remember is not to muddle the two columns; use either the metric measures or the Imperial measures, never a combination of the two. You will find on page 10 a chart of useful facts and figures relating to all the various conversions which I hope will help answer any queries you may have.

The book covers every aspect of cookery, from that never ending problem of 'what shall I give the family today' to those special occasions such as dinner parties and buffet receptions. I have also included some charts on meat roasting, Victoria sandwich and butter cakes, and a selection of jams, plus a comprehensive guide to the preparation and cooking of many vegetables, both common and unusual, with the relevant freezing instructions. And on the subject of freezing, wherever appropriate the recipes in this book carry their own special freezing instruction should you wish to cook ahead and store for the future.

While I was cookery editor of *Woman's Weekly*, I found that a large number of our readers were keen bakers, so much of the book is devoted to recipes for cakes, breads and scones. There are plenty of traybakes too – that marvellous cake tin filler which is a cross between a cake and a biscuit, often cooked in a Swiss roll tin so it can be cut into large or small pieces, depending on the number you need. You'll find beautiful gâteaux, rich and gorgeous for those special occasions, and I have also included a few novelty cakes for children's birthday parties, as well as a wedding cake should you feel that ambitious. There is a Simnel cake for Easter or Mother's Day plus a selection of Christmas cakes for the festive season.

The other aspect of the book which I hope you will find enjoyable as well as useful are the recipes taken from the Look and Learn series. This series started several years ago when approximately once a month I took one particular recipe and explained it step by step in easy to follow colour photographs. The subjects cover every area of cookery and I hope some of them will inspire you to tackle recipes which in the past you may have felt to be too complicated.

I spent many happy years working for *Woman's Weekly* and so when it came to compiling this cookery book recipe after recipe brought back memories – some amusing, some frustrating, some happy, some sad. Occasions such as Agricultural Shows when I had the opportunity to meet and talk to the readers; members of my staff I remember with affection; the problems of obtaining fruits and vegetables out of season; the time when the china got lost en route to a demonstration and we had to borrow dishes from the hotel.

All of these memories have just added to the enormous pleasure I have had in working on this book and I only hope you will find as much pleasure when working from it in the years to come.

Sue(?) Warren

Soups and Starters

Soups and their accompaniments, cold and hot hors d'oeuvres as well as pâtés, are to be found in this chapter. Serve them all attractively garnished. Hot crusty bread is good with soups and hot hors d'oeuvres, while freshly made toast goes best with the pâtés.

Saxon Soup

Serves 6

- 2 pig's trotters, split by the butcher
- ½ lb/225 g leeks
- 3 pints/1·75 litres water
- A bouquet garni (bought, or made from a bay leaf, sprig of thyme, parsley stalks and blade of mace, tied together with string)
- 1 bay leaf
- Salt and pepper
- 1 oz/25 g small pasta shells
- 6 oz/175 g carrots, peeled and grated
- 1 dessertspoon cornflour

Put the trotters into a bowl of cold salted water and leave them to soak while preparing the vegetables. Trim the leeks, then chop them into ¼-inch/5-mm cubes. Wash the pieces thoroughly so that they are free from dirt and sand. Put the trotters into a large pan with the water, prepared leeks, bouquet garni and bay leaf. Add plenty of seasoning and bring the soup to the boil. Skim the surface, then reduce the heat, cover and simmer for 2½ hours.

Remove the trotters, bay leaf and bouquet garni, then add the pasta and grated carrot to the soup and simmer for a further 20 minutes. Meanwhile, remove any meat from the trotters and shred it into small spoon-sized pieces. Stir the meat into the soup and check for seasoning.

In a small bowl, blend the cornflour to a smooth paste with a little cold water, then stir it into the soup. Bring the liquid back to the boil before serving.

Freezing Note *Freeze the soup for up to a month, thaw and reheat when required.*

Vichyssoise

Serves 6

- 1½ lb/675 g leeks
- 3 oz/75 g butter
- ½ lb/225 g potatoes
- 1 medium onion
- 1½ pints/900 ml chicken stock
- Salt and pepper
- ½ pint/300 ml milk
- 2–3 tablespoons single cream
- A few chopped chives
- Melba toast

Using a sharp knife, trim off the root, outer leaves and as much of the tops of the leeks as necessary; slit them lengthways and wash under cold running water, separating the leaves with the fingers to make sure every particle of grit and sand is removed. Chop the leeks into ½-inch/1-cm lengths.

Melt the butter in a large saucepan, add the leeks and cook slowly over a gentle heat for 10 to 15 minutes, stirring occasionally so they do not stick to the pan.

Meanwhile, peel and chop the potatoes and onion. Add them to the leeks and cook all the vegetables slowly for a few minutes more, then add the stock and salt and pepper. Cover the pan and simmer the soup for about 30 minutes, until all the vegetables are really soft.

Purée the soup through a sieve or Mouli vegetable mill, or liquidise in a blender. Rinse out the pan, return the soup to it and add the milk. Bring the Vichyssoise back to the boil then sieve again – this will give the soup a lovely smooth texture.

Chill the soup thoroughly before serving or serve it hot. In either case, just before it is to be eaten, swirl a teaspoonful of single cream into each serving and sprinkle with a few chopped chives. Serve accompanied by Melba toast.

Freezing Note *Freeze the soup for up to 6 months then reheat, even if the soup is to be served cold. Garnish and serve hot, or chill the soup well before serving, again garnished with cream and chives.*

Saxon Soup

English Broth with Dumplings

Serves 6

1 chicken carcass or 1 chicken leg and 1 chicken stock cube
3 pints/1·75 litres cold water
1 teaspoon salt
6 peppercorns
1 bay leaf
½ lb/225 g carrots, peeled and sliced
1 small turnip, peeled and cubed
1 onion, peeled and sliced
½ lb/225 g cabbage, shredded
For the Dumplings
4 oz/100 g self-raising flour
A pinch of salt
A pinch of dried mixed herbs
1 oz/25 g prepared shredded suet

Place the chicken carcass or leg in a large pan and cover with the cold water. If using a chicken leg instead of a carcass, add a chicken stock cube for flavour. Add the salt, peppercorns and bay leaf, bring to the boil, cover and simmer for 1 hour.

Strain the stock from the pan into a bowl, keeping the chicken carcass or leg on one side to cool. Return the stock to the pan, add the prepared carrots, turnip and onion and bring back to the boil. Cover and simmer very gently for a further 1 hour. Meanwhile, remove the chicken from the bones, cut into bite-sized pieces and keep on one side.

To make the dumplings, sift the flour, salt and herbs into a bowl. Stir in the suet and add sufficient water to make a fairly soft dough. Divide into eight pieces and, with floured hands, roll each into a ball.

Twenty minutes before the end of the cooking time, lower the dumplings into the soup with the chicken pieces and shredded cabbage, then bring back to the boil, cover and simmer for the remainder of the cooking time. Serve piping hot.

Freezing Note *Freeze the soup only, it will store for up to a month.*

English Broth with Dumplings, and Accompaniments: Celery Scones, Peanut Butter Bread, Crispy Norwich Rolls, Lemon and Parsley Rolls

French Onion Soup

Serves 6

1 lb/450 g onions
1 oz/25 g butter
1 tablespoon cooking oil
Salt and pepper
½ oz/15 g plain flour
2 pints/1·15 litres beef stock
1 bay leaf
6 thick slices French bread
2 oz/50 g butter
2 oz/50 g Cheddar cheese, grated

Peel and thinly slice the onions. Heat the butter and oil in a large saucepan over a gentle heat, then add the onions and plenty of salt. Fry the onions, turning them frequently, until golden brown and well cooked. Sprinkle over the flour and mix it in, then remove the pan from the heat and blend in the stock; add the bay leaf and return to the heat. Bring the soup to the boil, stirring occasionally, then cover and simmer gently for 30 minutes. Test and adjust for seasoning.

Meanwhile, toast the slices of bread on one side only. Spread the untoasted sides with the butter and sprinkle liberally with the grated cheese. Place under a preheated grill and cook until the cheese is golden brown, melted and bubbling.

Put the bread into a heated soup tureen, cheese sides uppermost. When the soup is ready, remove the bay leaf and pour over the bread, which should rise to the surface.

Serve the soup immediately, including a round of the cheesy bread with every serving.

Freezing Note *Freeze the soup only for up to 3 months then prepare the French bread when the soup is required for serving.*

Celery Soup

Serves 6

- 1 head celery
- ½ lb/225 g onions
- 1½ oz/40 g butter
- 1 tablespoon cooking oil
- 1½ pints/900 ml chicken stock
- Salt and pepper
- 1 bay leaf
- A blade of mace
- 2 tablespoons arrowroot
- ½ pint/300 ml milk

Wash and trim the celery sticks and cut into 1-inch/2·5-cm pieces. Peel and slice the onions. Heat the butter and oil in a large, heavy saucepan. Add the vegetables and cook over a low heat, stirring occasionally, until they have absorbed all the fat and oil and are tender but not brown. Add the stock, salt and pepper, bay leaf and mace, cover the pan and simmer over a low heat for about 30 minutes. Remove the bay leaf and mace, then purée the soup through a sieve or Mouli vegetable mill, or liquidise in a blender.

Put the arrowroot into the pan in which the soup was cooked, mix to a smooth paste with a little of the milk then stir in the rest of the milk and the soup. Return the pan to the heat and, stirring all the time, bring the soup to the boil for a few minutes to cook the arrowroot.

Check the soup for seasoning, then pour into individual bowls with a few croûtons (see page 18) in the centre.

Freezing Note *Freeze for up to 3 months, thaw and reheat.*

Peanut Butter Bread

Makes 1 loaf

- 4 oz/100 g self-raising flour
- 1 teaspoon salt
- 1 teaspoon baking powder
- 4 oz/100 g plain wholewheat flour
- 3 oz/75 g smooth peanut butter
- ½ oz/15 g dark soft brown sugar
- ½ pint/300 ml milk
- 1 oz/25 g salted peanuts, roughly chopped
- *A 1-lb/0·5-kg loaf tin, lightly greased*

Sift the self-raising flour, salt and baking powder into a mixing bowl and stir in the wholewheat flour. Rub in the peanut butter with the fingertips until evenly distributed, then mix in the sugar. Bind the ingredients together with the milk to make a soft consistency. Beat well, then pour the mixture into the prepared loaf tin.

Sprinkle the surface with the chopped peanuts and bake on the centre shelf of a moderate oven, gas mark 4 or 350°F/180°C, for 1 hour, or until the bread is starting to shrink away from the sides of the tin. It should be golden brown and well risen. Serve sliced and buttered.

Freezing Note *Freeze for up to 3 months.*

Crispy Norwich Rolls

Makes 20

- 2 oz/50 g Cheddar cheese, finely grated
- 2 teaspoons made mustard
- 2 oz/50 g butter
- 5 medium slices white bread

Mix the cheese and mustard well together in a small bowl. Melt the butter in a pan. Carefully remove the crusts from the bread and flatten each slice with a rolling pin. Spread evenly with the cheese mixture and roll up tightly. Cut into four even-sized rolls and secure in pairs with a wooden cocktail stick.

Place on a baking tray and brush with the melted butter. Bake in a fairly hot oven, gas mark 6 or 400°F/200°C, for 20 to 25 minutes, turning once to brown evenly.

Freezing Note *Freeze for up to 6 weeks, thaw then reheat in a moderate oven for 10 to 15 minutes before serving.*

Lemon and Parsley Rolls

Makes 8

- 8 oz/225 g plain flour
- 1½ teaspoons baking powder
- ½ teaspoon salt
- 1½ oz/40 g margarine
- Grated rind and juice of 1 lemon
- 1 tablespoon chopped parsley
- About 6 tablespoons milk
- Beaten egg for glaze

Sift the flour, baking powder and salt into a mixing bowl. Add the margarine and, using the fingertips only, rub in the fat, then stir in lemon rind and parsley. Make the lemon juice up to ¼ pint/150ml with milk and mix into the dry ingredients to make a fairly stiff dough.

Turn the dough on to a lightly floured surface and knead gently. Divide into eight equal pieces and roll into small balls. Place the rolls on a greased baking tray. Brush with egg glaze and bake in a fairly hot oven, gas mark 6 or 400°F/200°C, for 15 to 20 minutes, until golden brown. Serve immediately.

Freezing Note *Freeze for up to 6 weeks, thaw then reheat in a moderate oven for 10 to 15 minutes.*

Celery Scones

Makes 7

6 oz / 175 g self-raising flour
1 teaspoon celery salt
2 oz / 50 g margarine
¼ pint / 150 ml milk
Milk for glaze
Poppy seeds for decoration
A 2½-inch / 6-cm fluted cutter

Sift the flour and celery salt into a mixing bowl, add the margarine and, using the fingertips, rub it in until evenly distributed. Stir in the milk to make a fairly soft dough.

Turn the dough on to a lightly floured surface and knead it gently, then roll out to ½ inch / 1 cm thickness. Cut out seven scones with a fluted cutter and place on a lightly greased baking tray. Brush with milk, sprinkle over the poppy seeds and bake on the centre shelf of a fairly hot oven, gas mark 6 or 400°F / 200°C, for 15 to 20 minutes until well risen and golden.

Freezing Note *Freeze for up to 3 months, thaw then reheat in a moderate oven for 10 minutes before serving.*

Croûtons

Serves 6

3 thick slices white bread
Oil for deep frying

Remove the crusts and cut the bread into small cubes. Half fill a deep fat fryer with cooking oil and heat it well. Put the cubes of bread into the basket, lower into the oil and cook the croûtons for about 3 minutes, until golden brown. Drain them on absorbent paper and leave to cool.

Keep in an airtight container until required. Reheat in a hot oven for about 10 minutes before serving.

Liver Sausage and Egg Bake

Serves 4

¼ lb / 100 g liver sausage
1 large or 2 small tomatoes
4 large eggs (size 2)
4 teaspoons single cream
Salt and pepper
4 small ramekin dishes

Cut the liver sausage into four slices and lay one in the bottom of each dish. Cut the tomato into four slices and put one on top of each slice of liver sausage. Break an egg on top of each and spoon over the cream. Season, then bake the eggs on the centre shelf of a moderate oven, gas mark 4 or 350°F / 180°C, for 10 to 15 minutes, until the eggs are just set.

Liver Sausage and Egg Bake

Courgette and Ham Bake

Courgette and Ham Bake

Serves 4

1 lb/450 g small courgettes (baby marrows)
Salt and pepper
1 tablespoon cooking oil
1 oz/25 g butter
1 large onion, peeled and thinly sliced
1 clove garlic (optional)
$\frac{1}{4}$ lb/100 g ham, sliced
3 oz/75 g Cheddar cheese, grated
4 small ovenproof dishes, each of $\frac{1}{2}$ pint/300 ml capacity

Wipe the courgettes, slice them thinly and lay on a plate; sprinkle with salt and leave on one side to extract some of the moisture.

Heat the oil and butter in a pan, add the onion and fry it gently. Peel and chop the garlic, sprinkle with salt then crush to a smooth paste with the blade of a knife. Add the crushed garlic to the onion and continue frying until the onion is tender and just starting to colour.

Drain the courgettes and pat dry. Add them to the pan and fry until light brown. Chop the ham, add to the pan and heat through for a few minutes.

Season the mixture, then divide it between the dishes and sprinkle cheese over the top of each. Cook on the centre shelf of a moderately hot oven, gas mark 5 or 375°F/190°C, for about 20 minutes, until they are golden brown and the cheese has melted.

Serve with brown bread and butter.

Freezing Note *Freeze for up to a month, thaw then reheat in a moderate oven for about 20 minutes.*

Cheddar Eggs

Serves 4

8 oz/225 g Cheddar cheese, grated
4 tablespoons single cream
4 large eggs (size 2)
A shallow ovenproof dish, lightly greased

Spread the grated cheese into the ovenproof dish and make four depressions in it. Put a spoonful of cream into each hollow, then break an egg on top. Sprinkle a little of the cheese over the top of each egg. Bake the Cheddar Eggs on the centre shelf of a hot oven, gas mark 7 or 425°F/220°C, for 15 to 20 minutes, until the eggs are just set.

If preferred, the dish can be placed under a grill, when it will take 20 to 25 minutes.

Serve for a first course or light supper dish with brown bread and butter.

Egg Mousse

Serves 6

$\frac{3}{4}$ pint/450 ml milk
1 small onion, peeled and chopped
6 peppercorns
1 bay leaf
1 carrot, peeled and halved
2 hard-boiled eggs
2 large eggs (size 2), separated
4 tablespoons mayonnaise
$\frac{1}{2}$ teaspoon Worcestershire sauce
$\frac{1}{4}$ teaspoon Tabasco sauce
2 oz/50 g margarine
2 oz/50 g plain flour
$\frac{1}{2}$ oz/15 g powdered gelatine
4 tablespoons water
3$\frac{1}{2}$-oz/99-g can tuna fish
For the Garnish
2 hard-boiled eggs, shelled and sliced
A few sprigs of watercress
A 3-pint/1·75-litre ring mould

1 Pour the milk into a pan, add the onion, peppercorns, bay leaf and carrot, then bring the liquid to just below boiling point. Leave the pan to one side for 15 minutes for the flavours to penetrate into the milk.

2 Chop the hard-boiled eggs with the potato masher and add them to the egg yolks, mayonnaise, Worcestershire sauce and Tabasco sauce. Melt the margarine, stir in the flour then gradually blend in the strained milk.

3 Stirring all the time bring the sauce to the boil to thicken, then cover the surface with damp greaseproof paper and leave to cool. In a small pan sprinkle the gelatine over the water and dissolve it over a low heat.

4 Stir the gelatine into the sauce with the egg mixture and drained flaked tuna fish. Lightly oil the ring mould. Using a rotary or electric whisk, whisk the egg whites until they stand in soft peaks.

5 Using a metal spoon lightly and quickly fold the egg whites into the setting mixture. Carefully turn the mixture into the oiled mould. Spread the surface level then leave the mousse overnight to set.

6 Next day loosen the mousse from the sides of the mould, dip the ring into hot water for a quick count of 10, then turn on to a plate. Garnish the mousse with sliced eggs and watercress and serve with brown bread and butter.

Shrimp Cocktail

Serves 4

8-oz/226-g can pineapple tidbits
3$\frac{1}{4}$-oz/92-g can peeled shrimps
$\frac{1}{4}$ pint/150 ml salad cream
3 tablespoons tomato ketchup
A few drops of Worcestershire sauce
A pinch of caster sugar
Salt and pepper
Paprika pepper

Drain the pineapple and the shrimps and mix them together.

Blend the salad cream with the tomato ketchup and Worcestershire sauce, add the sugar and season to taste.

Serve the shrimp and pineapple mixture either in glasses on a bed of shredded lettuce, or in avocado pear halves. Spoon over the sauce just before serving and sprinkle the top with a little paprika pepper.

Egg Mousse

Melon and Tomato Cocktail

Melon and Tomato Cocktail

Serves 6

1 honeydew melon
3 large tomatoes
3 bananas
A little lemon juice
For the Herb Mayonnaise
1 large egg (size 2)
1 egg yolk (store the white in an airtight jar and use for meringues)
Salt and pepper
A pinch of caster sugar
A pinch of dry mustard
½ pint/300 ml cooking oil
1 dessertspoon white vinegar
1 dessertspoon chopped herbs or 1 teaspoon dried mixed herbs

Make the mayonnaise the day before it is required. Mix together the egg, egg yolk, salt, pepper, sugar and mustard. Add the oil, a drop at a time, beating well between each addition with a wooden spoon. As the mayonnaise starts to thicken, the oil can be added a little more quickly. When it is really thick, add the vinegar gradually until it returns to the right consistency. Mix in the herbs, cover and keep in a cool place.

Alternatively, put all the ingredients except the oil and herbs into the blender goblet and blend them for a second; add the oil slowly until the mayonnaise thickens. Mix in the herbs.

The following day, wipe the melon, then cut off the top about a quarter of the way down. Trim the ends of both pieces so that they stand upright. Remove the pips and, using a melon baller or a teaspoon, scoop out the flesh from inside both pieces. Skin the tomatoes, cut them into eight and remove the pips.

Slice the bananas and toss the pieces in lemon juice. Mix the tomatoes and bananas with the melon balls and fill the large melon shell with them. Spoon the mayonnaise into the melon lid for serving.

Orange and Tomato Ring

Serves 6

2 oranges
¼ pint/150 ml tomato juice
½ teaspoon Worcestershire sauce
1 tablespoon caster sugar
Salt and pepper
Just under ½ pint/300 ml chicken stock
¼ oz/7 g powdered gelatine
For the Garnish
1 orange
1 tomato
A 1½-pint/900-ml ring mould, lightly oiled

Grate the rind of one of the oranges into the tomato juice in a pan. Remove the peel and pith from the orange, divide it into segments and add to the tomato juice. Stir in the Worcestershire sauce, sugar and seasoning, and heat until the sugar has dissolved.

Cut the second orange in half lengthways, keep one half aside for decoration, and squeeze the juice from the other half into a jug, making the liquid up to ½ pint/300 ml with the chicken stock. Melt the gelatine in 3 tablespoons of chicken and orange stock in a small pan over a low heat. Stir it into the tomato and orange juice. Add the remaining stock, then pour the mixture into the ring mould and leave in a cool place overnight to set.

To serve, loosen the mixture from the sides of the ring mould, then turn it on to a plate. Peel and segment the whole orange, cut the tomato into thin wedges and arrange the orange and tomato around the bottom of the ring. Cut the remaining half orange into eight thin wedges and arrange these in the centre of the ring.

Cottage Pears

Serves 4

- 2 large ripe pears
- A little lemon juice
- 4 oz/100 g cottage cheese
- 1 oz/25 g chopped dates
- ½ oz/15 g walnuts, chopped
- 1 tablespoon mayonnaise or salad cream

For the Garnish

- 4 walnut halves
- 4 lettuce leaves

Wipe the pears, remove the stalks and cut each pear in half. Scoop out the cores with a teaspoon, then rub the cut surfaces with lemon juice to prevent the fruit discolouring.

Mix the cheese with the chopped dates and walnuts, then bind the ingredients together with the mayonnaise or salad cream. This can be made in advance and left in a cool place until required.

Arrange the lettuce leaves on a serving plate, put the pear halves on top, cutting a little off the base of each so that they stand level. Pile the filling into the centre of each pear and top with a walnut half.

Serve the Cottage Pears immediately.

Orange and Tomato Ring

Kipper Pâté

Serves 6

- 12-oz/340-g packet kipper fillets
- 2 oz/50 g fresh brown breadcrumbs
- 4 oz/100 g butter
- 1 small onion, peeled and finely chopped
- Juice of 1 lemon
- A little freshly ground pepper
- 1 bay leaf

Cook the kipper fillets following the instructions on the packet. Skin the fish, put it into a bowl and beat in the breadcrumbs.

Melt 3 oz/75 g butter in a pan, add the onion and cook it over a low heat until soft but not coloured. Beat the onion into the fish with the lemon juice and pepper to taste.

Turn the pâté into a serving dish and smooth the surface level. Melt the rest of the butter and pour it over the top, then place the bay leaf in the centre. Leave the pâté in a cool place for the butter to set.

Serve the pâté with freshly made toast.

Freezing Note *Freeze for up to 2 months, making sure it is well wrapped so the strong fish smell will not taint other foods.*

Tuna Pâté

Serves 4

- 7-oz/198-g can tuna fish, drained
- 4 tablespoons mayonnaise
- 6 drops of Tabasco sauce
- 1 teaspoon capers
- 1 teaspoon lemon juice
- Freshly ground black pepper
- 2 oz/50 g butter
- 1 bay leaf
- A few peppercorns
- *A ½-pint/300-ml shallow dish*

Place the drained tuna fish, mayonnaise, Tabasco sauce, capers, lemon juice, black pepper and 1 oz/25 g melted butter into the blender goblet. Put on the lid and turn on to high speed for 10 seconds, or until the ingredients are well mixed.

Alternatively break up the drained tuna fish with a fork in a bowl. Add the mayonnaise, Tabasco sauce, capers, lemon juice, black pepper and half the melted butter, then beat the mixture with the fork until smooth.

Spoon the mixture into the shallow serving dish, smoothing the surface with a knife.

Top with a bay leaf and peppercorns and pour over the remaining melted butter; leave the pâté to set in a cool place. Serve the Tuna Pâté with hot toast on a bed of lettuce leaves. Garnish with watercress sprigs and lemon slices.

Freezing Note *Freeze for up to 2 months. Make sure it is well sealed so the strong fish smell will not taint other foods.*

Country Pâté

Serves 8

- 1 lb/450 g belly of pork
- 1 lb/450 g ox liver
- 6 oz/175 g onions, peeled and coarsely chopped
- 1 large egg (size 2)
- 1 tablespoon tomato purée
- 1 teaspoon dried mixed herbs
- Salt and pepper
- 3 bay leaves
- ½-pint/300-ml packet aspic jelly powder
- *Three ½-pint/300-ml earthenware dishes*

Wipe the meat. Remove the bones and some of the fat from the pork before cutting it into pieces. Next, remove any sinews from the liver and slice the liver into pieces also. Mince the pork, liver and onions, using the coarse disc of the mincer, or chop very finely.

Stir the egg, tomato purée, herbs and plenty of seasoning into the meat until they are all well blended. Divide the pâté between the three dishes, pushing it down well with the back of a spoon. Place a bay leaf on top of each dish, then cover with lids or with foil. Stand the dishes on a baking tray and cook the pâté on the centre shelf of a moderately cool oven, gas mark 3 or 325°F/160°C, for about 2 hours, until the mixture is cooked. Remove from the oven and leave the pâté to cool in the dishes overnight.

Next day make up the aspic jelly according to the instructions on the

packet and pour it into each dish to cover the pâté.

Leave to set.

Freezing Note *Freeze without the aspic jelly for up to 3 months. Thaw overnight, cover with jelly then leave for 2 hours to set.*

Turkey Terrine

Serves 6

This is a delicious terrine to make using the leftovers from the Christmas lunch.

½ lb/225 g streaky bacon rashers
1 lb/450 g cooked turkey meat (white and dark meat)
1 medium onion, peeled
Any remaining stuffing, cranberry sauce and bread sauce
1 tablespoon chopped parsley
¼ pint/150 ml gravy
1 large egg (size 2), beaten
Salt and pepper
A 2-lb/1-kg loaf tin

Brush the tin with melted fat. Cut the rind and any small bones from the bacon, then line the base and sides of the tin with the rashers.

Using the medium disc on the mincer, mince the turkey, onion, stuffing and cranberry sauce into a bowl. Beat in the bread sauce with the parsley, gravy and beaten egg. Season the mixture well, turn into the lined tin and smooth over.

Cover the tin with foil and cook the terrine on the centre shelf of a moderately hot oven, gas mark 5 or 375°F/190°C, for 2 hours. Leave it in the tin to cool overnight.

Serve the Turkey Terrine either with a salad as a supper or lunch dish, or with hot crusty bread as a pâté.

Turkey Terrine

Freezing Note *Freeze for up to 2 months then thaw overnight.*

Fish

Fish is so adaptable and makes a welcome change for a main meal or supper dish. It is also very nutritious. Always ensure the fish is fresh and cook it as soon as possible after purchasing, so as to maintain its delicate flavour.

Herrings in Oatmeal

Serves 4

4 herrings, split and boned by the fishmonger
2 teaspoons salt
A generous pinch of pepper
4 oz / 100 g medium oatmeal
A little oil for frying
For the Garnish
Lemon slices
Sprigs of parsley

Wipe the fish with a damp cloth and remove any loose scales and fins.

Mix the salt and pepper with the oatmeal on a flat plate and coat the herrings on both sides, pressing the oatmeal firmly into the surface of the fish.

Heat a little oil in a frying pan and, when it is hot, put in the herrings, skin side uppermost. Fry them over a brisk heat for about 3 minutes, until they are light brown, then turn and cook the other side for the same time.

Lift the herrings on to a piece of absorbent paper to remove any excess oil, then arrange on a serving dish and garnish with slices of lemon and parsley sprigs.

Haddock and Prawn Mousse

Serves 6

1 lb / 450 g smoked haddock fillet
¼ pint / 150 ml milk
¼ pint / 150 ml water
½ bay leaf
1 pint / 600 ml fresh prawns
3 tablespoons cornflour
5 tablespoons mayonnaise
7-oz / 198-g can sweetcorn
¾ oz / 20 g powdered gelatine
2 tablespoons lemon juice
Pepper
A 2-pint / 1·25-litre ring mould

Wipe the haddock and place in an ovenproof dish. Pour over the milk and water, add the bay leaf then cover the dish with greaseproof paper. Poach the fish in a moderate oven, gas mark 4 or 350°F / 180°C, for about 15 minutes, until it is tender and will flake easily. Drain the fish, retaining the liquid, and remove the bay leaf. Using two forks, flake the fish. Peel all but seven of the prawns by pulling off the heads and the tails then removing the legs and the hard outside shell. Chop the prawns roughly and mix them with the flaked fish.

Mix the cornflour to a smooth paste with a little of the fish liquor, blend in the rest of the liquor and turn the sauce into a pan. Bring to the boil over a gentle heat, stirring all the time – the sauce will thicken as it boils. Leave to cool, then stir in the fish with the mayonnaise and drained sweetcorn.

Dissolve the gelatine slowly in a saucepan with the lemon juice, then stir it into the fish mixture. Check for seasoning, adding pepper if necessary.

Rub a little cooking oil around the inside of the mould, pour the mixture into it and leave the mousse to set in a cool place for at least 2 hours. It can be made the day before it is required if necessary.

Loosen the mousse from the sides of the mould, dip the ring quickly into hot water, then turn on to a serving plate. Pull the heads from the rest of the prawns and use to decorate the top of the mousse.

Freezing Note *The mousse is best frozen for only 2 weeks before the texture starts to deteriorate. Thaw in a cool place overnight.*

Herrings in Oatmeal

Haddock Gougère

Serves 4

For the Choux Pastry
2½ oz/65 g plain flour
2 oz/50 g margarine
¼ pint/150 ml water
2 large eggs (size 2)
For the Filling
½ pint/300 ml milk
1 oz/25 g margarine
1 oz/25 g plain flour
¾ lb/350 g smoked haddock or cod
Salt and pepper
3 small tomatoes, sliced
A 2½-pint/1·5-litre shallow ovenproof dish

1 Sift the flour for the pastry on to a piece of paper. Melt the margarine in a pan, then add the water. Bring the liquid to the boil over a high heat and shoot in the flour all at once.

2 Remove from the heat and beat the mixture thoroughly with a wooden spoon until it leaves the sides of the pan. Put the pan on one side for the mixture to cool slightly while making the filling.

Haddock Gougère

3 Put the milk, margarine and flour into a pan and heat it, whisking all the time until the sauce boils and thickens. Poach the fish in water for 7 to 10 minutes, then drain and flake. Stir the fish into the sauce and season.

4 Beat the eggs, then gradually add them to the choux pastry mixture, beating well between each addition until thoroughly incorporated.

5 Using a tablespoon, place the choux pastry around the inside edge of the dish to form a border. Turn the filling into the centre so it comes to the edge of the pastry ring.

6 Arrange the tomato slices slightly overlapping around the edge of the filling. Bake the Haddock Gougère in a fairly hot oven, gas mark 6 or 400°F/200°C, for 45 to 50 minutes.

Macaroni Haddock

Serves 4

4 oz/100 g short-cut macaroni
¾ lb/350 g smoked haddock fillet
For the Sauce
2 oz/50 g margarine
2 oz/50 g plain flour
1 pint/600 ml milk
A pinch of cayenne pepper
1 oz/25 g Cheddar cheese, grated
Salt and pepper
For the Topping
2 oz/50 g Cheddar cheese, grated
2 oz/50 g dried breadcrumbs
1 tomato, sliced
A few sprigs of watercress
A 2-pint/1·25-litre ovenproof dish

Cook the macaroni in boiling salted water for 15 minutes until soft. Drain the macaroni, then run hot water through the pasta to separate the pieces.

Meanwhile, melt the margarine in a pan. Remove the pan from the heat, stir in the flour and, when it is well blended, gradually mix in the milk to make a smooth sauce. Return the pan to the heat and, stirring all the time, bring the sauce to the boil so that it thickens. Stir the cayenne pepper, cheese and cooked macaroni into the sauce with seasoning.

Using a sharp knife, remove the skin from the fish, take out any small bones and cut the fish into 1-inch/2·5-cm cubes. Stir into the macaroni sauce and turn into the dish. Mix together the cheese and breadcrumbs for the topping and sprinkle over the Macaroni Haddock. Bake on the centre shelf of a moderate oven, gas mark 4 or 350°F/180°C, for 30 minutes until the top is golden brown and crispy.

Garnish with tomato and watercress.

Freezing Note *Store for up to a month. Thaw, then reheat in a moderate oven for 30 minutes.*

Haddock Flan

Serves 4

For the Pastry
6 oz/175 g plain flour
A pinch of salt
1½ oz/40 g lard
1½ oz/40 g margarine
For the Filling
¾ lb/350 g smoked haddock fillet
6 oz/175 g runner beans
2 large eggs (size 2)
¼ pint/150 ml milk
Salt and pepper
2 oz/50 g Cheddar cheese, grated
An 8-inch/20-cm flan ring

First make the pastry. Sift the flour and salt into a mixing bowl, add the fats cut into small pieces and, using the fingertips only, rub them in until evenly distributed and the mixture resembles fine breadcrumbs. Stir in sufficient cold water to make a fairly stiff dough then, on a lightly floured work surface, roll out to a circle just over 10 inches/25 cm in diameter. Stand the flan ring on a baking tray, lift the pastry into the centre and press it into the base and sides. Remove the excess dough by running the rolling pin over the top of the ring in both directions. Leave the flan case in a cool place while preparing the filling.

Wipe the fish and place in a shallow pan. Cover with water and cook gently for about 10 minutes, until the fish is tender. Drain the fish well, then discard any skin and bones and flake the fish.

Top, tail and string the beans and slice them thinly. Cook in boiling salted water for about 10 minutes, until tender. Drain the beans, then run cold water through the pieces until they are completely cool. Pat dry on absorbent paper. Spread the beans in the base of the flan and spoon the fish on top. Beat the eggs together, mix in the milk with plenty of seasoning and pour this mixture into the flan case. Sprinkle the cheese over the surface, then bake the flan on the centre shelf of a moderately hot oven, gas mark 5 or 375°F/190°C, for about 45 minutes, until the pastry is golden brown.

Serve the flan as a first course or with tomatoes and cucumber for a supper dish.

Freezing Note *Freeze for up to 1 month, heat from frozen in a moderate oven for 30 minutes before serving.*

Kedgeree

Serves 4–5

¾ lb/350 g smoked haddock
4 tablespoons water
4 tablespoons milk
2 oz/50 g butter or margarine
Salt and pepper
6 oz/175 g long-grain rice
3 hard-boiled eggs
1 tablespoon chopped parsley

Wipe the haddock, then place it in a shallow pan. Pour over the water and milk and add the butter or margarine with some pepper. Cover the pan and simmer the fish over a low heat for about 10 minutes, until tender.

Meanwhile, cook the rice. Tip it into a pan half-filled with boiling salted water and simmer for about 12 minutes, until a grain rubbed between the thumb and first finger feels soft to the centre. If you can feel a hard core, cook the rice for a little longer. Drain the rice and run hot water through the grains to separate them and remove any excess starch.

When the fish is cooked, remove it from the pan and reserve the liquor. Remove the skin and bones from the fish and separate the flesh into flakes. Mix the cooked rice with the fish and drained fish liquor. Shell the eggs, chop roughly and stir into the rice with the chopped parsley.

Check for seasoning then turn the Kedgeree into a heated dish and serve immediately with triangles of hot toast.

Fish and Chips

Serves 3

1 lb/450 g potatoes, peeled and cut into chips
1 large egg (size 2), beaten
2 tablespoons plain flour, seasoned with salt and pepper
Dried breadcrumbs
3 pieces cod (weighing about 1–1½ lb/450–675 g)
Cooking oil or fat for deep frying
For the Garnish
Lemon slices
Sprigs of parsley

Put sufficient oil or fat in the deep fat fryer pan to come halfway up.

Heat the fat to about 375°F/

190°C – when a small cube of bread slipped into the fat browns in about a minute. Dry the chips thoroughly, put them into the frying basket and lower it very gradually into the fat. Cook them over a moderate heat for about 5 minutes, shaking the basket occasionally so that the chips do not stick together. The chips are ready when they are cooked to the centre but still very pale in colour (this process is called blanching and results in finished chips which are golden and crisp). Leave them on one side to refry later.

Put the beaten egg and seasoned flour on to separate plates and the breadcrumbs on to a piece of greaseproof paper. Dust the fish with flour, then brush all over with beaten egg and lastly coat thoroughly with the breadcrumbs, pressing them well into the surface. Leave the fish on one side.

Reheat the fat and fry the chips quickly until they are crisp and golden brown. Turn them on to absorbent paper to remove excess fat, then transfer them to a serving dish. Sprinkle the chips with salt and keep warm while frying the fish.

Reheat the fat to 375°F/190°C. Fry the fish one piece at a time, so that the temperature of the fat is not lowered by too much food. Cook the fish for about 5 to 8 minutes, then drain the pieces on absorbent paper. Serve them piled on the chips, garnished with lemon and parsley and accompanied by a tartare sauce.

Freezing Note *The chips can be frozen after the first cooking. The fish will not freeze satisfactorily cooked.*

Cod and Bacon Corkscrews

Makes 8

- ½ lb/225 g smoked haddock or cod fillet
- 1 lb/450 g potatoes, peeled, cooked and creamed
- 1 tablespoon gherkins, finely chopped
- 1 small onion, peeled and grated
- 1 large egg (size 2), beaten
- Salt and pepper
- ½ lb/225 g streaky bacon rashers
- 2 oz/50 g browned breadcrumbs
- 4 slices lemon, halved, for garnish

Put the fish into a pan, and just cover it with cold water. Bring to the boil, then reduce the heat and simmer the fish for about 5 minutes, until tender. Remove from the pan and, using two forks, flake the fish into pieces, discarding any skin and bones.

Mix the potato with the chopped gherkin, grated onion and beaten egg, then mix in the fish and check for seasoning. Divide the mixture into eight pieces and form each one into a sausage shape. Using a pair of scissors, remove the rind and any small bones from the bacon rashers, then stretch them out with the back of a knife. Wrap one rasher around each sausage shape then toss in browned breadcrumbs. Put them close together in a baking tin so they retain their shape during cooking, and bake on the centre shelf of a moderate oven, gas mark 4 or 350°F/180°C, for 45 minutes.

Put one piece of lemon on each corkscrew and serve as a supper dish with peas and sauté potatoes.

Freezing Note *Freeze the corkscrews before or after cooking. They will keep for about 1 month. Thaw, then cook as in the recipe or reheat in a moderate oven for 15 to 20 minutes.*

Fish and Chips

Fish Crispies

Serves 3–4

1 lb/450 g cod or haddock fillet
1 oz/25 g plain flour, seasoned with salt and pepper
Cooking oil or fat for deep frying
For the Batter
4 oz/110 g plain flour
A pinch of salt
1 large egg (size 2), beaten
1 tablespoon cooking oil
¼ pint/150 ml milk
¼ pint/150 ml water
1 teaspoon baking powder

First make the batter. Sift the flour and salt into a mixing bowl and make a well in the centre. Add the beaten egg and cooking oil and, using a wooden spoon, gradually work in the flour from around the sides of the bowl. When the egg has been mixed in, add the milk and water. Beat the batter for a minute to incorporate as much air as possible, then cover it and leave the bowl on one side while preparing the fish.

Lay the fillets, skin side down, on a board and hold the tail firmly in the fingers (a little salt on them will help you to grip). Separate the flesh from the skin by sawing with a sharp knife from side to side, keeping the knife almost upright as you work. Cut the fish into 1½-inch/3·5-cm squares and toss the pieces in the seasoned flour.

Half-fill a deep fat fryer with fat and heat to 375°F/190°C, or when a cube of bread slipped into the fat browns in 1 minute. Remove the basket from the fryer. Stir the baking powder into the batter. Coat the pieces of fish with the batter and lower them into the hot fat. Cook the Fish Crispies for about 5 minutes, until golden brown. Lift them out of the fat and drain on absorbent paper while cooking the other fish pieces.

Cod and Mushroom Pies

Makes 4

For the Pastry
6 oz/175 g plain flour
A pinch of salt
5 oz/150 g margarine (in a hard block straight from the refrigerator)
Beaten egg for glaze
For the Filling
2 oz/50 g mushrooms
1 oz/25 g margarine
1 oz/25 g plain flour
½ pint/300 ml milk
1 tablespoon chopped parsley
Salt and pepper
1 lb/450 g cod or haddock fillet
Four ½-pint/300-ml individual oven-proof pie dishes
A 2-inch/5-cm plain cutter

First make the pastry. Sift the flour and salt into a mixing bowl. Grate the margarine coarsely and mix it into the flour. Stir in sufficient water to make a fairly stiff dough, wrap in greaseproof paper and leave in a cool place while preparing the filling.

Wipe the mushrooms – there is no need to peel them, just trim the stalks and chop roughly. Melt the margarine in a pan over low heat, then add the mushrooms and fry until tender. Remove the pan from the heat and stir in the flour, then gradually blend in the milk and, when the sauce is smooth, return to the heat. Stirring all the time, bring the sauce to the boil and cook it for a minute so that it thickens. Stir in the

Fish Crispies, Cod and Mushroom Pies, Cod and Bacon Corkscrews

parsley and check the sauce for seasoning. Skin the fish as described in the recipe for Fish Crispies (see above), then cut into 1-inch/2·5-cm pieces and stir into the sauce. Divide the mixture between the dishes.

Roll out the pastry on a lightly floured work surface then, using one of the dishes as a guide, cut out four circles. Moisten the edges and put them on top of the dishes, pressing lids firmly to the rim. Gather up the scraps and reroll the pastry fairly thinly then cut out 12 rounds using the plain cutter. Fold them in half, then form each one into a crescent shape. Brush the pastry tops with egg glaze and arrange three crescents in the centre of each pie. Bake the pies on the centre shelf of a fairly hot oven, gas mark 6 or 400°F/200°C, for 30 minutes, until the pastry is golden brown.

Serve the pies immediately – they are delicious with a coleslaw salad.

Freezing Note *Freeze the cooked pies for up to 2 months. Thaw overnight and reheat in a moderate oven, gas mark 4 or 350°F/180°C, for 20 minutes.*

Crunchy Fishcakes

Crunchy Fishcakes

Makes 6

1 lb/450 g white fish fillet – cod, haddock or coley
4 tablespoons milk
4 tablespoons water
Salt and pepper
1 lb/450 g potatoes, peeled, cooked and creamed
1 tablespoon chopped parsley
Plain flour, seasoned with salt and pepper
1 large egg (size 2), beaten
2 oz/50 g cornflakes, crushed to crumbs
Cooking oil or fat for deep frying

Wipe the fish and put into a shallow pan with the milk and water. Add a little seasoning then bring slowly to the boil. Reduce the heat, cover the pan and simmer the fish for 10 to 15 minutes, until tender. Drain the fish well and, using a pair of forks, flake the flesh, removing any skin or bones.

Carefully stir the fish into the potatoes with the parsley and plenty of seasoning. Divide the mixture into six equal portions and, using floured hands and working on a floured surface, shape each portion into a round, 3 inches/7·5 cm in diameter and ½ inch/1 cm deep.

Put the seasoned flour on to one plate, the beaten egg on to another plate, and the cornflake crumbs on to a third plate. Coat each fishcake first in the flour, then in the egg and finally in the crumbs, so that the surface is completely covered. (The egg and crumbing process may be repeated to ensure a really good covering.)

Half-fill a deep fat fryer with cooking oil and heat it to 375°F/190°C – that is when a piece of bread slipped into the oil browns in just 1 minute. Cook the fishcakes for 10 to 15 minutes until golden, then drain on absorbent paper and serve.

Freezing Note *Fishcakes are a good standby to keep in the freezer. Separate them with waxed discs, then pile them up and freeze either in polythene bags or in a rigid container. Store for up to 3 months. Grill or fry the fishcakes from frozen, using a slightly lower than normal heat.*

Fish Pie

Serves 6

$1\frac{1}{2}$ lb/675 g cod fillet
$\frac{3}{4}$ pint/450 ml milk
1 bay leaf
Salt and pepper
$\frac{1}{4}$ lb/100 g mushrooms, quartered
1 medium onion, peeled and sliced
2 oz/50 g butter
2 oz/50 g plain flour
7-oz/198-g can sweetcorn, drained
2 tablespoons chopped parsley
3 tomatoes, sliced
$1\frac{1}{2}$ lb/675 g potatoes, peeled, cooked and creamed with 2 oz/50 g butter
A $2\frac{1}{2}$-pint/1·5-litre ovenproof dish
A large piping bag with No 10 star pipe attached

Poach the fish in the milk with the bay leaf and seasoning for 15 minutes. When it is tender, drain, reserving the liquid for the sauce, and flake the fish, removing any skin or bones.

Sauté the mushrooms and onion in the butter until soft then remove from the heat. Mix in the flour then gradually blend in the reserved fish liquor. Bring the sauce to the boil, stirring all the time, until smooth and thickened. Add the sweetcorn, flaked fish and parsley. Check the sauce for seasoning then turn the mixture into the dish, spread the surface level and cover it with sliced tomatoes.

Spoon the creamed potato into the piping bag and cover the surface of the pie with piped potato. Either heat the pie immediately in a fairly hot oven, gas mark 6 or 400°F/200°C, for 30 minutes until golden brown or, if the pie is left till cold, allow about 1 hour to reheat and brown.

Freezing Note *Freeze for up to 6 weeks, thaw and heat as for the cold pie; or reheat from frozen when the pie will take about 2 hours.*

Somerset Fish Pie

Serves 4

1 lb/450 g cod fillet
$1\frac{1}{2}$ oz/40 g plain flour, seasoned with salt and pepper
1 oz/25 g butter
1 medium onion, peeled and sliced
$\frac{1}{4}$ pint/150 ml water
5 tablespoons dry cider
2 oz/50 g frozen peas
Salt and pepper
$7\frac{1}{2}$-oz/212-g packet frozen puff pastry, thawed
Milk for glaze
A $1\frac{1}{2}$-pint/1-litre pie dish

Using a sharp knife, remove the skin from the fish, then cut the flesh into 1-inch/2·5-cm pieces, discarding any bones. Put the seasoned flour on to a plate and toss the fish in it. Melt the butter in a pan, add the onion and fry it until beginning to soften, then add the fish and quickly fry the pieces until they are sealed on all sides; transfer the fish to the pie dish. Stir the remaining seasoned flour into the pan and, off the heat, gradually blend in the water and then the cider. Return the pan to the heat and, stirring all the time, bring the sauce to the boil and cook it for a minute until it thickens. Mix the peas and a little extra seasoning into the sauce and pour it over the fish.

On a lightly floured work surface, roll the pastry into an oval 1 inch/2·5 cm larger than the pie dish. Place the dish in the centre of the pastry and cut round it, then remove the dish from the pastry. Moisten the rim of the dish with

Fish Pie

water and lift the border of pastry into position on the rim. Moisten the pastry rim, then lift the pastry lid into place and press the edges well together. Trim the edges with a sharp knife, knock them together, then flute into scallops. Reroll the pastry trimmings and cut out five diamonds for leaves. Place the leaves in the centre of the pie, then brush the surface with milk and leave the pie in a cool place to rest for 10 minutes.

Bake the Somerset Fish Pie on the centre shelf of a fairly hot oven, gas mark 6 or 400°F/200°C, for 40 to 45 minutes, until the pastry is golden brown and well risen. Serve at once.

Freezing Note *Store the cooked pie for up to a month. Thaw overnight and reheat in a moderate oven, gas mark 4 or 350°F/180°C, for 30 minutes.*

Corsican Cod

Serves 4

4 cod steaks
1 oz/25 g margarine
2 medium onions, peeled and sliced
8-oz/227-g can tomatoes
1 teaspoon dried marjoram
Salt and pepper
A 2-pint/1·25-litre ovenproof dish

Place the cod steaks in the ovenproof dish.

Melt the margarine in a pan over low heat, add the onions and fry gently for a few minutes, until they are soft but not coloured. Scatter the onions over the fish.

In the same pan, heat the tomatoes with the marjoram and seasoning, then pour this mixture over the fish. Cover the dish with foil and bake on the centre shelf of a moderately hot oven, gas mark 5 or 375°F/190°C for 45 minutes, or until the fish is tender.

Freezing Note *Freeze for up to a month. Thaw, then reheat covered in a moderate oven for 15 to 20 minutes.*

Sole Véronique

Sole Véronique

Serves 3–6

6 lemon or Dover sole fillets (plaice can also be used if sole is not available)
½ pint/300 ml water
4 tablespoons white wine
1 tablespoon lemon juice
A blade of mace
6 peppercorns
1 bay leaf
2 oz/50 g margarine
2 oz/50 g plain flour
Salt and pepper
A small knob of butter
¼ lb/100 g small seedless grapes
A 2-pint/1·25-litre ovenproof dish

First prepare the fish. If the fishmonger has not removed the skin, lay the fillets skin side down on a work surface. Hold the tail end firmly in the fingers (a little salt on them will help you to grip), and using a sharp knife separate the flesh from the skin with a sawing action, keeping the knife almost upright as you work.

Roll up the fillets starting at the thicker end, and with the side that has had the skin removed inside. Place the rolls in the ovenproof dish, add the water, wine, lemon juice, mace, peppercorns and bay leaf. Cover with foil or greaseproof paper and cook on the centre shelf of a moderate oven, gas mark 4 or 350°F/180°C, for about 20 minutes, until the fish is tender. It is ready when the surface is covered with a milky white liquid. Carefully lift the fish rolls out of the dish, arrange in a serving dish and keep warm.

Melt the margarine in a pan over low heat. Remove from the heat and mix in the flour, then strain the fish liquor and gradually blend it in. When the sauce is smooth, place the pan over a low heat and, stirring all the time, bring the sauce to the boil, to thicken. Check for seasoning and stir in the butter to make the sauce really glossy. Using a large spoon, carefully coat the fish fillets with the sauce.

Wash the grapes and scatter them over the centre of the dish, before serving it as a first or main course.

Note If the grapes contain pips, the best way to remove them and still keep the grape whole is to use the curved end of a hair grip. Make sure it is perfectly clean, then push it into the grape and hook out the pips.

Greek Eggs

Serves 4

3 oz/75 g smoked cod's roe
2 oz/50 g butter, softened
4 large hard-boiled eggs (size 2)
2 tablespoons milk
1 teaspoon tomato ketchup
A little pepper and salt
1 teaspoon lemon juice
A few sprigs of watercress for garnish
For the Sauce
2 teaspoons tomato ketchup
¼ pint/150 ml mayonnaise

Cut the hard skin from the cod's roe and beat the roe to a soft consistency with the butter. Cut the hard-boiled eggs in half lengthways, remove the yolks and sieve them into the cod's roe. Add the milk, tomato ketchup, pepper and lemon juice and beat them all together until well combined. Check for seasoning, then spoon the mixture back into the egg whites, shaping it so that each half looks like a whole egg.

Beat the tomato ketchup into the mayonnaise, and, at the last minute, spoon the sauce over the eggs to completely cover them. Garnish the dish with a few sprigs of watercress, then serve the Greek Eggs as a first course with thinly sliced brown bread and butter.

Kipper Potato Bake

Serves 4–6

1 pair kippers
1 oz/25 g butter
1¾ lb/800 g potatoes, peeled and thinly sliced
Grated rind and juice of ½ lemon
A little pepper
½ pint/300 ml water
A 2-pint/1·25-litre shallow ovenproof dish

Kipper Potato Bake, Greek Eggs

Using a sharp pointed knife, remove the backbone from the kippers, then cut off the head and tail and remove the fins. Run the knife under the skin and pull it away. Cut the fish into 2-inch/5-cm pieces.

Grease the dish with a little of the butter and arrange a layer of potatoes in the base, then some of the fish. Sprinkle over a little grated lemon rind and juice with some pepper. Continue layering the ingredients, ending with a neat layer of potatoes, slightly overlapping.

Dot the surface with the remaining butter and pour in the water. Bake the dish on the centre shelf of a moderately hot oven, gas mark 5 or 375°F/190°C, for about 1 to 1½ hours, until the potatoes are golden brown and tender.

Serve the Kipper Potato Bake for supper with sliced bread and butter.

Dawlish Mackerel

Serves 4

4 medium mackerel, cleaned by the fishmonger
¾ pint/450 ml milk
1 bay leaf
5 peppercorns
1 oz/25 g butter
1 onion, peeled and grated
1 oz/25 g plain flour
2 teaspoons horseradish sauce
Salt and pepper
For the Garnish
3 tomatoes, sliced
1 small bunch watercress
A 3-pint/1·75-litre shallow ovenproof dish

Trim the tails off the mackerel, then wash the fish thoroughly. Lay the fish in the ovenproof dish, pour over the milk and add the bay leaf and peppercorns. Cover with a piece of foil and poach the mackerel on the centre shelf of a moderately hot oven, gas mark 5 or 375°F/190°C, for 20 to 30 minutes, until the flesh is opaque and any liquid seeping out of the fish is milky white in colour. Lift the fish carefully on to a plate and keep warm while making the sauce. Strain and reserve the fish liquor.

Melt the butter in a pan, add the onion and fry gently over a low heat until soft but not coloured. Remove the pan from the heat and stir in the flour, then gradually blend in the fish liquor. When the sauce is smooth, return to the heat and, stirring all the time, bring to the boil. Stir in the horseradish sauce and seasoning to taste.

Arrange the cooked mackerel in the dish and coat them with the sauce. Garnish the dish with sliced tomatoes and sprigs of watercress.

Tuna Fish Pancakes

Serves 4

For the Pancakes
4 oz/110 g plain flour
A pinch of salt
1 large egg (size 2)
¼ pint/150 ml milk
¼ pint/150 ml water
A little oil for frying
For the Filling
1 oz/25 g butter
1 oz/25 g plain flour
½ pint/300 ml milk
2 oz/50 g cheese, grated
7-oz/198-g can tuna fish
Salt and pepper
For the Topping
4 oz/100 g Cheddar cheese, grated
Sprigs of watercress to garnish
A shallow 1½-pint/900-ml dish, lightly greased

Sift the flour and salt for the pancakes into a bowl, make a well in the centre and break in the egg. Using a wooden spoon, gradually work the flour from around the sides into the egg, adding the milk and water at the same time to make a smooth batter.

Heat a frying pan with a little oil and, when it is really hot, drain off as much oil as possible. Reheat the pan, then pour in a little of the batter and swirl the pan so that the base is thinly coated. Put the pan back over the heat and, when the underside of the pancake is brown, turn to cook the other side. Cook the rest of the batter in the same way, piling the pancakes one on top of the other when cooked. The pan will need to be re-greased between every fifth or sixth pancake. Keep the pancakes warm while you make the filling.

Melt the butter in a pan, remove it from the heat and stir in the flour, then gradually blend in the milk. When smooth, return the pan to the heat and, stirring all the time, bring the sauce to the boil. Cook it for 1 minute to thicken. Remove the pan from the heat and stir in the cheese. Drain any oil from the tuna and stir the fish into the sauce, breaking it into pieces. Check the mixture for seasoning.

Place a spoonful of the filling on each pancake and roll it up. Place the pancakes side by side in the dish. Scatter the cheese over the surface, and if they are to be served immediately, brown the pancakes under a preheated grill. They can also be stored overnight in a cool place, then reheated in a moderate oven, gas mark 4 or 350°F/180°C, for 30 to 40 minutes. Garnish with watercress.

Freezing Note *Freeze, label and store the filled or unfilled pancakes. Unfilled pancakes will store for 6 months, filled ones for 3 months. Do not scatter with cheese before they are frozen.*

Thaw the unfilled pancakes at room temperature – they will take about 4 hours – then serve them sweet or savoury.

The filled pancakes can be heated straight from the freezer, still in their foil container. Scatter the surface thickly with the cheese, then place them on the centre shelf of a moderate oven, gas mark 4 or 350°F/180°C, for 50 to 60 minutes. If the filled pancakes are thawed follow normal cooking instructions for heating.

Taunton Tuna

Serves 4

7-oz/198-g can tuna fish
¼ lb/100 g mushrooms
1 oz/25 g butter
1½ oz/40 g plain flour
½ pint/300 ml milk
¼ pint/150 ml cider
3 tablespoons chopped parsley
Salt and papper

Wipe the mushrooms – there is no need to peel them – trim the stalks, then cut into slices. Melt the butter in a pan, add the mushrooms and fry gently until they are just cooked. Remove the pan from the heat and stir in the flour, then carefully blend in the milk and cider.

Drain the oil from the tuna and break the fish into large flakes, then stir the pieces into the sauce mixture. Return the pan to the heat and, stirring all the time, bring the sauce to the boil. Stir in the parsley and check the mixture for seasoning.

Serve Taunton Tuna immediately with crusty bread.

Meat

Make the most of meat, whether it is beef, pork, lamb, poultry, bacon or one of the offals, by choosing the best cut available for the dish to be cooked. The cheaper cuts are ideal for long slow cooking in casseroles and stews. The middle-priced cuts make delicious pies and pot roasts, while the more expensive cuts are perfect for roasting and special meals.

Roasts and Bakes

Glazed Pork Bake

Serves 6

½ oz/15 g butter
1½ lb/675 g potatoes, peeled and thinly sliced
Salt and pepper
½ lb/225 g carrots, peeled and thinly sliced
¼ pint/150 ml stock
8 strips of belly of pork (about 2½ lb/1·25 kg in weight)
3 oz/75 g demerara sugar
2 tablespoons honey
1 teaspoon made French mustard
Grated rind and juice of 1 lemon
A 3-pint/1·75-litre ovenproof dish

Rub the butter over the base and sides of the ovenproof dish. Place half the potato slices in the bottom, season, then spread over all the carrots; season again and top with the remaining potato slices, then pour over the stock.

Carefully cut the rind from the pork belly strips and arrange on top of the potatoes. Mix the sugar with the honey, mustard and lemon rind and juice in a small bowl.

Coat the meat thoroughly with this mixture then cover the dish with foil. Bake on the centre shelf of a fairly hot oven, gas mark 6 or 400°F/200°C, for 1½ hours. Remove the foil for the final 15 minutes so the meat turns brown and crispens.

The dish can be served as a complete meal but it is also perfect accompanied by buttered cabbage.

Pale Ale Pork

Serves 6

2½–3-lb/1·25–1·5-kg blade joint of pork
2 tablespoons cooking oil
½ lb/225 g onions, peeled and sliced
¼ lb/100 g mushrooms, wiped, trimmed and sliced
1 large orange
½ pint/300 ml pale ale
1 teaspoon brown sugar
Salt and pepper
Orange wedges for garnish

Cut the rind from the joint of pork, using a sharp knife. Heat the oil in a roasting tin, then brown the joint on all sides over a fairly high heat; transfer it to a plate.

Add the onions to the tin and, when they start to soften, stir in the mushrooms. Fry the two ingredients together for about 5 minutes.

Using a potato peeler, remove the rind from the orange and cut it into thin strips. Squeeze the juice from the orange and add to the roasting tin with the orange peel strips and the pale ale. Bring the mixture to the boil, stir in the sugar and season to taste.

Return the meat to the tin and cover with foil. Bake on the centre shelf of a moderate oven, gas mark 4 or 350°F/180°C, for 1½ hours. Remove the foil, baste the meat and return the joint to a fairly hot oven, gas mark 6 or 400°F/200°C, for a further 15 minutes.

Transfer the pork to a heated serving dish and spoon over the vegetables. Garnish the dish with wedges of orange, and serve the cooking juices separately.

Accompany the pork with Brussels sprouts and Duchesse potatoes.

Glazed Pork Bake, Home-Made Sausages (see recipe page 74), Pale Ale Pork

Curried Cider Chops

Curried Cider Chops

Serves 4

$\frac{3}{4}$ pint/450 ml dry cider
1 large egg (size 2)
3 oz/75 g fresh white breadcrumbs
1 teaspoon powdered sage
Salt and pepper
4 pork chops
1 oz/25 g butter
1 medium onion, peeled and finely chopped
1 tablespoon curry powder
2 tablespoons sweet chutney
A shallow ovenproof dish, buttered

Heat the cider in a saucepan and boil to reduce it by one-third.

Beat the egg and pour it on to a plate, then mix the breadcrumbs with the sage and seasoning on another plate. Trim the chops to remove any excess fat. Dip each chop first in the beaten egg, then in the crumbs and arrange them in the ovenproof dish.

Melt the butter in a frying pan. Fry the onion and curry powder gently until the onion is soft, then stir in the chutney and pour in the cider. Add seasoning to taste, then pour this sauce over the chops. Bake in the centre of a moderately hot oven, gas mark 5 or 375°F/190°C, for about 1 hour, until tender.

Serve the chops with Duchesse potatoes and a tossed cucumber and celery salad.

Oriental Roast Pork

Serves 6

$3\frac{1}{2}$-lb/1·5-kg piece of spare rib of pork
Salt
2 oz/50 g lard
8 oz/225 g vermicelli
For the Sauce
$\frac{1}{2}$ oz/15 g margarine
1 medium onion, peeled and sliced
4 tablespoons malt vinegar
3 tablespoons cornflour
1 tablespoon soy sauce
4 tablespoons honey
1 pint/600 ml chicken stock
4 oz/100 g dried apricots, soaked overnight
4 oz/100 g dried prunes, soaked overnight

Wipe the meat with a damp cloth, score the skin with a sharp knife and sprinkle with salt. Weigh the joint and calculate the cooking time by allowing 25 minutes per pound/per half kilo plus an extra 25 minutes. Melt the lard in a roasting tin then roast the joint on the centre shelf of a fairly hot oven, gas mark 6 or 400°F/200°C, for the calculated time. Baste it twice during cooking.

Meanwhile, make the sauce. Melt the margarine in a pan, add the sliced onion and cook it gently until tender but not coloured. Mix the vinegar and cornflour to a paste, then stir in the soy sauce and honey. When the onion is tender, remove the pan from the heat and stir in the cornflour mixture together with the stock. Return the pan to the heat and, stirring all the time, bring it to the boil. Reduce the heat, add the drained apricots and prunes and simmer the sauce slowly for about 15 minutes.

Put the vermicelli into a pan half-filled with boiling salted water and cook for about 3 minutes as instructed on the packet. Drain thoroughly, then run hot water through it to separate the strands.

Turn the vermicelli on to a large heated serving dish, pushing it to the edges. Place the pork in the centre, spoon some of the sauce around the joint and serve the remainder separately.

Freezing Note *Freeze the sauce for up to a month then reheat when required.*

Gorgeous Gammon

Serves 12

6 lb/2·75 kg middle cut gammon
Demerara sugar
Sprigs of watercress for garnish
For the Decoration
12 dried prunes, soaked overnight
1 lb 13-oz/825-g can peach halves
12 maraschino cherries

Soak the joint in cold water for up to 6 hours to remove the excess salt.

Calculate the cooking time at 25 minutes per pound/per half kilo.

Rinse the joint, dry the surface then rub the cut surfaces with demerara sugar. Wrap the joint in foil and place in a roasting tin. Roast in a moderately hot oven, gas mark 5 or 375°F/190°C, for the calculated cooking time.

Meanwhile, prepare the decoration. Drain the prunes and cut out the stones. Drain the peaches also. Place each prune in the hollow of a peach half and a cherry in each prune, then spear them with a wooden cocktail stick.

Ten minutes before the end of the cooking time, take the joint out of the oven and remove the foil. Peel off all the skin then garnish the top of the joint with the filled peach halves. Return the joint to the oven for the rest of the cooking time. Garnish with watercress and serve hot with Cumberland Sauce.

Cumberland Sauce

4 tablespoons redcurrant jelly
¼ pint/150 ml inexpensive red wine
Grated rind and juice of 1 orange
Grated rind and juice of 1 lemon
1½ teaspoons cornflour

Melt the redcurrant jelly in the wine over a low heat, then add the grated rind and juice of the orange and lemon.

Blend the cornflour with a little cold water to make a smooth paste and stir it into the sauce. Bring to the boil to thicken, stirring all the time. Leave to cool before serving.

Gorgeous Gammon

Crown Roast of Lamb

Serves 6

2 pieces of best end neck of lamb (7 bones each), chined by the butcher
Salt and pepper
2 oz/50 g lard
For the Stuffing and Decoration
4 oz/100 g long-grain rice
1 oz/25 g lard
1 medium onion, peeled and chopped
1 teaspoon curry powder
15-oz/425-g can apricot halves
2 oz/50 g walnuts, chopped
Salt and pepper
1 lb/450 g new carrots, cooked
1 lb/450 g broad beans, cooked
½ lb/225 g peas, cooked
2 oz/50 g butter, melted
Trussing needle and a length of string
14 cutlet frills

Using a sharp knife, cut out the ends of the shoulder blade which are sometimes still left in the thicker end of the joints, then remove the chine bone. Make a cut along each joint about 1½ inches/3·5 cm from the tip of the bones and remove the meat as close to the bones as possible, then trim away the meat between the cutlet bones, using a smaller knife.

Scrape away any meat still on the tips of the bones, so that they are quite clean – any meat left on will burn during cooking and spoil the appearance of the crown. Finally, using a trussing needle and string, tie the two joints together by pushing the needle through the bottom of the two joints and securing them together, then join the two pieces of meat at the top as well. It may be necessary to make small slits at the base of each cutlet, no more than ½ inch/1 cm in length, to give the joint a true round crown shape.

Weigh the joint and allow 20 minutes cooking time per lb/per half kilo, then add an extra 20 minutes to the total time. Sprinkle the inside of the joint with salt and pepper, rub the outside with the lard and put the joint into a roasting tin. Leave in a cool place while preparing the stuffing.

Wash the rice, put into a pan of boiling salted water and simmer gently for 9 minutes. Drain well in a sieve, then pour hot water through the rice to separate the grains and remove any excess starch. Place in a mixing bowl.

Melt the lard in a frying pan and gently cook the chopped onion with the curry powder until the onion is tender. Turn into the bowl with the rice. Drain the apricot halves, reserve eight for decoration, then chop the rest and add to the rice with the chopped walnuts. Mix the ingredients well together, check for seasoning, then fill the centre of the lamb with the stuffing, packing it fairly loosely. Cover the top of the

Crown Roast of Lamb

joint with a piece of foil so the stuffing does not dry out during cooking.

Roast the joint on the centre shelf of a moderately hot oven, gas mark 5 or 375°F/190°C, for the calculated cooking time, basting the outside once or twice.

When the joint is cooked, remove the foil and fork up the rice stuffing. Arrange the apricot halves around the top and slip a frill on the end of each cutlet. Lift the joint on to a heated meat dish. Toss the hot vegetables in the melted butter, arrange a few around the joint and mix the remainder together to serve separately.

Stuffed Shoulder of Lamb

Serves 6–8

4–4½-lb/1·75–2-kg shoulder of lamb
2 oz/50 g dripping
A little salt
2 sprigs of rosemary for garnish
For the Stuffing
1 onion, peeled and thinly sliced
1 oz/25 g butter
4 oz/100 g lamb's liver, diced
2 tablespoons raisins, cleaned
1 teaspoon chopped mixed herbs
3 oz/75 g cooked long-grain rice (1½ oz/40 g uncooked rice)
Salt and pepper
Trussing needle and a length of string

1 Using a small, sharp knife and starting at the wide end of the joint, cut the meat away from the bone, keeping the knife as close to the bone as possible.

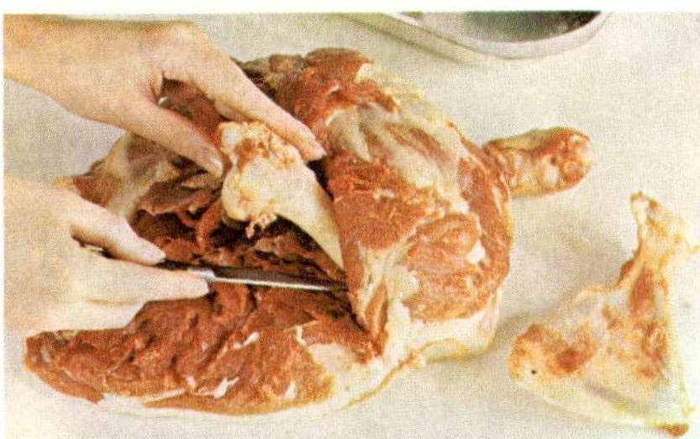

2 Work along both sides of the bone to the ball and socket joint and, when the joint is revealed, cut through it to release the bone. Keep this bone for making stock.

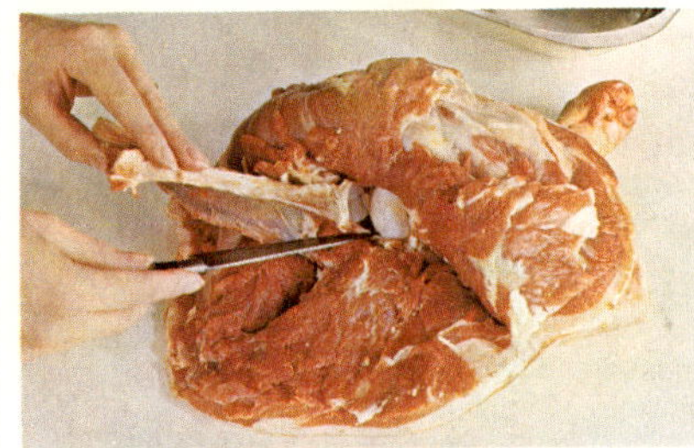

3 Continue in the same way along the next bone to the hinge joint and cut through it also to release the bone, leaving the shin bone in place. Fry the onion in the butter till soft.

4 Add the liver and, when it is sealed, stir in the raisins, herbs, rice and seasoning. Leave the stuffing to cool. Open up the cavity in the lamb left from removing the bones.

5 Pack in the stuffing then reshape the joint. Starting at one end of the opening, thread the string and sew the two edges together to keep the stuffing in.

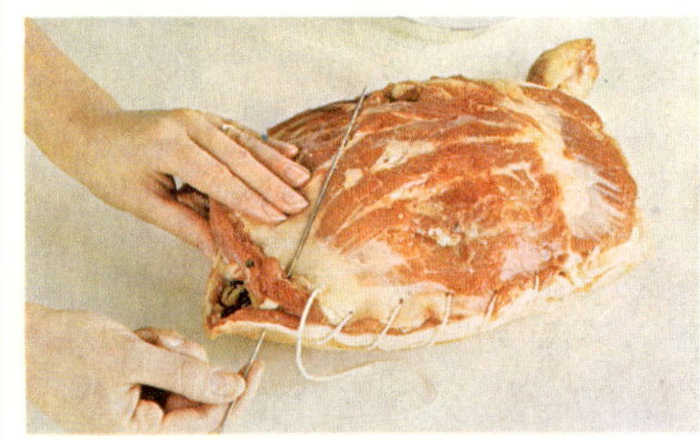

6 Calculate the cooking time – 20 minutes per lb/per half kilo plus 20 minutes. Baste, sprinkle with salt, then cook at gas mark 6 or 400°F/200°C, for 20 minutes, then at gas mark 5 or 375°F/190°C, for the rest of the time.

Freezing Note *The stuffed shoulder can be frozen uncooked for up to 2 months. Thaw overnight in a cool place then cook as above.*

Meat Roasting Chart

Cuts	Roasting time	Temperature	Ounces/grams per serving	Accompaniments
Beef	Cooking time is given for a medium roasted joint. If you prefer rare beef, allow 5 minutes less per lb/per half kilo; for a well-done joint allow 5 minutes more per lb/per half kilo.			
Topside *Large*	25 mins. per lb/per half kilo plus 25 mins.	20 mins. at gas mark 7 or 425°F/220°C, turned down to gas mark 5 or 375°F/190°C for rest of cooking time	6 oz/175 g	Horseradish sauce, Yorkshire pudding, mustard, gravy
Small	20 mins. per lb/per half kilo plus 20 mins.	20 mins. at gas mark 7 or 425°F/220°C, turned down to gas mark 5 or 375°F/190°C for rest of cooking time	As above	As above
Wing rib	25 mins. per lb/per half kilo	As above	8 oz/225 g	As above
Brisket *Large or Small*	45 mins. per lb/per half kilo plus 45 mins.	Gas mark 3 or 325°F/160°C for all the cooking time	6 oz/175 g	As above
Lamb				
Shoulder *Half and Whole*	20 mins. per lb/per half kilo plus 20 mins.	Gas mark 5 or 375°F/190°C for all the cooking time	6 oz/175 g	Mint sauce, redcurrant jelly, onion sauce, stuffing
Leg *Half and Whole*	As above	As above	As above	As above
Best end of neck	As above	As above	As above	As above
Pork				
Leg	30 mins. per lb/per half kilo	30 mins, at gas mark 7 or 425°F/220°C, turned down to gas mark 5 or 375°F/190°C for rest of cooking time	6 oz/175 g	Apple sauce, sage and onion stuffing balls, gravy
Thick end of belly	30 mins. per lb/per half kilo plus 30 mins.	Gas mark 3 or 325°F/160°C until last 15 mins., then increase to gas mark 6 or 400°F/200°C	As above	As above
Hand and spring	30 mins. per lb/per half kilo plus 30 mins.	30 mins. at gas mark 7 or 425°F/220°C, turned down to gas mark 5 or 375°F/190°C for rest of cooking time	8 oz/225 g	As above
Loin	25 mins. per lb/per half kilo plus 25 mins.	25 mins. at gas mark 7 or 425°F/220°C, turned down to gas mark 5 or 375°F/190°C for rest of cooking time	As above	As above

Preparation for Roasting

Beef

1 Melt 2–3 tablespoons of lard or dripping in a roasting tin in a preheated oven.

2 Prick the fat of the joint all over with a fork then rub salt into it.

3 Place the joint in the roasting tin, baste with the fat, then cook for the calculated time.

Lamb

As for beef, but leaving out point 2.

Pork

As for beef, but do not prick the skin before rubbing in salt. Ask the butcher to score the rind when you purchase the joint.

Chicken and Capon

1 Melt 2–3 tablespoons of lard in a roasting tin in a preheated oven.

2 Remove the giblets from inside the bird and if it is frozen, ensure that it thaws completely before cooking. An average-sized chicken (3–4 lb/1·5–1·75 kg) will need about 12 hours at room temperature.

3 Stuff the bird (see recipes page 48), weigh, then calculate cooking time.

4 Place the chicken in the roasting tin, baste with melted lard and roast for the required length of time.

Duck

1 Remove the giblets and thaw the bird, if necessary. A 4-lb/1·75-kg duck will thaw in about 12 hours at room temperature.

2 Stuff the duck with the desired stuffing, weigh, then calculate the cooking time. Preheat the oven.

3 Prick the surface all over with a fork, place the duck in the roasting tin and cook for the calculated time. No additional fat is required.

Goose

1 Follow the instructions given for duck, but insert a whole lemon

(unpeeled) with the stuffing to help counteract the richness of the bird.

Turkey

1 Remove the giblets and thaw the bird, if necessary – about 36 hours at room temperature for an average 12-lb/5·5-kg turkey – then weigh and calculate the cooking time.
2 Stuff the turkey.
3 Melt 2–3 tablespoons of fat in a roasting tin in a preheated oven.
4 Completely cover the legs and breast of the bird with rashers of fat bacon (about 1 lb/450 g will be needed), then place in the tin and cover loosely with foil before roasting.
5 Thirty minutes before the end of the cooking time, remove the foil and bacon to allow the bird to brown.

Pheasant

1 Melt 1–2 tablespoons of fat in a roasting tin in a preheated oven.
2 Cover the bird completely with rashers of streaky bacon (about 4 oz/100 g will be needed), then roast for the required length of time.
3 Fifteen minutes before the end of the cooking time remove the bacon, pour over ¼ pint/150 ml stock and return the pheasant to the oven.
4 When ready, remove the pheasant from the tin, skim the fat from the surface of the stock left in the tin, then pour the stock into a gravy boat for serving.

Poultry Roasting Chart

	Roasting time	Temperature	Ounces/grams per serving	Accompaniments
Chicken				
Fresh	20 mins. per lb/per half kilo	Gas mark 5 or 375°F/190°C	8–10 oz/225–275 g	Stuffing, bacon rolls and sausages, bread sauce, gravy
Frozen	20 mins. per lb/per half kilo plus 20 mins.	As above	As above	As above
Capon				
Fresh or frozen	20 mins. per lb/per half kilo	As above	8 oz/225 g	As above
Duck				
Fresh or frozen	25 mins. per lb/per half kilo	30 mins. at gas mark 6 or 400°F/200°C. Rest of time at gas mark 4 or 350°F/180°C	14–16 oz/400–450 g	Stuffing (traditionally sage and onion), apple sauce, orange salad, gravy
Goose				
Fresh or frozen	*Up to 6 lb/2·75 kg* 20 mins. per lb/per half kilo. *Over 6 lb/2·75 kg* 20 mins. per lb/per half kilo plus 20 mins.	Gas mark 5 or 375°F/190°C	12–14 oz/350–400 g	Stuffing, gooseberry sauce, bread sauce, gravy
Turkey				
Fresh or frozen	20 mins. per lb/per half kilo plus 20 mins.	*Up to 12 lb/5·5 kg* 1 hour at gas mark 6 or 400°F/200°C; rest of time at gas mark 4 or 350°F/180°C. *Over 12 lb/5·5 kg* 1 hour at gas mark 6 or 400°F/200°C; rest of time at gas mark 2 or 300°F/150°C	8–10 oz/225–275 g	Chestnut stuffing, bread sauce, cranberry sauce, boiled bacon, gravy
Pheasant				
Hen	50–60 mins.	Gas mark 4 or 350°F/180°C	6 oz/175 g	Fried breadcrumbs, game chips, bacon rolls, bread sauce, clear gravy
Cock	70–80 mins.	As above	As above	As above

Accompaniments for Roast Meat

Beef

Yorkshire Pudding

Serves 4–6

4 oz/110 g plain flour
A pinch of salt
1 large egg (size 2)
¼ pint/150 ml milk
¼ pint/150 ml water
2 tablespoons dripping from the roast
Small patty tins

Sift the flour and salt into a mixing bowl, break the egg into the centre and add the milk. Beating from the centre, gradually incorporate the flour into the liquid. Add a little of the water and continue beating until the batter is smooth and shiny, then add the rest of the water.

Spoon a little dripping in the base of each tin and fill them almost full with batter. Bake them on the top shelf of a fairly hot oven, gas mark 6 or 400°F/200°C, for about 20 to 25 minutes, until they are golden brown and well risen. Serve around the joint.

A large Yorkshire Pudding is cooked at the same temperature for 40 minutes.

Lamb

Mint Sauce

Mint leaves, removed from the stalks
Granulated sugar
2 tablespoons boiling water
Vinegar

Put the mint leaves on to a chopping board, sprinkle them with sugar, then chop very finely with a sharp knife – the sugar will enhance the flavour of the mint and make it easier to chop the leaves.

Put the chopped mint into a small bowl or sauceboat and stir in the boiling water. (This extracts the flavour from the mint and also dissolves the sugar.) Add the vinegar to suit your own taste.

The sauce can be stored in a small jar until required, but do not keep it for too long or the colour will deteriorate.

Pork

Sage and Onion Stuffing Balls

Makes 14

8 oz/225 g fresh white breadcrumbs
2 oz/50 g prepared shredded suet
Salt and pepper
1 medium onion, peeled and finely chopped
1 tablespoon chopped sage or 1 dessertspoon dried sage
1 large egg (size 2)
1 tablespoon milk

Mix the breadcrumbs with the suet and season with salt and pepper. Cook the chopped onion in boiling salted water for 2 to 3 minutes until it has softened slightly, then drain it thoroughly and stir into the breadcrumbs with the sage.

Beat the egg and milk together and use this to bind the dry ingredients. Divide the stuffing into 14 even pieces and roll each piece into a ball. Place around the roasting pork 45 minutes before the end of the cooking time.

To serve, arrange the Sage and Onion Stuffing Balls around the joint.

Roasts

Gravy

After the joint has been removed, drain almost all the dripping from the roasting tin. Stir a tablespoon of flour into the fat and cook it over a gentle heat until lightly browned. Remove the tin from the heat and very gradually blend in 1 pint/600 ml stock. When the gravy is smooth return the tin to the heat then, stirring all the time, bring it to the boil.

Check for seasoning, then turn the gravy into a sauceboat for serving.

Note Instead of stock the water from the vegetables can be used but do adjust the seasoning.

How to Joint a Chicken

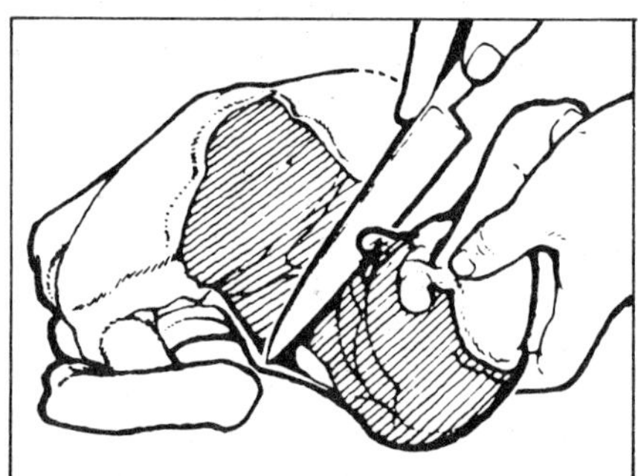

1 Using a sharp knife, first cut off the legs by cutting through the skin between the leg and breast on each side. Then pull back the leg to reveal the thigh bone and cut through the joint.

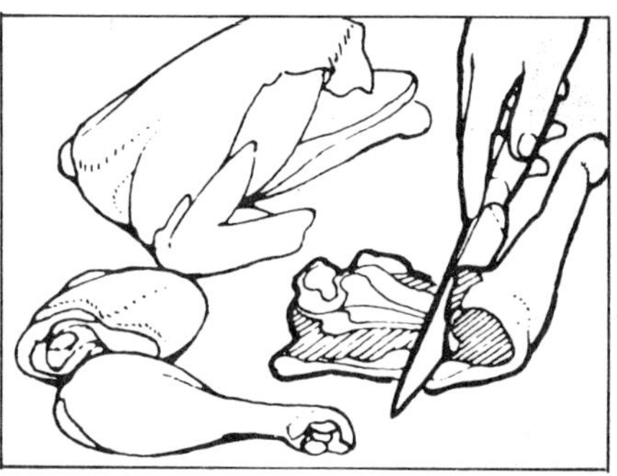

2 Cut each leg into two at the joint, between the thigh and drumstick.

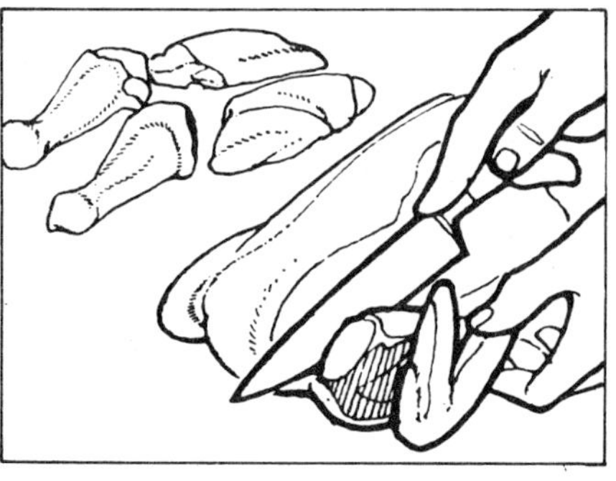

3 Remove the wings from the bird, cutting off a piece of breast with each.

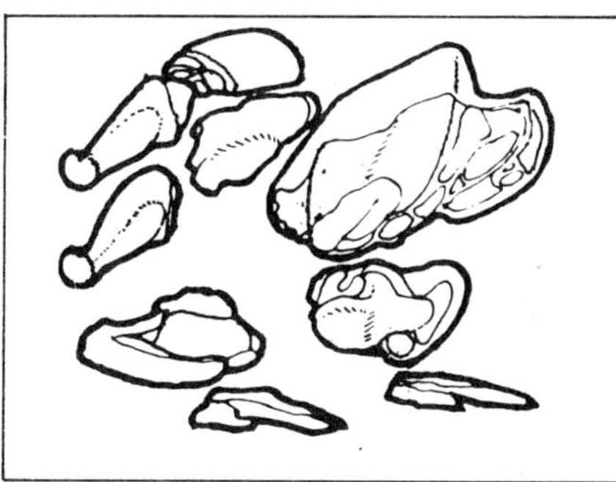

4 When both legs and wings have been removed, the chicken looks like this. Remove the wing tips from each wing and discard.

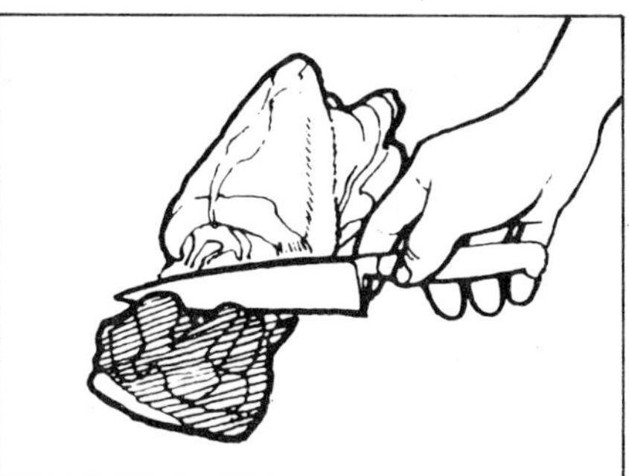

5 Take off the skin from the breast, then cut off the wishbone which is situated at the wing end of the breast; take some breast meat with the wishbone as you cut.

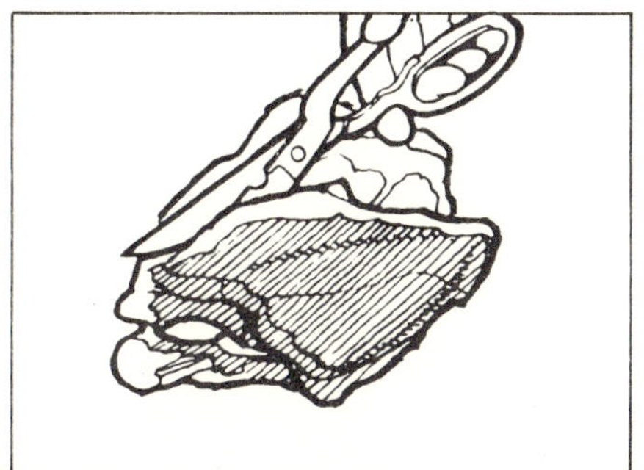

6 Turn the carcass on its side and, using a pair of scissors, cut through the rib cage to separate it from the breast meat. Turn the carcass over and cut the meat away from the backbone in one piece. Repeat with the other side.

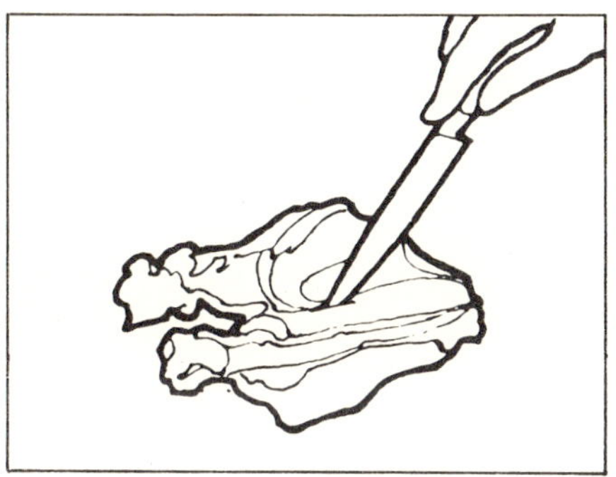

7 Finally, cut the breast meat in half down the centre. Use the carcass and bones for stock.

Capricorn Chicken

Capricorn Chicken

Serves 4

3–3½-lb/1·5-kg roasting chicken (trussed weight)
Salt and pepper
A generous pinch of dried rosemary
1 oz/25 g butter
¾ pint/450 ml cider
For the Sauce
½ pint/300 ml milk
1 small onion, peeled and sliced
1 small carrot, peeled and sliced
1 bay leaf
3 peppercorns
2 oz/50 g butter
2 oz/50 g flour
4 oz/100 g Cheddar cheese, grated
Salt and pepper

Wipe the chicken. Season the inside with salt, pepper and rosemary. Rub the butter over the breast of the chicken, then place in a roasting tin and pour over the cider. Roast the chicken in the centre of a moderately hot oven, gas mark 5 or 375°F/190°C, for about 1¼ hours, until cooked.

Pour the milk into a saucepan and add the onion, carrot, bay leaf and peppercorns and bring slowly to the boil. Remove the pan from the heat and leave it on one side for the milk to extract the flavours from the vegetables and seasoning.

When the chicken is cooked, remove from the tin and place on a board, reserving the chicken juices in the tin. Cut the chicken into nine joints as instructed on page 46. Arrange the joints in a heated flameproof dish and keep warm.

Remove any excess fat from the chicken juices. Strain the milk and make up to 1 pint/600 ml with the juices. Melt the butter in a pan, stir in the flour and add the milk. Bring to the boil, stirring all the time, and cook for 2 to 3 minutes. Remove the pan from the heat, stir in half the cheese, and check the sauce for seasoning.

Pour the sauce over the chicken and sprinkle the rest of the cheese over the top. Place the dish under a preheated grill and cook until golden brown and bubbly.

Serve immediately, garnished with watercress.

Freezing Note *Freeze the chicken after it has been coated with sauce for up to a month. Thaw, sprinkle with cheese then heat through in a moderate oven for 30 minutes or until golden brown.*

Chicken Pilau

Serves 4–6

3½-lb/1·5-kg roasting chicken (trussed weight)
2 oz/50 g butter
1 tablespoon curry powder
For the Rice Pilau
½ lb/225 g onions, peeled and sliced
2 oz/50 g butter
1 bay leaf
6 cloves
1 cinnamon stick
½ teaspoon turmeric powder
1 lb/450 g long-grain rice
2 pints/1·15 litres chicken stock
Salt and pepper
4 oz/100 g raisins, cleaned
2 oz/50 g salted peanuts
2 large hard-boiled eggs (size 2), shelled

Wipe the chicken and put into a roasting tin. Spread the butter over the legs and breast of the bird and sprinkle all over with the curry powder.

Roast the chicken in the centre of a fairly hot oven, gas mark 6 or 400°F/200°C, for 1¼ hours, until tender. Baste the bird several times so that the curry flavour penetrates into it.

Fry the onions in the butter until golden brown. Stir in the bay leaf, cloves, cinnamon stick and turmeric. Rinse the rice in cold water, add to the pan and, when it has absorbed the fat, pour in the boiling stock. Season the mixture, then cover tightly and cook the rice slowly, stirring occasionally until the rice has absorbed all the liquid and feels soft to the centre. Add the raisins.

Remove the chicken from the roasting tin and stir the curry flavoured juices into the rice. Using a sharp knife and a pair of scissors, cut the chicken into nine manageable joints as instructed on page 46.

Turn the rice on to a heated serving dish and nestle the chicken joints on top. Scatter over the peanuts, quarter the eggs and arrange on top of the rice. Accompany with a green salad.

Lemon and Herb Stuffing

Sufficient for a 3–4-lb/1·5–1·75-kg chicken

4 oz/100 g fresh white breadcrumbs
Grated rind of ½ lemon
1 dessertspoon chopped parsley
1 teaspoon chopped thyme or a pinch of dried thyme
1 oz/25 g prepared shredded suet
Salt and pepper
1 small onion
1 large egg (size 2), well beaten

Mix the breadcrumbs with the lemon rind, parsley, thyme, suet and seasoning. Peel and finely chop the onion, then stir into the ingredients and bind together with the egg. Use as required.

Oriental Stuffing

Sufficient for a 3–4-lb/1·5–1·75-kg chicken

3 oz/75 g long-grain rice
1 oz/25 g walnuts, chopped
1 oz/25 g raisins, cleaned
Salt and pepper
½ oz/15 g margarine
1 dessertspoon curry powder
1 small egg (size 4), well beaten

Cook the rice in a pan of boiling salted water for 12 minutes, or until a grain rubbed between the thumb and first finger feels soft to the centre. Drain the rice well then run cold water through the grains to separate them. Mix the walnuts and raisins into the rice and season to taste.

Melt the margarine in a pan over a low heat, add the curry powder and fry it for 2 minutes to develop the flavour. Mix this into the rice then bind the ingredients together with the egg. Use the stuffing as required.

Apricot and Ham Stuffing

Sufficient for a 3–4-lb/1·5–1·75-kg chicken

1 oz/25 g dried apricots
2 oz/50 g ham, chopped
3 oz/75 g fresh white breadcrumbs
Salt and pepper
1 small egg (size 4), well beaten

Cover the apricots with cold water and leave them to soak overnight.

Next day, drain the apricots, chop them finely and mix with the ham, breadcrumbs and plenty of season-

ing. Bind the ingredients together with the egg, then use as required.

Middle Eastern Chicken

Serves 4–5

5-oz/142-g can tomato purée
$\frac{1}{2}$ pint/300 ml water
2 teaspoons ground coriander
$\frac{1}{4}$ teaspoon salt
Pepper
4-lb/1·75-kg roasting chicken (trussed weight)
1 large aubergine, thickly sliced
1 lb/450 g courgettes, cut into chunks
1 large onion, peeled and sliced
1 green pepper, seeded and cut into strips
A large roasting tin

Duck à l'Orange, Roast Chicken with Lemon and Herb Stuffing, Oriental Stuffing and Apricot and Ham Stuffing

Mix the tomato purée with the water and leave to stand for 2 hours, then stir in the coriander, salt and pepper.

Season the inside of the chicken, then arrange the prepared vegetables in the base of the roasting tin and place the chicken on top. Pour the tomato purée mixture over the chicken, turn the vegetables over, then add a further $\frac{1}{4}$ pint/150 ml water if the liquid is not sufficient to coat them.

Bake the chicken, uncovered, just above the centre of a moderate oven, gas mark 4 or 350°F/180°C, for $1\frac{1}{4}$ to $1\frac{1}{2}$ hours, until the bird is cooked. Baste the chicken, turning the vegetables over in the tomato liquid two or three times during cooking.

Serve the chicken on a platter surrounded by the vegetables.

Duck à l'Orange

Serves 4

4–$4\frac{1}{2}$-lb/1·75–2-kg roasting duck (trussed weight)
For the Sauce
3 large oranges
$14\frac{1}{2}$-oz/411-g can consommé soup
2 tablespoons cornflour
1 dessertspoon malt vinegar
1 dessertspoon demerara sugar
1 tablespoon sherry
Salt and pepper

Prepare and roast the duck as instructed on page 44.

Pare the rind thinly from one orange (a potato peeler is ideal for this) and cut it into very thin strips. Pour the soup into a pan with the orange rind, bring to the boil, then reduce and simmer for 15 minutes.

Meanwhile, peel the remaining oranges by working spirally around each one, cutting just below the rind but above the flesh. Divide the oranges into segments between the membranes, removing the pith, and keep to one side.

Blend the cornflour to a paste with the vinegar, stir in a little of the hot soup then add it to the soup in the pan. Bring the sauce to the boil over a low heat, stirring all the time, and cook until it thickens. Stir in the sugar, sherry, juice from the pared orange and seasoning.

When the duck is cooked, cut it into quarters by first cutting across the centre and down between the leg and wing on each side. Cut along the centre of the breast bone and slip the knife down between the meat and bone. Sever the wings and legs at their joints to make four pieces, and arrange them on a serving plate, keeping them warm. Strain the fat from the tin and stir any sediment left in the bottom into the sauce. Reheat the sauce, pour it over the duck and garnish each portion with orange segments. Any extra sauce can be served separately, along with an orange salad.

Casseroles and Stews

Beef with Dumplings

Serves 4–5

2 lb / 1 kg shin of beef
1 oz / 25 g plain flour, seasoned with salt and pepper
1 oz / 25 g dripping or lard
1½ pints / 900 ml beef stock
1 lb / 450 g potatoes
½ lb / 225 g carrots
¼ lb / 100 g parsnips
½ lb / 225 g onions
Chopped parsley for garnish
For the Dumplings
9 oz / 250 g self-raising flour
Salt and pepper
4 oz / 100 g prepared shredded suet
A 4-pint / 2·25-litre flameproof casserole dish

Using a sharp knife, remove any fat from the beef. Cut the meat into pieces about 1-inch / 2·5-cm square and toss them in the seasoned flour.

Melt the fat in a frying pan and add a few pieces of meat at a time, browning them quickly on all sides. Transfer them to the casserole dish when they are ready. When all the meat is browned, remove the pan from the heat and stir in the rest of the seasoned flour, then gradually blend in the stock. Return to the heat and, stirring all the time, bring the sauce to the boil and boil for a few moments to cook the flour. Check the sauce for seasoning before pouring it over the meat. Cover the casserole, place over a low heat and simmer for about 2 hours.

Meanwhile, peel the potatoes, carrots and parsnips and cut them all into quarters. Peel the onions and leave them whole if they are not too large, otherwise halve them. After the casserole has simmered for 2 hours, add all the vegetables and continue cooking for a further 30 minutes.

Beef with Dumplings

Make the dumplings. Sift the flour, salt and pepper into a mixing bowl and stir in the shredded suet with enough cold water to make a soft but not sticky dough. Divide the dough into six even pieces and roll them into balls between floured hands. Bring the casserole to the boil and place the dumplings in the liquid, then replace the lid and cook the dumplings for about 15 minutes without removing the lid.

Serve the casserole immediately, garnished with a little chopped parsley.

Note The casserole can be cooked in the oven but, in this case, add all the vegetables at the beginning. Cook at gas mark 3 or 325°F / 160°C, for about 2½ hours before adding the dumplings, which will take a further 30 minutes to cook.

Freezing Note *Freeze the casserole after it has cooked for 2 hours, that is before the vegetables and dumplings are added. It will keep for up to 3 months. Thaw, then bring back to the boil, add the vegetables and continue to cook as in the recipe.*

Boeuf Stroganoff

Serves 5

$1\frac{3}{4}$ lb / 800 g chuck steak
2 medium onions
$\frac{1}{2}$ lb / 225 g button mushrooms
1 oz / 25 g butter
3 tablespoons cooking oil
Salt and pepper
8 oz / 225 g long-grain rice
5-fl oz / 142-ml carton soured cream
1 tablespoon chopped parsley

Using a sharp knife, remove any fat and gristle from the meat then cut it into thin strips about $1\frac{1}{2}$–2 inches / 3·5–5 cm long. Peel and finely chop the onions, and wipe and slice the mushrooms.

Heat half the butter and oil in a saucepan, add the onions and fry gently until they are tender and lightly browned. Add the sliced mushrooms and continue to fry for a further 3 to 4 minutes; remove from the pan and put to one side.

Heat the rest of the butter and oil in the same pan, add the meat and fry it briskly over a high heat for about 5 minutes, turning it frequently until brown. Return the vegetables to the pan, season with salt and pepper and cover the pan. Reduce the heat and simmer the Boeuf Stroganoff for about 30 minutes, stirring it occasionally, until the meat is tender (you will find as the ingredients cook their juices will form the sauce).

While the meat is cooking, boil the rice. Have ready a saucepan half-filled with boiling salted water. Wash the rice, then put it in the pan, reduce the heat and simmer for about 12 minutes. To test if the rice is cooked, rub a grain between the thumb and first finger; if you can feel a hard core the rice is not ready and should be cooked for a little longer, but if the rice feels soft, drain it thoroughly, then run hot water through to separate the grains. Turn the rice into a heated serving dish.

When the meat is tender, stir in all but 2 tablespoons of the soured cream and turn the Boeuf Stroganoff into a heated serving dish. Spoon the rest of the cream on top and sprinkle with the chopped parsley. Serve immediately.

Boiled Beef and Carrots

Boiled Beef and Carrots

Serves 6

4 lb / 1·75 kg salt brisket of beef
1 bay leaf
$1\frac{1}{2}$ lb / 675 g carrots, peeled and quartered if too large
1 lb / 450 g small onions, peeled
$\frac{3}{4}$ lb / 350 g parsnips or swedes, peeled and cut into pieces
For the Dumplings
12 oz / 350 g self-raising flour
A generous pinch of salt
5 oz / 150 g prepared shredded suet

Cover the beef with cold water and leave to soak overnight.

Weigh the joint and calculate the cooking time by allowing 30 minutes per pound / per half kilo, plus an extra 30 minutes.

Put the beef into a pan with the bay leaf, cover the meat with water and slowly bring to the boil. Cover the pan and simmer the meat for the required cooking time, starting from the time when the liquid boils. Add the prepared vegetables $1\frac{1}{2}$ hours before the beef is ready.

Sift the flour and salt into a mixing bowl, stir in the shredded suet and mix in enough cold water to make a soft dough. Flour your hands, divide the dough into 12 portions and roll each into a ball. Twenty minutes before the end of the cooking time, bring the liquid to the boil and put in the dumplings. Cover the pan, reduce the heat and simmer for about 20 minutes, until the dumplings are well risen and cooked.

To serve, lift out the meat and arrange it on a serving plate with the vegetables and dumplings.

Note The liquor in which the meat was cooked can be used as the gravy, but check the flavour for seasoning before serving.

Beef Olives

Serves 4

1 lb/450 g topside of beef, cut into 4 slices
2 oz/50 g lard

For the Stuffing

3 oz/75 g fresh white breadcrumbs
1 oz/25 g prepared shredded suet
2 oz/50 g mushrooms
1 tomato (reserved from the can used in the sauce)
Salt and pepper
1 large egg (size 2)

For the Sauce

1½ oz/40 g plain flour
¾ pint/450 ml beef stock
1 tablespoon tomato purée
8-oz/227-g can tomatoes
2 oz/50 g mushrooms
Salt and pepper
A bouquet garni (bought, or made from a bay leaf, sprig of thyme and some parsley, tied together with string)
Wooden cocktail sticks
A 2½-pint/1·5-litre casserole dish

Place the slices of beef, one at a time, between two sheets of wet greaseproof paper and, using a rolling pin, bang the meat so that it doubles in size. Cut each slice in half to make eight pieces in all.

Mix the breadcrumbs for the stuffing with the suet. Wipe the mushrooms, trim the stalks and chop into small pieces. Chop the reserved tomato from the can. Stir these ingredients into the stuffing with seasoning to taste and bind all together with the egg.

Lay the slices of meat on a work surface and divide the stuffing between them. Roll up each piece and secure it firmly with a cocktail stick. Melt the lard in a pan and fry the Beef Olives quickly so that they brown evenly. When each one is cooked transfer it to the casserole dish.

Stir the flour into the fat remaining in the pan, off the heat, and gradually blend in the stock. When the sauce is smooth, return the pan to the heat and, stirring all the time, bring it to the boil. Stir in the tomato purée and the tomatoes. Wipe and trim the mushrooms, cut into slices and stir into the sauce. Check the sauce for seasoning, pour over the Beef Olives, then add the bouquet garni and cover the dish.

Cook the Beef Olives on the centre shelf of a moderate oven, gas mark 4 or 350°F/180°C, for 1½ hours, until the meat is tender. Serve with potatoes and peas.

Freezing Note *Store cooked for up to 3 months. Thaw, then reheat in a moderate oven for about 30 minutes, stirring occasionally.*

Aunt Emily's Casserole

Serves 4–5

8 oz/225 g noodles
1 lb/450 g minced beef
½ lb/225 g sausagemeat
1 medium onion, peeled and chopped
15¼-oz/432-g can tomato soup
2 oz/50 g cream cheese
1 tablespoon Worcestershire sauce
Salt and pepper
¼ lb/100 g mushrooms, wiped and sliced
A 4-pint/2·25-litre casserole dish

Cook the noodles in a pan of boiling salted water for 10 to 15 minutes, until they feel soft. Drain them well and run hot water through the strands to separate them.

Fry the minced beef and sausagemeat in a pan, mixing them together as they cook. Add the onion and continue cooking until the meats change colour. Stir in the soup with the cheese, cut into cubes, the Worcestershire sauce, seasoning and sliced mushrooms. Bring to the boil so that the cheese melts.

Turn the noodles into the casserole dish and ease them to the sides. Pour the mince mixture on top and bake the casserole, covered, on the centre shelf of a moderate oven, gas mark 4 or 350°F/180°C, for about 30 minutes, until tender.

Hungarian Goulash

Hungarian Goulash

Serves 4

$1\frac{1}{2}$ lb/675 g shin of beef
2 medium onions
1 clove garlic
Salt
2 oz/50 g lard
2 tablespoons plain flour
2 tablespoons paprika pepper
1 teaspoon dried mixed herbs
8-oz/227-g can tomatoes
$\frac{1}{2}$ pint/300 ml beef stock or water
$\frac{1}{2}$ teaspoon caraway seeds
1 lb/450 g potatoes, peeled and cut into chunks
5-fl oz/142-ml carton natural yogurt
1 green pepper, seeded and sliced
A 3-pint/1·75-litre casserole dish

1 Cut the meat into 1-inch/2·5-cm pieces, removing any excess fat. Peel and chop the onions. Peel the garlic and crush it to a paste with plenty of salt.

2 Melt the fat in a pan and fry the meat quickly and lightly in two batches until evenly brown. Transfer the meat to the casserole dish, then fry the onion and garlic in the remaining fat.

3 Mix the flour, paprika pepper and herbs together then stir them into the onion and garlic. When they are mixed, blend in the tomatoes and carefully stir in the stock or water.

4 Bring the mixture to the boil, stirring all the time. When it has thickened, pour it over the meat and sprinkle with the caraway seeds. Cover the dish.

5 Cook the Goulash in a moderately cool oven, gas mark 3 or 325°F/160°C, for 1 hour 50 minutes, then remove from the oven and stir in the potatoes.

6 Cook the Goulash, covered, for a further 45 minutes. Just before serving, mix in the yogurt and green pepper. Sprinkle with a little extra paprika and serve the dish with creamed potatoes or plain boiled rice.

Spanish Casserole

Serves 6–8

$2\frac{1}{2}$–3 lb/1·25–1·5 kg spare rib of pork
1 oz/25 g lard
1 large onion, peeled and sliced
$\frac{1}{4}$ lb/100 g mushrooms
3 dessertspoons plain flour
$\frac{3}{4}$ pint/450 ml stock
$\frac{1}{4}$ pint/150 ml white wine or dry cider
Salt and pepper
$\frac{1}{4}$ lb/100 g ham, sliced
12 stuffed green olives
A 3-pint/1·75-litre casserole dish

Using a sharp knife, remove the rind, any excess fat and all the bones from the meat, then cut it into 1-inch/2·5-cm pieces.

Heat the lard in a pan, add the meat a third at a time and brown the pieces over a high heat. Transfer them to the casserole dish when they are ready. Next, fry the onion over a fairly high heat. Wipe, trim and slice the mushrooms, add them to the onion and fry the two ingredients together until they start to colour. Remove the pan from the heat and stir in the flour, then gradually blend in the stock and wine or cider. When the sauce is smooth, return the pan to the heat and, stirring all the time, bring the sauce to the boil and check it for seasoning. Cut the ham into strips and stir into the sauce with the olives. Pour the sauce over the meat, cover the casserole and cook on the centre shelf of a moderate oven, gas mark 4 or 350°F/180°C, for $1\frac{1}{4}$ hours, until the pork is tender.

Check for seasoning, then serve with creamed potatoes and peas.

Freezing Note *Freeze for up to 4 months. Thaw, then reheat in a moderate oven, gas mark 4 or 350°F/180°C, for about 30 to 45 minutes, stirring occasionally.*

Pennywise Hot Pot

Serves 4

$\frac{3}{4}$ lb/350 g belly of pork
1 oz/25 g dripping
$\frac{1}{2}$ lb/225 g onions, peeled and sliced
1 lb/450 g cabbage, washed and shredded
2 tablespoons plain flour
2 tablespoons vinegar
$\frac{1}{2}$ pint/300 ml stock
Salt and pepper
2 tablespoons demerara sugar
$1\frac{1}{2}$ lb/675 g potatoes, peeled and halved
1 oz/25 g butter, melted
A 3-pint/1·75-litre casserole dish

Cut the pork into $\frac{1}{2}$-inch/1-cm pieces, removing the rind and any pieces of bone. Melt the dripping in a deep saucepan and fry the meat quickly until brown all over, then remove from the pan.

Add the onion to the fat remaining in the pan and fry it slowly so that it starts to cook but does not turn brown. Stir in the cabbage and continue frying gently, turning occasionally, until all the fat has been absorbed. Mix in the flour, vinegar, stock, seasoning and sugar, and bring to the boil. Stir in the meat and transfer it all to the casserole dish. Cover with the halved potatoes and brush them completely with the melted butter.

Bake the Pennywise Hot Pot on the centre shelf of a moderate oven, gas mark 4 or 350°F/180°C, for $1\frac{1}{2}$ hours, until the potatoes are golden brown.

Serve piping hot.

Pennywise Hot Pot

Lancashire Hot Pot

Ploughman's Casserole

Serves 1

$\frac{1}{2}$ lb/225 g belly of pork
1 tablespoon plain flour
Salt and pepper
$\frac{1}{2}$ teaspoon dried mixed herbs
1 tablespoon cooking oil
1 small onion, peeled and sliced
1 small apple, peeled, cored and sliced
1 oz/25 g seedless raisins, cleaned
1 oz/25 g small pasta shells
$\frac{1}{2}$ pint/300 ml stock
A 1-pint/600-ml casserole dish

Using a sharp knife, remove the bones and any excess fat from the pork and cut the meat into $\frac{1}{2}$-inch/1-cm pieces. Mix the flour with the salt, pepper and herbs and toss the pieces of meat in it to coat them.

Heat the oil in a frying pan, add the onion and fry it over a low heat until the slices start to soften, then add the meat and cook the pieces quickly to seal them. Turn the onion and meat into the casserole dish, mix in the apple slices, raisins and pasta, then pour in the stock. Cover and cook on the shelf below the centre of a moderately hot oven, gas mark 5 or 375°F/190°C, for 1 hour, until the meat is tender.

Lancashire Hot Pot

Serves 5–6

2–2$\frac{1}{2}$ lb/1–1·25 kg best end neck of lamb, chopped by the butcher
2 lamb's kidneys
Salt and pepper
1 teaspoon curry powder
1$\frac{1}{4}$ lb/575 g potatoes, peeled
$\frac{3}{4}$ lb/350 g onions, peeled and sliced
$\frac{1}{2}$ pint/300 ml stock
A little melted butter
A 4-pint/2·25-litre casserole dish

Trim the meat, cutting off any excess fat, and remove the white spinal cord that runs along the backbone. Put a layer of meat in the casserole dish. Peel the skin off the kidneys, then cut them in half and remove the cores. Cut each half into thin slices. Lay some of the kidney slices over the meat and season with salt and pepper and curry powder.

Cut six small potatoes in half and slice the rest fairly thinly. Arrange a layer of sliced potato and onion on top of the kidneys. Season once again with more salt, pepper and curry powder, and continue layering all the ingredients into the dish until they are used up. Pour over the stock. Top with the halved potatoes and brush them with the melted butter.

Do not cover the dish but cook on the centre shelf of a moderate oven, gas mark 4 or 350°F/180°C, for 2$\frac{1}{4}$ to 2$\frac{1}{2}$ hours.

Irish Stew

Serves 4

1$\frac{1}{2}$ lb/675 g potatoes, peeled and sliced
Salt and pepper
1 lb/450 g onions, sliced
2 tablespoons chopped parsley
8 middle neck of lamb chops
1 chicken stock cube
$\frac{1}{4}$ pint/150 ml hot water
$\frac{1}{4}$ pint/150 ml milk
Parsley for garnish
A 4-pint/2·25-litre casserole dish

Layer half the potatoes in the bottom of the casserole dish and season generously. Cover with half the onions and sprinkle over half the parsley. Arrange the chops on top, sprinkle with seasoning and the rest of the parsley. Top with the remaining onions and then the potatoes, seasoning well.

Dissolve the stock cube in the water, then stir in the milk and pour into the casserole dish. Cover with the lid or foil and cook for 2 hours in a moderately cool oven, gas mark 3 or 325°F/160°C, until the potatoes and meat are tender.

Garnish the Irish Stew with parsley, if liked.

Romany Lamb Casserole

Serves 4–5

2 lb/1 kg middle neck of lamb, chopped by the butcher
1 oz/25 g dripping or lard
1 medium onion, peeled and sliced
2 tablespoons plain flour
1 teaspoon ground cinnamon
2 tablespoons demerara sugar
1 lb 12-oz/793-g can tomatoes
Salt and pepper
1 bay leaf
A 4–5-pint/2·25–3-litre casserole dish

Cut off any excess fat and gristle from the meat. Melt the fat in a frying pan, add the meat and fry the pieces over a fairly high heat so that they brown quickly. Turn the meat frequently and, when it is evenly browned, transfer the pieces to the casserole dish.

Add the onion to the fat remaining in the pan and fry it slowly so that the slices start to cook but do not brown. Stir in the flour, cinnamon, sugar and tomatoes and bring the mixture to the boil. Check for seasoning, add the bay leaf and pour it over the meat. Cover the casserole with a tight-fitting lid and cook on the centre shelf of a moderately cool oven, gas mark 3 or 325°F/160°C, for 1½ to 1¾ hours, until the meat is really tender.

Freezing Note *Freeze for up to 2 months. Thaw, then reheat gently for about 20 minutes, stirring occasionally until thoroughly hot.*

Lamb Curry

Serves 6

2½ lb/1·25 kg shoulder of lamb
½ lb/225 g onions, peeled and sliced
1½ oz/40 g margarine
1 tablespoon turmeric powder
2 tablespoons curry powder
1 teaspoon ground ginger
¼ pint/150 ml beef stock
1½ teaspoons salt
5-fl oz/142-ml carton soured cream
2 oz/50 g blanched almonds
10 oz/275 g long-grain rice

Cut the meat from the bones, removing any excess fat, then cut it into 1-inch/2·5-cm pieces.

Cook the onions slowly in 1 oz/25 g margarine until they start to soften. Stir in the turmeric, curry powder and ginger, then add the rest of the margarine and, when it has melted, stir in the meat. Increase the heat and, stirring occasionally, brown the meat on all sides. Remove from the heat and stir in the stock and salt. Bring the liquid to the boil, then reduce the heat, cover the pan and simmer the curry for 45 minutes, until the meat is tender. Stir in the soured cream and almonds, then cook the curry for 10 minutes more.

Meanwhile, cook the rice in boiling salted water for about 12 minutes. Drain and run hot water through the grains, then turn the rice into a heated serving dish and spoon the lamb curry into the centre.

Serve the curry with a selection of accompaniments.

Freezing Note *Store the curry before the cream and almonds are added. It will keep for up to 3 months. Thaw, then reheat and continue as in the recipe.*

Romany Lamb Casserole

Coq au Vin

Serves 4–6

4–5-lb/1·75–2·25 kg roasting chicken (trussed weight)
1 oz/25 g butter
1 tablespoon cooking oil
1 clove garlic
Salt and pepper
¼-lb/100-g gammon rasher
½ lb/225 g small pickling onions, peeled (or larger onions, peeled and sliced)
¼ lb/100 g mushrooms
A bouquet garni (bought, or made from a bay leaf, blade of mace, parsley stalk and sprig of thyme, tied together with string)
1 oz/25 g plain flour
½ bottle inexpensive red wine
7½ fl oz/225 ml chicken stock

For the Garnish

2 slices white bread
A little lard
A 4-pint/2·25-litre casserole dish

First joint the chicken as instructed on page 46. Cook the giblets gently in water to make stock.

Heat the butter and oil in a frying pan, add the chicken joints a few at a time, and fry briskly until golden brown. Transfer them to the casserole dish when they are ready.

Peel the clove of garlic and, using a palette knife, crush the clove to a paste with plenty of salt. Cut the gammon into 1-inch/2·5-cm pieces and add to the frying pan with the garlic and prepared onions. Fry until golden brown. Wipe and trim the mushrooms – there is no need to peel them – and put them into the casserole dish with the bouquet garni and onion mixture.

Stir the flour into the fat remaining in the pan and gradually blend in the wine and strained stock. Return the pan to the heat and, stirring all the time, bring the sauce to the boil. Check for seasoning, then pour it over the chicken. Cover and cook on the centre shelf of a moderately cool oven, gas mark 3 or 325°F/160°C, for 1½ to 2 hours, until the chicken is tender.

Just before the dish is ready, cut the crusts off the bread and cut each

Coq au Vin

slice into four triangles. Melt the lard in a frying pan and fry the bread triangles until they are golden brown on both sides.

When the Coq au Vin is cooked, remove it from the oven, take out the bouquet garni and scatter the bread triangles over the surface. Serve with Duchesse potatoes and peas.

Freezing Note *Freeze the cooked casserole for up to a month. Thaw, then reheat on the top of the stove or in a moderate oven, gas mark 4 or 350°F/180°C, for 30 minutes. Prepare the bread for garnish as described in the recipe.*

London Time Casserole

Serves 4

- 3–3½-lb/1·5-kg roasting chicken (trussed weight)
- 1 tablespoon oil
- 4 sticks celery
- 2 tablespoons plain flour
- ¾ pint/450 ml chicken stock
- Salt and pepper
- 7½-oz/213-g can prunes
- 1 oz/25 g walnuts, roughly chopped
- *A 2-pint/1·25-litre casserole dish*

First joint the chicken as instructed on page 46.

Heat the oil in a frying pan, add the chicken joints a few at a time, and fry the pieces quickly and lightly so they brown on all sides. Transfer the chicken pieces to the casserole dish when ready.

Trim and chop the celery and add the pieces to the fat still in the pan. When they start to soften, stir in the flour. Remove the pan from the heat and gradually blend in the stock to make a smooth sauce. Return to the heat and stir the sauce constantly until it boils and thickens. Check for seasoning, then pour over the chicken and cover the dish. Cook on the centre shelf of a moderately cool oven, gas mark 3 or 325°F/160°C, for 1 hour.

Meanwhile, drain the prunes, reserving 3 tablespoons of the juice, then carefully remove the stones. When the cooking time is up for the chicken, remove the dish from the oven and stir in the prunes, reserved juice and the chopped walnuts. Check the sauce for seasoning, then recover the dish and return to the oven for a further 15 minutes, until the chicken is tender.

Freezing Note *Store the chicken before the prunes and nuts are added. Keep for up to 3 months. Thaw, then reheat and continue as in the recipe.*

Liver and Apricot Casserole

Serves 4–5

- 1 lb/450 g lamb's liver
- 1 oz/25 g plain flour, seasoned with salt and pepper
- 1 oz/25 g margarine
- ¼ lb/100 g streaky bacon rashers
- 2 medium onions, peeled and sliced
- ¾ pint/450 ml stock
- 2 oz/50 g dried apricots, soaked overnight
- Salt and pepper
- *A 3-pint/1·75-litre casserole dish*

Trim the liver, cut it into 1-inch/2·5-cm pieces, then toss them in the seasoned flour. Melt the margarine in a pan. Cut the rind and any small bones from the bacon, then dice the rashers and fry them for 1 minute. Add the onions and fry for a further minute, then add the liver and fry all the ingredients until the liver is brown.

Gradually blend in the stock and bring the mixture to the boil. Stir in the apricots and add seasoning to taste. Turn the mixture into the casserole and cook it on the centre shelf of a moderately hot oven, gas mark 5 or 375°F/190°C, for about 45 minutes, until the liver is tender.

Oxtail Stew

Serves 4

- 2–3 lb/1–1·5 kg oxtail, cut into pieces by the butcher
- 1 oz/25 g dripping
- 1 lb/450 g leeks
- 1 lb/450 g carrots
- 1 stick celery
- 2 oz/50 g plain flour
- 1 pint/600 ml beef stock
- Salt and pepper
- *A 4-pint/2·25-litre casserole dish*

Using a sharp knife, trim off any fat from the pieces of oxtail. Melt the dripping in a large frying pan, add the oxtail and fry the pieces over a fairly high heat until brown all over. Transfer them to a plate.

Meanwhile, prepare the vegetables. Trim the leeks, removing any damaged leaves, then split them down the centre nearly to the root and run cold water through the leaves to remove any particles of dirt or sand. Cut the leeks into 1-inch/2·5-cm lengths. Wash, peel and slice the carrots, and scrub and slice the celery. Put all the vegetables into the casserole with the browned oxtail on top.

Remove the frying pan from the heat and stir the flour into the remaining fat, then gradually blend in the stock. When the sauce is smooth, return to the heat and, stirring all the time, bring to the boil. Check for seasoning then pour the sauce over the meat and vegetables. Cover the casserole and cook the Oxtail Stew on the centre shelf of a moderate oven, gas mark 4 or 350°F/180°C, for 1 hour, then reduce the heat to gas mark 2 or 300°F/150°C, for a further 2 hours, or until the meat is really tender.

Serve the Oxtail Stew with potatoes and Brussels sprouts.

Freezing Note *Store for up to 3 months. Thaw, then reheat in a moderate oven for about 1 hour, stirring occasionally.*

Puddings and Pies

Steak and Kidney Pie

Serves 5

For the Rough Puff Pastry
6 oz / 175 g plain flour
A pinch of salt
2 oz / 55 g margarine
2 oz / 55 g lard
Beaten egg for glaze
For the Filling
1½ lb / 675 g chuck steak
6 oz / 175 g ox kidney
2 tablespoons plain flour, seasoned with salt and pepper
1 large onion, peeled and sliced
¼ pint / 150 ml beef stock
A 2½-pint / 1·5-litre pie dish
A pie funnel

Sift the flour and salt into a mixing bowl. Cut the fats into pieces about the size of a walnut and *stir* them into the flour, then mix in enough cold water to make a fairly soft dough. Turn the dough on to a well floured work surface and, using a floured rolling pin, roll the dough into a long and narrow rectangle. Fold the two shorter ends to the centre and then fold one half over the other. Seal the edges and turn the pastry once anti-clockwise, then roll it out again and fold it once more in the same way. Wrap the pastry in a piece of greaseproof paper and leave it in a cool place to rest for about 20 minutes. Repeat the process of rolling, folding and chilling twice more, by which time the pastry should be very smooth in appearance and ready to use.

Using a sharp knife, remove the fat from the meat and cut it into 1-inch/2·5-cm pieces. Remove the core from the kidney and cut into fairly small pieces. Put the seasoned flour into a polythene bag, add the meats and shake until well coated with the flour. Stand a pie funnel in the centre of the pie dish, and arrange the meat and onion around it. Pour over the stock.

Roll out the pastry 1 inch/2·5 cm larger all round than the top of the dish. Cut off a 1-inch/2·5-cm wide strip from around the edges, moisten the rim of the dish with a little water and lay the strip on it. Lift the lid over the pie to make sure it is large enough to allow for a ¼-inch/5-mm overlap – if too small roll the pastry out a little more (but do not try to stretch it or it will shrink during cooking). Brush the pastry rim with a little water and lift the lid into position, pressing the edges firmly together. Trim off any surplus pastry with a sharp knife. Knock up the edges with the back of a knife, then flute them at 1½-inch/3·5-cm intervals. Reroll the trimmings into a 1-inch/2·5-cm wide strip and cut out five diamond shapes for leaves. Brush the entire surface of the pie with beaten egg, then arrange the leaves in the centre and glaze these with beaten egg as well.

Leave the pie in a cool place for at least 30 minutes as this will help to prevent the pastry from shrinking during cooking. Bake the pie on the centre shelf of a hot oven, gas mark 7 or 425°F/220°C, for 20 minutes, then reduce the heat to gas mark 2 or 300°F/150°C, for a further 1½ hours, or until the meat is tender when tested with a skewer. If, after the first hour the top of the pie is becoming too brown, cover it with a double layer of greaseproof paper.

Freezing Note *Freeze the cooked pie for up to a month. Thaw, then reheat at gas mark 6 or 400°F/200°C for 20 to 30 minutes, to heat the filling and crisp the pastry.*

Steak and Kidney Pie

Steak and Kidney Pudding

Serves 5–6

For the Suet Crust Pastry
12 oz/350 g self-raising flour
A pinch of salt
5 oz/150 g prepared shredded suet
For the Filling
$1\frac{1}{2}$ lb/675 g chuck steak
$\frac{1}{4}$ lb/100 g ox kidney
2 tablespoons plain flour, seasoned with salt and pepper
4 tablespoons beef stock
A $2\frac{1}{2}$-pint/1·5-litre pudding basin, greased

1 Using a sharp knife, cut the meat into very thin slices and the kidney into small pieces. Roll a strip of meat around each piece of kidney, then toss the rolls in the seasoned flour.

2 Sift the flour and salt together, stir in the suet and add enough water to make a fairly soft dough. On a lightly floured surface, roll the dough into a large circle and cut out a quarter.

Steak and Kidney Pudding

3 Grease the pudding basin, then, using the larger piece of dough, carefully line the base and sides, so the pastry extends just above the rim. Fill with the meat and stock.

4 Roll the remaining quarter of dough into a circle the diameter of the top of the basin, moisten the rim of the pastry then lift the lid into place, pressing the edges together really well.

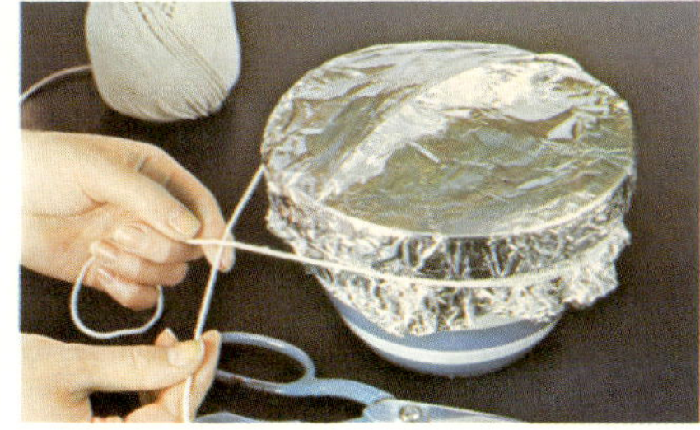

5 Make a $1\frac{1}{2}$-inch/3·5-cm pleat down the centre of a piece of foil and fasten it over the pudding. Make a string handle so the basin can be easily removed from the steamer.

6 Cook the pudding in a saucepan of boiling water that comes only half-way up the sides of the basin, or in a double steamer, for $3\frac{1}{2}$ hours. Refill with boiling water when needed.

Raised Pork Pie

Serves 6–8

For the Hot Water Crust Pastry

5 oz / 150 g lard

½ pint / 300 ml cold water

1 lb / 450 g plain flour

1½ teaspoons salt

Beaten egg for glaze

For the Filling

1½ lb / 675 g pie pork, trimmed and finely chopped

1 medium onion, peeled and finely chopped

1 tablespoon dried mixed herbs

Salt and pepper

1 teaspoon powdered gelatine

¼ pint / 150 ml chicken stock

A 6-inch / 15-cm round loose-bottomed tin

Melt the lard, add the water and bring to the boil. Then, using a fork, stir the liquid into the sifted flour and salt to make a dough that is soft in consistency.

When the dough is cool enough to

handle, knead until smooth and leave a quarter of it covered in the bowl so it remains warm. Line the base and sides of the cake tin with the remainder.

Mix together the pork, onion, herbs and seasoning, turn into the tin and spread level. Roll the reserved pastry to make a lid and place it in position.

Seal the edges firmly then, using scissors, trim off the surplus pastry and make it into a tassel for decoration. Crimp the edges with the thumb and two fingers. Put the tassel on top. Make two holes to allow steam to escape then brush the pastry with beaten egg. Bake the pie in a hot oven, gas mark 7 or 425°F/220°C, for 30 minutes, then reduce to gas mark 5 or 375°F/190°C for 1½ hours, until golden brown.

Cool in the tin for about 2 hours then leave on a wire rack to get completely cold.

Lastly, dissolve the gelatine in the stock. Carefully pour it through the steam vents into the centre of the pie to fill up any gaps around the meat. Leave to set then serve with a salad.

Pork and Prune Pie

Serves 4

For the Quick Flaky Pastry
- 8 oz/225 g plain flour
- A pinch of salt
- 6 oz/175 g margarine (in a hard block straight from the refrigerator)
- Beaten egg for glaze

For the Filling
- 4 oz/100 g dried prunes
- 1½ lb/675 g lean pork
- 1 tablespoon flour, seasoned with salt and pepper
- 1 medium onion, peeled and finely chopped
- 1 oz/25 g blanched almonds
- ¼ pint/150 ml stock
- *A 1½-pint/900 ml pie dish*

Put the prunes into a bowl, cover with boiling water and leave to soak for about 10 minutes while making the pastry.

Sift the flour and salt into a bowl. Grate the margarine into the flour, using the coarse side of the grater, and stir it through. Add enough cold water to make a soft but not sticky dough. Wrap the dough in greaseproof paper and leave in a cool place while making the filling.

Trim the pork, removing any excess fat, and cut it into 1-inch/2·5-cm pieces. Put the meat into a bowl and toss in the seasoned flour. Drain the prunes, halve them and remove the stones. Put the prune halves into the bowl with the meat, add the onion and almonds and mix all together. Turn the filling into the pie dish and pour over the stock.

On a floured surface, roll out the pastry 1 inch/2·5 cm larger than the dish all round, and to a thickness of about ½ inch/1 cm. Place the dish in the centre of the pastry then, using a sharp knife, cut round the dish. Moisten the rim of the dish with water and lift the pastry border on to it. Moisten the pastry border with water and lay the pastry lid in place. Press the edges firmly together so that they stick to the pie dish. Trim the edges with a sharp knife and then knock them up using the back of the knife. Flute the edges into small scallops. Reroll the pastry trimmings and cut into four diamonds for the leaves. Mark veins on the leaves with a knife.

Arrange the leaves on top of the pie, sticking them with water, then rest the pie in a cool place for about 10 minutes.

Brush the surface of the pie with beaten egg glaze and bake on the centre shelf of a fairly hot oven, gas mark 6 or 400°F/200°C, for 1½ hours, covering with greaseproof paper halfway through cooking to prevent the pastry from becoming too brown.

Freezing Note *Freeze the pie uncooked for up to 2 months. Thaw, glaze then cook as in the recipe.*

Lemony Pork Pudding

Serves 4

For the Suet Crust Pastry
- 6 oz/175 g self-raising flour
- A pinch of salt
- 2 oz/55 g prepared shredded suet

For the Filling
- 1½ lb/675 g spare rib of pork
- 2 tablespoons plain flour, seasoned with salt and pepper
- 1 small onion, peeled and thinly sliced
- 2 tablespoons tomato ketchup
- Grated rind of 1 lemon
- ¼ lb/100 g mushrooms, wiped, trimmed and quartered
- A pinch of dried marjoram
- 4 tablespoons stock
- 1 small bay leaf
- *A 1½-pint/900-ml pudding basin*

Sift the flour and salt into a bowl, stir in the suet and add enough cold water to make a fairly soft dough. On a lightly floured surface, roll out three-quarters of the dough into a large circle. Use to line the base and sides of the pudding basin so that the pastry extends just above the rim.

Trim the meat, removing the bones and any excess fat. Cut the meat into 1-inch/2·5-cm pieces. Put the seasoned flour into a bowl then add the meat and toss the pieces in it to coat them. Stir the onion, tomato ketchup, lemon rind, mushrooms and marjoram into the meat.

Turn this meat mixture into the lined basin, pour over the stock and add the bay leaf. Cover the pudding with the last quarter of pastry, rolled out to fit. Make a pleat in a piece of greased foil, tie it over the top of the pudding and make a handle from the string so that the basin can be removed from the steamer.

Cook the Lemony Pork Pudding for 3¼ hours, replenishing the steamer with more hot water as it is needed.

Veal and Ham Pie

Serves 4

For the Quick Flaky Pastry
8 oz/225 g plain flour
A pinch of salt
6 oz/175 g margarine (in a hard block straight from the refrigerator)
Beaten egg for glaze
For the Filling
1 lb/450 g pie veal
½-lb/225-g gammon rasher
1 medium onion, peeled and finely chopped
2 teaspoons chopped fresh sage or 1 teaspoon dried sage
Pepper
2 large hard-boiled eggs (size 2), shelled
¼ pint/150 ml water
A 1¾-pint/1-litre pie dish

1 Sift the flour and salt into a bowl. Grate in the margarine and stir it through. Add enough water to make a soft but not sticky dough. Wrap in greaseproof paper and leave to rest for 10 minutes.

2 Trim the veal, removing any excess fat, and cut into 1-inch/2·5-cm pieces. Using a pair of scissors, remove the rind from the gammon rasher then snip the rasher into ½-inch/1-cm strips.

3 Mix together the meats, onion, sage and pepper and put half this mixture into the dish. Lay the eggs on the meat, cover with the remaining meat mixture and pour over the water.

4 On a floured surface, roll out the pastry 1 inch/2·5 cm larger than the dish, then place the dish in the centre of the pastry and cut round it. Press the pastry border on to the dampened edge of the dish.

5 Dampen the pastry border and lift the lid into place. Press the edges together well and trim off excess pastry. Knock up the edges with the back of a knife and mark into scallops.

6 Roll out the trimmings and cut four diamonds for leaves. Decorate the pie and make a hole to release steam. Glaze with beaten egg and bake in a fairly hot oven, gas mark 6 or 400°F/200°C, for 1 hour.

Cutlet Pie

Serves 4–6

For the Quick Flaky Pastry
8 oz/225 g plain flour
A pinch of salt
6 oz/175 g margarine (in a hard block straight from the refrigerator)
Beaten egg for glaze
For the Filling
6 best end neck of lamb cutlets
1 onion, peeled and chopped
¼ lb/100 g mushrooms, wiped, trimmed and quartered
Salt and pepper
2 lamb's kidneys
3 tablespoons plain flour
2 tablespoons redcurrant jelly
½ pint/300 ml stock
A 1½-pint/900-ml pie dish

Sift the flour and salt into a bowl. Grate in the fat then bind the ingredients with sufficient cold water to make a fairly stiff dough. Wrap in greaseproof paper and rest in a cool place for 10 minutes.

Trim the cutlets, removing the white milky spinal cord, and clean about 1 inch/2·5 cm at the end of each cutlet. Keep any meat trimmings to add to the pie.

Arrange the cutlets around the pie dish so the bones are evenly spaced, protruding over the rim. Add the onion, mushroom, seasoning and any meat trimmings. Remove the skin and core from the kidneys and cut each half into four. Add to the pie dish, sprinkle over the flour then add the redcurrant jelly and stock.

On a lightly floured surface roll out the pastry to 1 inch/2·5 cm larger than the pie dish and trim off the excess strip. Moisten the rim of the pie dish and place the pastry strip around the edge, underneath the cutlet bones. Moisten the strip and lift the pastry lid into place, pressing the edges well together. Knock up the edges using the back of a knife and mark into flutes. Brush the pie with beaten egg glaze.

Cutlet Pie

Gather up the pastry trimmings, reroll them and cut out three diamond leaves. Mark with veins then place in the centre of the pie. Brush the leaves with beaten egg then allow the pie to rest in a cool place for 10 minutes. Bake in a fairly hot oven, gas mark 6 or 400°F/200°C, for 1½ hours, covering the pastry if it becomes too brown.

Just before serving, put a cutlet frill on the end of each cutlet bone.

Freezing Note *Store uncooked for up to 2 months, thaw then cook as in the recipe.*

Shepherd's Pie

Serves 4

1½–2 lb/675–900 g potatoes
¾ lb/350 g cooked meat (lamb or beef)
1 oz/25 g dripping or lard
2 onions, peeled and sliced
1 oz/25 g flour
½ pint/300 ml stock or water
1 teaspoon dried mixed herbs
Salt and pepper
1 oz/25 g butter or margarine
2 tablespoons top of the milk
A 2½-pint/1·5-litre pie dish or shallow ovenproof dish

Peel the potatoes and cut into fairly large pieces. Cook in boiling salted water until tender – about 15 minutes. Meanwhile, cut the meat into cubes.

Melt the dripping or lard in a frying pan and fry the onions until golden brown. Stir in the flour, then add the stock or water and bring to the boil, stirring all the time. Remove from the heat and add the meat, herbs and seasoning to taste. Spoon the mixture into the dish.

Drain the cooked potatoes. Add the butter or margarine, top of the milk and seasoning, and mash thoroughly. Spread the potato over the top of the meat.

Bake in a moderate oven, gas mark 4 or 350°F/180°C, for 30 to 40 minutes, until the mixture is piping hot and the potato browned.

Freezing Note *Store the pie once topped with potato for up to 3 months. Thaw, then reheat as in the recipe.*

Chicken and Mushroom Cobbler

Serves 6

4-lb/1·75-kg roasting chicken (trussed weight)
2 tablespoons cooking oil
2 oz/50 g margarine
2 medium onions, peeled and sliced
¼ lb/100 g mushrooms
2 oz/50 g plain flour
¾ pint/450 ml chicken stock
¼ pint/150 ml milk
1 tablespoon chopped parsley
Salt and pepper
For the Dumplings
12 oz/350 g self-raising flour
A pinch of salt
4 oz/110 g prepared shredded suet
4 oz/110 g Lancashire cheese, crumbled
A 5-pint/3-litre casserole dish

Cut the chicken into joints and remove any loose skin, as instructed on page 46. Heat the oil and margarine in a pan, add the chicken pieces and fry briskly until golden brown. Transfer the pieces to the casserole dish.

Reduce the heat and fry the onions in the pan until tender but not coloured. Add to the chicken. Wipe, trim and quarter the mushrooms. Fry for a few minutes, then add to the chicken.

Remove the pan from the heat, mix the flour into the melted fat, then gradually blend in the stock and milk. When the sauce is smooth, return to the heat and, stirring all the time, bring the sauce to the boil and cook until it thickens. Stir in the parsley, check the sauce for seasoning, then pour it over the chicken pieces. Cover the casserole and cook for 45 minutes on the centre shelf of a moderately hot oven, gas mark 5 or 375°F/190°C.

Meanwhile, make the dumplings. Sift the flour and salt into a bowl, stir in the suet and cheese, then bind with enough cold water to make a fairly soft dough. Divide into 12 pieces and roll each one into a ball.

After the 45 minutes cooking time place the dumplings on top of the casserole. Return the dish, uncovered, to the oven for 15 minutes, then reduce the heat to gas mark 4 or 350°F/180°C, for a further 30 minutes, to brown the dumplings.

Open Turkey Pie

Serves 4–6

13-oz/368-g packet frozen puff pastry, thawed
Beaten egg for glaze
For the Filling
2 oz/50 g margarine
2 oz/50 g plain flour
½ pint/300 ml chicken stock
½ pint/300 ml milk
¼ lb/100 g mushrooms, wiped, trimmed and sliced
8-oz/227-g packet frozen mixed vegetables
12 oz/350 g cooked turkey, chopped

On a lightly floured work surface roll the pastry into a 9 × 11-inch/23 × 28-cm rectangle; trim the edges with a sharp knife then cut a 7½ × 9½-inch/19 × 24-cm rectangle from the centre, to leave a 1½-inch/4-cm border all round. Leave this border on one side. Reroll the rectangle to its original size, 9 × 11 inches/23 × 28 cm, and lift it carefully on to a baking tray. Using a little water, moisten the edges and lift the border in position on top, pressing together. Prick the centre of the pastry case with a fork so it rises evenly and, with the back of a knife, decorate the border with a criss-cross pattern. Brush the border with a little beaten egg then leave in a cool place for 15 minutes to rest.

Bake on the centre shelf of a hot oven, gas mark 7 or 425°F/220°C, for 15 to 20 minutes, until it is golden brown and well risen.

Meanwhile, prepare the filling. Melt the margarine in a pan over a gentle heat, remove the pan from the heat and stir in the flour, then gradually blend in the stock and milk. When the sauce is smooth return the pan to the heat and, stirring all the time, bring to the boil. Stir in the sliced mushrooms and mixed vegetables and simmer the sauce for about 3 minutes, until the vegetables are tender. Finally stir in the meat and heat thoroughly.

Lift the pastry case carefully on to a large serving dish and pour the turkey filling into the centre.

Freezing Note *Freeze the pastry case and the filling separately for up to 2 months. Reheat the filling then turn it into the frozen pastry case and warm through in a moderate oven for about 15 minutes.*

American Chicken Pie

Serves 4–5

For the Quick Flaky Pastry
6 oz/175 g plain flour
A pinch of salt
4 oz/110 g margarine (in a hard block straight from the refrigerator)
Beaten egg for glaze
For the Filling
3-lb/1·5-kg roasting chicken (trussed weight)
2 oz/50 g margarine
2 oz/50 g plain flour
¾ pint/450 ml milk
11-oz/312-g can sweetcorn
1 bay leaf
Salt and pepper
A 3-pint/1·75-litre pie dish

Sift the flour and salt for the pastry into a mixing bowl. Using a coarse grater, grate the margarine into the flour and stir it in with a knife, then mix in enough cold water to make a fairly stiff dough. Wrap the pastry in greaseproof paper and leave in a cool place until needed.

Joint the chicken as instructed on page 46, and place the pieces in the pie dish. Melt the margarine in a pan, remove from the heat, stir in the flour and gradually blend in the milk. When the sauce is smooth, return to the heat and, stirring all the time, bring it to the boil. Cook the sauce for a few minutes to thicken, then stir in the sweetcorn, add the bay leaf and check the sauce for seasoning. Pour the sauce over the chicken in the pie dish.

On a lightly floured work surface, roll the pastry into an oval 1 inch/2·5 cm larger than the pie dish. Stand the dish in the centre and cut round it to leave a border of pastry for the rim of the dish. Damp the rim of the dish with a little cold water. Lift the pastry border on to it and brush this with water. Lift the pastry top, with the help of a rolling pin, on to the dish and press it into the pastry rim. Hold the pie on one hand and, with a sharp knife in the other, trim off the excess pastry. Gather all the pastry strips together and roll them out to ⅛ inch/3 mm thick and cut four diamonds for leaves. Mark them with veins and place on top of the pie. Cut a strip just under 1 inch/2·5 cm wide and roll it up to resemble a flower. Place this in the centre of the leaves. Finally, with the back of a knife, knock up and flute the edges of the pie. Brush the entire surface with beaten egg to glaze it.

Freezing Note *Freeze for up to 2 months when cooked. Thaw, then reheat in a moderately hot oven, gas mark 5 or 375°F/190°C, for 30 minutes, covering the pastry with foil if it becomes too brown.*

Open Turkey Pie

Rabbit Pie

Serves 5

7½-oz/212-g packet frozen puff pastry, thawed
Beaten egg for glaze
For the Filling
¼ lb/100 g streaky bacon rashers
1 rabbit (1½ lb/675 g), skinned and jointed
3 large hard-boiled eggs (size 2)
Salt and pepper
¼ teaspoon ground mace
¼ pint/150 ml chicken stock
A 3-pint/1·75-litre pie dish
A pie funnel

Using a pair of scissors, cut the rind and any small bones from the bacon rashers, then lay half of them in the pie dish with half the prepared rabbit. Shell the eggs, cut in half lengthways and lay them in the dish. Season the filling, sprinkle over the mace, then add the remaining rabbit and bacon. Pour over the stock, and place the pie funnel in position.

On a lightly floured work surface, roll the pastry into an oval about 1 inch/2·5 cm larger all round than the dish. Place the dish in the centre and, with a sharp knife, cut round the rim to make the top. Lift the dish off the pastry and brush the rim of the dish with a little water.

Place the pastry border around the edge of the dish, then brush the border with water. Using a rolling pin, carefully lift the pastry for the top into position, pushing the funnel through the centre and pressing the edges firmly together. Trim off the surplus pastry with a sharp knife then, using the back of the knife, knock up the edges. Brush the pastry top with beaten egg glaze and leave the pie in a cool place for about 15 minutes to rest the pastry.

Bake the pie on the centre shelf of a hot oven, gas mark 7 or 425°F/220°C, for 20 minutes, then reduce the heat to gas mark 4 or 350°F/180°C, for a further 1½ hours, covering the pastry if necessary.

Suppers and Snacks

Supper and snack dishes are in fact so versatile that they fit many other occasions. Serve a supper dish with a salad or a green vegetable and it makes a marvellous main course for lunch. Or a snack followed by a selection of cakes is perfect for high teas and, of course, such dishes as pizzas and sandwiches are splendid as picnic fare.

Toad-in-the-Hole

Serves 4–5

4 oz/110 g plain flour
Salt and pepper
1 large egg (size 2)
¼ pint/150 ml milk
¼ pint/150 ml water
1 lb/450 g pork sausages
A 2-pint/1·25-litre ovenproof dish

Sift the flour with the salt and pepper into a mixing bowl and make a well in the centre. Break the egg into it and, using a wooden spoon, carefully work in the flour from around the sides. Gradually beat in half the milk and water and continue beating the batter for at least a minute to incorporate as much air as possible. Mix in the rest of the liquid to make a smooth consistency without dispelling any air.

Arrange the sausages in the dish to resemble the spokes of a wheel and bake on the centre shelf of a hot oven, gas mark 7 or 425°F/220°C, for 10 minutes. Remove from the oven and pour the batter over the sausages. Return to the oven and cook for a further 30 to 35 minutes, until the batter is well risen and the sausages are golden brown. Serve with a green vegetable.

Moussaka

Serves 4–5

2 medium aubergines
5 tablespoons cooking oil
2 medium onions, peeled and sliced
1 lb/450 g minced beef
2 tablespoons tomato purée
¼ pint/150 ml beef stock
1 teaspoon dried mixed herbs
Salt and pepper
½ lb/225 g cooked potatoes
2 tomatoes
For the Sauce
1 oz/25 g margarine
1 oz/25 g plain flour
½ pint/300 ml milk
2 large eggs (size 2), separated
1 oz/25 g Cheddar cheese, grated
A 4-pint/2·25-litre ovenproof dish

Wipe the aubergines, cut into slices and spread out on a plate. Sprinkle the surface with salt and leave for 15 minutes to extract some of the water. Rinse and pat dry.

Fry the aubergine slices in a little of the oil until brown on both sides. Drain on absorbent paper and leave on one side until needed.

Heat the remaining oil and fry the sliced onion until golden, then add the meat and fry quickly to seal it. Stir in the tomato purée, stock, herbs and seasoning; cover and simmer for 15 minutes.

Meanwhile, slice the cooked potatoes and the tomatoes.

Put a layer of aubergines in the dish, spoon over half the meat mixture and cover with sliced tomatoes. Add the rest of the aubergines and the meat then top with the sliced potatoes.

Next make the sauce. Melt the margarine, stir in the flour and gradually blend in the milk. Stirring all the time, bring the sauce to the boil and cook until smooth and thickened. Beat in the egg yolks and the grated cheese. Whisk the egg whites until stiff and fold into the sauce.

Pour the sauce over the Moussaka then bake on the centre shelf of a moderately hot oven, gas mark 5 or 375°F/190°C, for 45 minutes, until golden.

Freezing Note *Store when cooked for up to 2 months. Thaw then reheat as in the recipe.*

Moussaka

ΜΥΤΙΛΗΝΗΣ
PRODUCT OF GREECE
SPENTZAS & SON

Spaghetti Bolognese

Spaghetti Bolognese

Serves 2–3

6 oz / 175 g spaghetti
1 oz / 25 g butter
2 oz / 50 g cheese, grated
For the Sauce
1 clove garlic
Salt and pepper
1 oz / 25 g dripping
1 large onion, peeled and finely chopped
$\frac{1}{2}$ lb / 225 g minced beef
1 tablespoon plain flour
2 tablespoons tomato purée
2 teaspoons dried mixed herbs
$\frac{1}{2}$ pint / 300 ml beef stock

Peel the garlic and crush it to a paste with plenty of salt. Melt the dripping in a frying pan and fry the onion with the garlic until the onion starts to soften. Add the minced beef and brown it over a fairly high heat.

Remove the pan from the heat and stir in the flour, tomato purée, seasoning, herbs and stock. Return to the heat and bring to the boil; simmer, uncovered, for 30 minutes.

Meanwhile, cook the spaghetti. Have ready a large pan half-filled with boiling salted water. Hold the spaghetti in a bunch in one hand, then put the other end into the water. As the pasta softens, curl it around the pan until it is completely immersed. Cook for 10 to 15 minutes, until a strand of spaghetti feels soft to the centre. Drain it well and run hot water through the strands to remove the excess starch. Return the pasta to the pan and stir in the butter.

When the sauce is cooked, pile the spaghetti into a hot dish and pour over the sauce. Serve at once with grated cheese.

Freezing Note *Store the sauce only for up to 3 months. Thaw, then reheat slowly until piping hot.*

Stuffed Marrow

Serves 5–6

1 marrow (about $2\frac{3}{4}$ lb / 1·25 kg)
For the Filling
$\frac{1}{4}$ lb / 100 g minced beef
$\frac{1}{4}$ lb / 100 g sausagemeat
1 medium onion, peeled and chopped
1 large egg (size 2)
2 oz / 50 g fresh white breadcrumbs
2 teaspoons dried mixed herbs
Salt and pepper
For the Sauce
1 small onion, peeled and chopped
$\frac{1}{2}$ oz / 15 g butter
1 tablespoon plain flour
A generous pinch of caster sugar
Salt and pepper
$\frac{1}{4}$ pint / 150 ml beef stock
8-oz / 227-g can tomatoes
2 tablespoons tomato ketchup

Put the minced beef, sausagemeat, onion, egg, breadcrumbs, herbs and seasoning into a bowl and mix well together.

Peel the marrow and cut out a 3-inch / 7·5-cm wide square wedge from the top. Keep this lid on one side and, using a spoon, scoop out the seeds from inside the marrow and from the lid.

Spoon the stuffing into the cavity of the marrow, pressing it well down with a spoon so that it reaches both ends of the cavity and fills the centre.

Put the marrow on to a large piece of aluminium foil and replace the lid, then wrap it up and seal the ends. Bake the Stuffed Marrow in a fairly hot oven, gas mark 6 or 400°F / 200°C, for 1 hour.

Meanwhile, make the sauce. Fry the onion in the butter in a small pan. Stir in the flour, sugar and seasoning then gradually blend in the stock, tomatoes and tomato ketchup. Bring the sauce to the boil and simmer for 5 minutes. When the marrow is cooked remove the foil and lift carefully on to a serving dish. Pour over the tomato sauce and serve immediately.

Lasagne

Serves 4–5

4 oz/100 g lasagne verdi
½ oz/15 g butter
For the Filling
1 clove garlic
Salt and pepper
3 rashers streaky bacon, derinded and chopped
1 large onion, peeled and chopped
1 lb/450 g minced beef
2 medium carrots, peeled and grated
3 dessertspoons tomato purée
½ pint/300 ml beef stock
For the Sauce
2 oz/50 g margarine
2 oz/50 g plain flour
1 pint/600 ml milk
6 oz/175 g strong Cheddar cheese, grated
A 4-pint/2·25-litre ovenproof dish

1 Add the sheets of lasagne to a pan of boiling salted water, one at a time, counting to 15 between each one so they do not stick together. Cook for 15 minutes, then drain and separate on to a plate for later.

2 Taking one clove from the head of garlic, remove the peel and, using a stainless steel knife, crush it to a paste with plenty of salt. Fry the bacon pieces over a high heat until they start to brown, then add the onion and garlic.

3 When the onion is tender, add the beef and brown quickly, then stir in the carrot, tomato purée, stock and seasoning to taste. Bring to the boil, reduce the heat and simmer for 30 minutes, until the liquid has reduced.

4 Melt the margarine in a pan, stir in the flour then gradually blend in the milk off the heat. When the sauce is smooth, return to the heat and, stirring all the time, bring it to the boil. Stir in two-thirds of the cheese and season to taste.

5 Grease the dish with the butter, then arrange half the lasagne over the base. Cover it with half the meat filling, then half the cheese sauce. Repeat the layers once more so all the ingredients are used.

6 Scatter the rest of the cheese over the top of the Lasagne, then bake on the centre shelf of a moderately hot oven, gas mark 5 or 375°F/190°C, for 25 minutes, until golden brown. Serve with a salad.

Freezing Note *Store without the final layer of cheese for up to 2 months. Thaw, scatter with cheese then bake as above for about 45 minutes.*

Pressed Tongue

1 ox tongue (3–5 lb/1·5–2·25 kg in weight, bought already salted by the butcher)
1 medium onion, peeled
6 peppercorns
1 bay leaf

Weigh the tongue and calculate the cooking time – 1 hour per pound/per half kilo.

Soak the tongue for 3 to 4 hours then put into a large pan, cover with cold water and add the onion, peppercorns and bay leaf. Bring the water very slowly to the boil, then reduce the heat and simmer the tongue, covered, until ready. (The cooking time is taken from the very beginning.)

Leave the tongue to cool slightly in the liquid, then transfer it carefully on to a board. Remove any small bones and gristle from around the throat and peel off the outer skin. Ease the tongue, tightly curled, into a cake tin – it must fit tightly to ensure a good shape. Lay a saucer or small plate on top, inside the rim of the tin, and weigh it down with heavy objects such as kitchen weights or cans of food. Enough liquid will be pressed out of the meat to surround it and set into a jelly when cold. Leave overnight in a cool place.

Freezing Note *Store for up to 2 months uncooked or, once cooked, slice and wrap well then store for up to a month.*

Chicken Fricassée

Chicken Fricassée

Serves 4

2 oz/50 g butter or margarine
¼ lb/100 g mushrooms, wiped, trimmed and sliced
2 tablespoons plain flour
¾ pint/450 ml milk
12 oz/350 g cooked chicken, chopped
Salt and pepper
8 oz/225 g long-grain rice
For the Garnish
3–4 rashers streaky bacon
2 slices white bread, crusts removed
1 oz/25 g butter
1 tablespoon cooking oil
A 2½-inch/6-cm round cutter

Heat the butter or margarine in a pan and fry the mushrooms until starting to cook. Stir in the flour and when it has absorbed all the fat remove from the heat and gradually blend in the milk. When the sauce is smooth, return to the heat and bring it to the boil, stirring all the time. Cook the sauce for a minute to thicken it then stir in the chicken with plenty of seasoning. Simmer for 5 to 10 minutes to heat the chicken thoroughly.

Meanwhile, cook the rice in plenty of boiling salted water for 12 minutes, until a grain of rice rubbed between the fingers feels soft to the centre. Drain and run hot water through the grains to separate them.

Cut the rind and any bones from the bacon rashers, then stretch them with the back of a knife to twice their length. Cut each rasher in half and roll up.

Using the edge of the round cutter, cut eight crescents from each slice of bread. Heat the butter and oil in a frying pan and fry the crescents until golden brown. Drain on absorbent paper then fry the bacon rolls until crispy.

Turn the rice into a heated serving dish, spreading it over the base and round the sides. Spoon the Chicken Fricassée into the centre then arrange the bread crescents around the edge of the dish and the bacon rolls down the centre.

Freezing Note *Store the fricassée part only for up to 2 months. Thaw, then reheat slowly and simmer for 10 minutes until thoroughly hot. Meanwhile, cook the rice and garnish and serve as above.*

Traditional Pizza

Serves 4

For the Base
2 tablespoons milk
2 tablespoons water
½ teaspoon dried yeast
½ teaspoon caster sugar
6 oz/175 g strong plain white flour
½ teaspoon salt
1 small egg (size 4)
1 oz/25 g butter
For the Topping
3 medium tomatoes, sliced
½ teaspoon dried marjoram
Salt and pepper
4 oz/100 g Edam cheese
2-oz/56-g can anchovy fillets
6 black olives
2 tablespoons oil

Traditional Pizza

Warm the milk and water to blood heat and mix into the yeast and sugar. Leave to dissolve in a warm place – it will take about 10 minutes.

Form the flour and salt into a ring on the work surface. Beat the egg into the yeast mixture and pour into the centre of the flour.

Gradually mix the flour into the yeast liquid and when the ingredients have formed a dough, knead for at least 5 minutes. Finally spread the dough out a little, place the butter in the centre and knead it in until the dough is smooth again and the butter evenly distributed.

Put the dough into a greased bowl, cover with a damp tea towel and leave in a warm place for 40 minutes to rise, until doubled in size. Knead the dough again lightly so that it returns to its original size and form into a 9-inch/23-cm round.

Place the dough in a shallow-sided tin. Arrange the tomato slices on top, keeping a ½-inch/1-cm border free around the edge. Scatter the marjoram over the tomatoes then season with a little salt and pepper.

Cut the cheese into thin slices and arrange over the tomatoes. Soak the anchovy fillets in a little milk for about 10 minutes to remove any excess salt then cut each fillet into two lengthways and arrange over the cheese in a trellis pattern. Cut the olives in half, remove the stones then place in between the trellis. Pour the oil around the pizza then leave in a warm place to rise for 15 minutes. Bake on the centre shelf of a fairly hot oven, gas mark 6 or 400°F/200°C, for 30 minutes, until golden brown.

Freezing Note *Store the well-wrapped Pizza for up to a month. Thaw then reheat at gas mark 4 or 350°F/180°C for 15 to 20 minutes.*

Quiche Lorraine

Serves 4

For the Pastry
5 oz/150 g plain flour
A pinch of salt
1 oz/30 g margarine
1½ oz/45 g lard
For the Filling
4 oz/100 g streaky bacon rashers
1 small onion, finely chopped
2 large eggs (size 2)
½ pint/300 ml milk
Salt and pepper
2 oz/50 g Cheddar cheese, grated
An 8-inch/20-cm flan ring

Stand the flan ring on an upturned baking tray. Sift the flour and salt into a mixing bowl, add the fats, cut into small pieces, and, using the fingertips only, rub them in until evenly distributed. Stir in enough cold water to make a fairly stiff dough, then roll out the pastry on a lightly floured work surface. Lift the pastry into the flan ring and press it firmly into the base and sides. Trim the top by running the rolling pin over it in both directions, then leave the flan case in a cool place.

Cut the rind and any small bones from the bacon, then cut the rashers into pieces and fry in a pan until they start to brown. Add the onion and fry the two ingredients together until they are both almost cooked. Transfer to the flan case. Beat the eggs with the milk, add plenty of seasoning and half the cheese, then pour into the flan case. Sprinkle over the rest of the cheese.

Bake the flan on the centre shelf of a moderately hot oven, gas mark 5 or 375°F/190°C, for about 40 minutes, until the pastry is golden brown and the filling well risen.

Slip off the flan ring and serve the Quiche Lorraine piping hot.

Freezing Note *Store for up to 3 months then reheat from frozen in a moderate oven, gas mark 4 or 350°F/180°C, for 30 to 40 minutes.*

Home-Made Sausages

Makes 15

1 lb/450 g minced pork
4 oz/100 g fresh white breadcrumbs
1 teaspoon salt
Pepper
¼ teaspoon dry mustard
½ teaspoon dried mixed herbs
4 tablespoons milk
Cooking oil for frying

Put the minced pork into a bowl with the breadcrumbs, salt, pepper, mustard and herbs. Stir in the milk and mix all the ingredients together so they are well combined. Shape them into sausages in one of two ways: either divide the mixture into five portions, roll out each on a lightly floured work surface into a 12-inch/30-cm length and cut into three to make 15 sausages in all; or fill a piping bag with a ¾-inch/1·5-cm plain pipe attached with some of the mixture at a time, then pipe 12-inch/30-cm lengths on to a floured surface and cut them into three to make 15 sausages.

Fry the sausages a few at a time in the oil for about 12 minutes, turning them as they cook so they brown all over. Serve with mashed potatoes.

Freezing Note *If the pork is fresh the sausages can be made and frozen raw. Freeze them loose on a tray then pack into a polythene bag when solid. Store for up to 3 months, thaw then cook as in the recipe.*

Ham and Potato Pasties

Makes 4

13-oz/368-g packet frozen puff pastry, thawed
Beaten egg for glaze
For the Filling
4 oz/100 g mashed potato
4 oz/100 g cooked bacon
½ 1-pint/600-ml packet ham and pea soup powder

On a lightly floured work surface roll the pastry into a 10-inch/25-cm square. Trim the edges, then divide the pastry into four 5-inch/12·5-cm squares.

Mix the mashed potato with the cooked bacon and dry soup mix, then divide it between the pastry squares. Damp the edges with cold water and fold over to form a triangle, pressing the edges together to seal securely.

Sprinkle a little water over a baking tray to help the puff pastry to rise, before placing the pasties on it. Leave in a cool place for about 15 minutes to rest.

Brush the pasties with egg glaze, then bake on the centre shelf of a hot oven, gas mark 7 or 425°F/220°C, for 20 to 25 minutes, until golden brown. Serve hot or cold.

Freezing Note *Store when cooked for up to a month. Thaw then reheat if liked in a moderate oven for 15 minutes.*

Lancashire Grill

Serves 3–4

2 oz/50 g butter
10 thin slices white bread
8 oz/225 g Lancashire cheese, grated
1 large egg (size 2)
A few drops of Worcestershire sauce
1 teaspoon dry mustard
Salt and pepper
4 tablespoons milk
2 tablespoons tomato pickle
6 slices ham
A large Swiss roll tin

Melt the butter and brush a little over the base and sides of the tin.

Toast five slices of bread on one side only, cut in half and place, toasted side down, in the tin.

In a pan, mix together the cheese, egg, Worcestershire sauce, mustard, seasoning and milk, heating gently until they are well blended, then lightly mix in the tomato pickle. Lay the slices of ham on top of the bread in the tin and spread over half the cheese mixture. Cover this with the five remaining bread slices, also cut in half, and finally spread the rest of the cheese mixture on top.

Place the tin under a preheated grill for about 5 minutes, until the cheese has melted and turned golden brown.

Cut the Lancashire Grill into slices and serve hot with tomatoes and watercress.

Ham and Potato Pasties

Ribbon Sandwiches

Makes 20

5 slices white bread and butter
5 slices brown bread and butter
For the Fillings
Layer 1
2 oz/50 g liver sausage
½ bunch watercress, chopped
Layer 2
¼ lb/100 g mushrooms, sliced
1 oz/25 g margarine
1 tablespoon soy sauce
Layer 3
4 oz/100 g cooked chicken, chopped
2 tablespoons cranberry sauce
Layer 4
2 tomatoes, thinly sliced
1 teaspoon lemon juice
Salt and pepper

Make two stacks, using alternate slices of brown and white bread – butter-side up except for the top slice. Cover with fillings as follows.

Layer 1 mashed liver sausage, covered with watercress.

Layer 2 cold fried mushroom slices, mixed with soy sauce.

Layer 3 chicken mixed with cranberry sauce.

Layer 4 sliced tomatoes, sprinkled with lemon juice and seasoning.

Cover with the top slice of bread, butter-side down, and press lightly.

Wrap each stack in foil or cling film and chill for at least 2 hours or overnight in the refrigerator.

To serve, remove crusts and cut each stack into five slices; cut each slice in half again.

Salmon Party Rolls

Makes 16

8 slices bread and butter
For the Filling
4 oz/100 g salmon paste or spread
8 spring onions

Spread all the slices of bread with salmon paste, cut off the crusts and lay a cleaned spring onion along one side of the bread before rolling up, as described for Curried Cheese Party Rolls. Chill and serve as for these.

Ribbon Sandwiches, Salmon and Curried Cheese Party Rolls

Curried Cheese Party Rolls

Makes 16

8 slices bread and butter
For the Filling
4 oz/100 g cream cheese
½ teaspoon curry paste
4 gherkins, quartered

Mix the cheese and curry paste together. Spread one-eighth of the cheese mixture evenly over each slice of bread and remove the crusts.

Lay two pieces of gherkin along one edge of each slice then roll the bread up from this end. Wrap each roll in foil and chill for at least 1 hour. Cut in half to serve.

Egg and Tomato Sandwiches

Makes 2 rounds

6 slices granary bread and butter
For the Fillings
2 large eggs (size 2)
1 tablespoon milk
Salt and pepper
½ oz/15 g margarine
1 tablespoon mayonnaise
1 spring onion, thinly sliced
2 tomatoes, thinly sliced

Beat the eggs with the milk and plenty of seasoning. Melt the margarine, add the egg mixture and stir continually until lightly scrambled. Cool, then stir in the mayonnaise.

Cover two slices of bread with the spring onion and sliced tomato and season well. Place another slice of bread on top of each and spread it with scrambled egg. Cover with a third slice of bread. Press down firmly before cutting the sandwiches in half to serve.

Tuna and Bean Pop-Ins

To Freeze Sandwiches

Sandwiches are a marvellous standby to have in the freezer, especially if the family takes packed lunches. However, there are a few fillings to avoid, such as hard-boiled eggs, those based on salad cream or mayonnaise, and salad ingredients.

Leave the crusts on the bread to give more protection and freeze in small packs.

Thaw sandwiches in their wrapping for 3 hours at room temperature, then remove the crusts if preferred.

Tuna and Bean Pop-Ins

Makes 4

4 long bread rolls
butter
For the Filling
3½-oz/99-g can tuna fish
2 oz/50 g cooked French beans, roughly chopped
1 small onion, thinly sliced and separated into rings
1 teaspoon vinegar
Salt and pepper
2 oz/50 g cucumber, thinly sliced

Drain the tuna fish, reserving 1 tablespoon of oil. Flake the flesh.

Cut each roll downwards to within ½ inch/1 cm of its base and spread softened butter over the cut surfaces.

Mix the tuna with the chopped beans, onion rings, vinegar, reserved tuna oil and seasoning. Pile the mixture into the rolls and garnish with twists of cucumber.

Cottage Cheese and Prawn Rounds

Makes 4

4 slices French bread and butter
For the Topping
1 tablespoon seafood dressing
6 oz/175 g cottage cheese
Salt and pepper
2 oz/50 g peeled prawns
Chives
8 thin slices lemon

Spread each slice of buttered French bread with a little seafood dressing. Season the cottage cheese generously with salt and pepper and divide between the slices of bread. Toss the prawns in the remaining seafood dressing and press lightly into the cottage cheese. Garnish with snipped chives and slices of lemon.

Cottage Cheese and Prawn Rounds

Vegetables and Salads

The art of good vegetable cooking and salad preparation is to choose produce at the peak of its condition. Use vegetables as soon as possible after picking, when they are bright in colour and crisp in texture, or purchase them from a shop with fast turnover to ensure complete freshness.

Ratatouille

Serves 6

- 1 aubergine
- 1 lb/450 g tomatoes
- 1 green pepper
- 1 red pepper
- 1 lb/450 g courgettes
- ¾ lb/350 g onions, peeled and sliced
- 1 clove garlic, crushed
- 4–6 tablespoons oil
- A pinch of caster sugar
- Salt and pepper
- *A 3-pint/1·75-litre casserole dish*

Slice the aubergine, sprinkle the slices with salt and leave for 30 minutes to draw out some of the water. Drain and pat dry.

Peel the tomatoes by plunging them into boiling water for 20 seconds then transfer to a bowl of cold water and slip off the skins. Cut into quarters. Cut the peppers in half, remove the seeds and cores then cut into slices. Wipe the courgettes and cut into diagonal slices. Mix all the vegetables together and add the crushed garlic.

Heat the oil in a large frying pan and cook the vegetables for 8 to 10 minutes, then transfer to the casserole dish. Stir in the sugar and plenty of seasoning, cover and cook in a moderately cool oven, gas mark 3 or 325°F/160°C, for 1½ to 2 hours, until the vegetables are soft.

Ratatouille is delicious served as a vegetable dish or cold sprinkled with grated cheese for a first course.

Freezing Note *Ratatouille freezes very well, sealed and labelled in a rigid container. Keep for up to 3 months and thaw at room temperature.*

Savoury Cabbage Rolls

Serves 4–5

- 1 medium cabbage
- 8-oz/227-g can tomatoes

For the Filling

- 1 oz/25 g margarine
- 3 oz/75 g long-grain rice
- 1 tablespoon cooking oil
- 1 medium onion, peeled and finely sliced
- 1 oz/25 g walnuts, chopped
- Salt and pepper
- *A shallow 1½-pint/900-ml ovenproof dish*

Grease the dish with half the margarine. Trim the cabbage, removing any damaged leaves, then simmer it whole in a pan of boiling salted water for 6 to 7 minutes, until the leaves are just starting to soften. Drain the cabbage and leave to cool slightly.

Meanwhile, cook the rice in boiling salted water for 12 minutes, until tender, then drain thoroughly. Heat the oil and remaining margarine in a frying pan, add the onion and cook it gently until soft but not coloured. Stir in the walnuts with the drained rice and check the stuffing for seasoning.

Carefully remove the whole cabbage leaves from the base, cutting out any thick stalks as you work. Lay the leaves on a work surface and divide the stuffing between them. Roll each leaf around the filling, tucking in the sides, and put the parcels in the dish, packing them close together so that they do not unroll during cooking. Pour over the tomatoes, cover the dish with foil and bake on the centre shelf of a moderately hot oven, gas mark 5 or 375°F/190°C, for 20 to 25 minutes, until the cabbage leaves are completely cooked and the filling is piping hot. Serve with creamed potatoes.

Freezing Note *Store for up to 1 month. Thaw, then reheat as described in the recipe.*

Savoury Cabbage Rolls

Crispy Cheddar Chips

Serves 3–4

- 1 lb/450 g potatoes
- 1 oz/25 g butter
- 4 oz/100 g Cheddar cheese, grated
- Salt and pepper
- *A ¾-pint/450-ml ovenproof dish*

Peel the potatoes and cut them into chips. Melt the butter in a saucepan, add the grated cheese and plenty of salt and pepper, then add the chips. Put the lid on the pan and shake it so the chips are well coated with the buttery cheese.

Turn the potatoes into the ovenproof dish and bake on the centre shelf of a moderately hot oven, gas mark 5 or 375°F/190°C, for about 1¼ hours, until tender but crispy. Serve immediately.

Greek Beans

Serves 4

- 8 oz/225 g butterbeans, soaked overnight
- 3 tablespoons oil
- 1 clove garlic
- Salt and pepper
- 1 bay leaf
- 1 lb 12-oz/793-g can tomatoes
- 1 small onion, peeled and finely chopped

Drain the soaked beans well. Heat the oil in a large pan. Peel the garlic and crush it to a paste with some salt, then stir into the pan with the beans and bay leaf. Simmer the beans gently for 10 minutes, then stir in the tomatoes with plenty of seasoning. Pour over sufficient boiling water to cover the beans by 1 inch/2·5 cm. Cover the pan and simmer the ingredients gently for about 2 hours, until the beans are completely cooked. Ten minutes before the end of the cooking time, add the chopped onion.

Freezing Note *Cook until the onion is to be added then cool, freeze and store for up to 2 months. Thaw and reheat gently on top of the cooker, add the onion and cook for a further 10 minutes.*

Spinach and Potato Flan

Serves 6

For the Pastry

- 8 oz/225 g plain flour
- A pinch of salt
- 3 oz/85 g margarine
- 1 oz/25 g lard

For the Filling

- 2 × 11-oz/312-g packets frozen chopped spinach, thawed
- ¼ lb/100 g mushrooms
- ½ oz/15 g butter
- 1½ lb/675 g potatoes, peeled and cooked
- 2 large eggs (size 2)
- ¼ pint/150 ml milk
- A generous pinch of ground nutmeg
- Salt and pepper
- *An 8-inch/20-cm plain flan ring*

First make the pastry. Sift the flour and salt into a mixing bowl, add the margarine and lard cut into small pieces and, using the fingertips only, rub in the fats until they are evenly distributed. Stir in sufficient cold water to make a fairly stiff dough, then wrap the pastry and leave in a cool place for about 15 minutes.

When the pastry is ready, roll it out on a lightly floured work surface to a circle 2 inches/5 cm larger than the flan ring. Put the ring on to a baking tray then lift the pastry on the rolling pin into the ring. Press it into the base and up the sides and trim off any excess pastry by rolling the pin over the top of the ring, first one way then the other. Place the lined ring in a cool place while preparing the filling.

Cook the spinach according to the instructions on the packet, then leave to drain and cool. Wipe, trim and slice the mushrooms, and sauté in the melted butter until tender. Slice the cooked potatoes.

Spread the spinach over the base of the flan case and cover with the mushrooms. Lay the potatoes on top, overlapping them slightly. Beat the eggs with the milk, nutmeg and seasoning, and pour into the flan case.

Bake the flan on the shelf above the centre of a moderately hot oven, gas mark 5 or 375°F/190°C, for 45 minutes, until the top is lightly browned.

Serve hot or cold.

Freezing Note *Store cooked for up to a month. Reheat at gas mark 5 or 375°F/190°C for 35 to 45 minutes.*

Savoy Special

Serves 4

- 1 small Savoy cabbage (1 lb/450 g)
- 15¾-oz/447-g can baked beans
- ½ lb/225 g streaky bacon rashers
- ½ oz/15 g margarine
- Salt and pepper
- *A 2-pint/1·25-litre serving dish*

Remove any damaged leaves from the cabbage, then shred and wash it thoroughly. Cook in boiling salted water for 10 minutes, until just tender. Drain well and keep warm.

Heat the beans in the pan in which the cabbage was cooked. Remove the rind and any small bones from the bacon, cut the rashers in half and fry or grill them until golden brown.

Grease the inside of the serving dish with the margarine. Lay half the cabbage in the base and pour over half the beans. Season, then repeat the layers, using the rest of the cabbage and beans. Cover the surface with the bacon and serve Savoy Special with creamed potatoes.

Vegetable Pudding, Savoy Special

Vegetable Pudding

Serves 6

For the Suet Crust Pastry
12 oz/350 g self-raising flour
A pinch of salt
5 oz/150 g prepared shredded suet
For the Filling
1 lb/450 g Brussels sprouts
3 leeks
1 lb/450 g carrots, peeled and diced
2 oz/50 g butter
Salt and pepper
A 3-pint/1·75-litre pudding basin

Wash the sprouts and remove any damaged leaves. Trim the leeks, again removing any damaged leaves, then slit them to the base and wash under running water to remove all the grit. Cut the leeks into 2-inch/5-cm strips.

Put the diced carrots, sprouts and leeks into a pan of cold water. Bring to the boil then drain them immediately and run cold water through to help the vegetables cool quickly, as they should not be added to the pastry case while hot.

Sift the flour and salt into a mixing bowl. Stir in the suet with enough cold water to make a fairly soft dough. Grease the pudding basin, then roll out two-thirds of the dough to line the base and sides of the basin, extending it just above the rim. Pack in the vegetables, adding knobs of butter and seasoning well. Roll the remaining piece of pastry into a round a little larger than the top of the basin, moisten the edges of the pastry with water, then lift the lid into position and press the edges together. Trim off any excess dough with a pair of scissors. Make a pleat along the centre of a piece of foil large enough to cover the basin and extend well down the sides, to allow the pudding to rise. Place the foil over the pudding, securing it with string.

Steam the pudding for 2½ hours, replenishing the water in the steamer whenever necessary with more hot water.

Vegetable Pudding is delicious served with a parsley sauce or gravy made using the vegetable water.

Winter Salad

Serves 4–6

1 lb/450 g red cabbage
½ lb/225 g carrots, peeled and grated
2 oz/50 g raisins
1 large apple
For the Dressing
4 tablespoons salad cream
Grated rind and juice of ½ orange

Using a sharp knife, shred the cabbage and put it into a large bowl, then mix in the grated carrot and the raisins. Quarter, core and chop the apple and stir the pieces through the other ingredients.

Just before the salad is to be served, mix in the salad cream and the grated orange rind and juice. This salad makes a delicious accompaniment to cheese or hard-boiled eggs.

Salad Niçoise

Serves 5–6

2 × 7-oz/198-g cans tuna fish
1 lb/450 g runner or French beans
1 lb/450 g tomatoes
½ large cucumber
2-oz/56-g can anchovy fillets
8 black olives, stoned
For the French Dressing
2 tablespoons cooking oil
1 tablespoon vinegar
1 teaspoon salt
A pinch of pepper
A generous pinch of caster sugar
½ teaspoon dry mustard
A few finely chopped herbs

Drain the fish then flake it with a fork and put in a serving dish. Top and tail the beans. If using runner beans, slice them thinly, but cut French beans into 2-inch/5-cm lengths. Have ready a pan of boiling salted water and cook the beans for about 10 minutes, until tender. Drain them in a sieve or colander and run under cold water to cool before spreading over the tuna fish.

Peel the tomatoes – if you plunge them into boiling water for the count of 20, then transfer them immediately into cold water, the skins should come off easily. Cut the tomatoes into quarters and remove the pips and the centres. Keep several pieces aside for decoration and arrange the rest on top of the beans. Slice the cucumber thinly, peeling it if preferred, and arrange a layer over the tomatoes.

To decorate the salad, first briefly soak the anchovy fillets in a little milk to remove any excess saltiness then halve each fillet lengthways and arrange in a criss-cross design over the salad. Halve the olives and lay them in each diamond shape. Place the reserved tomatoes around the edge of the dish.

To make the French Dressing, place all the ingredients in a screw-topped jar. Shake well, then pour the dressing over the salad about 15 minutes before it is required. This dressing keeps very well in a screw-topped jar, but always shake it well before using.

Salad Niçoise

Scotch Egg Salad

Serves 4

For the Scotch Eggs
4 hard-boiled eggs
Flour
$\frac{3}{4}$ lb/350 g sausagemeat
1 egg, beaten
Dried breadcrumbs
Deep fat or oil for frying
For the Salad
4 medium oranges
$\frac{1}{2}$ lb/225 g tomatoes
3 tablespoons corn oil
1 tablespoon vinegar
1 teaspoon demerara sugar
1 teaspoon made mustard
Salt and pepper
A few sprigs of watercress

1 Shell the eggs and dust them lightly with a little flour. Divide the sausagemeat into four and, on a floured work surface, flatten each piece into an oval to cover one egg.

2 Flour your hands and work the sausagemeat around the eggs so that they are completely enclosed. The surface of the sausagemeat should be smooth with no cracks.

3 Pour the beaten egg on to a plate and spread the breadcrumbs on to greaseproof paper. Brush the Scotch Eggs with the beaten egg and roll them in the breadcrumbs.

4 Coat the eggs again, if liked. Half-fill a deep fat fryer with cooking oil and heat it to 360°F/182°C. Lower the eggs into the fat and cook for 5 to 6 minutes. Drain on absorbent paper and cool.

5 Using a sharp knife, remove the rind from the oranges by cutting spirally around them just below the pith. Slice the oranges and tomatoes and arrange on a serving dish.

6 Put the oil, vinegar, sugar, mustard and seasoning into a screw-topped jar and shake well. Sprinkle the dressing over the salad and arrange the eggs and watercress in the centre.

Artichoke (Globe)
AVAILABLE During the summer
AMOUNT PER PERSON One

Appearance Resembles a very large green prickly bud (it is, in fact, a member of the thistle family).

To Cook Soak the artichoke in cold, salted water for 15 minutes, then cook in boiling, salted water for about 30 minutes, or until the leaves will pull away easily. Drain.

To Serve Serve hot as a first course, with melted butter or Hollandaise sauce, or cold with vinaigrette dressing. It is eaten with the fingers by pulling off a leaf and dipping it in the sauce. Only the base of the leaf and the centre of the stalk is eaten; the round furry choke in the centre is discarded.

Freezing Note *Not recommended for freezing.*

Artichoke (Jerusalem)
AVAILABLE November to February
AMOUNT PER PERSON
6–8 oz/175–225 g

Appearance Looks like a very knobbly potato.

To Cook Scrub, peel and keep until required covered with water which has a little lemon juice added. Cook in boiling salted water – also with lemon juice – for 30 minutes, until tender. Alternatively, the artichokes can be fried.

To Serve Toss in melted butter, or coat with a white or cheese sauce.

Freezing Note *Freeze as a purée. Store for up to 3 months. Reheat gently and serve as a vegetable or dilute with milk and stock to serve as a soup.*

Aubergine (or Eggplant)
AVAILABLE All the year round
AMOUNT PER PERSON
Approx. 6 oz/175 g

Appearance An oval or pear-shaped vegetable with a very dark purple shiny skin.

To Cook Cut off the stalk and surrounding leaves. Wipe the vegetable, then cut it diagonally into ½-inch/1-cm slices. Lay the slices on a plate, sprinkle them liberally with salt and leave for at least 30 minutes to draw off some of the water content. Rinse and dry thoroughly, then fry the slices in equal quantities of butter and oil. Drain on absorbent paper before serving.

To Serve As an accompanying vegetable, or halved and stuffed with meat for a supper dish.

Freezing Note *Freeze only as part of a vegetable dish such as Ratatouille (see page 78). Thaw, then reheat over a moderate heat.*

Beans (French and Runner)
AVAILABLE French from May to July; Runner from June to August
AMOUNT PER PERSON
4–8 oz/100–225 g

Appearance The French bean is about 4–6 inches/10–15 cm long and fairly round. The runner bean is much longer and tends to be broader and flatter.

To Cook Top, tail and string the beans. Keep French beans whole, but thinly slice the runners. Cook the beans in boiling salted water for 15 to 20 minutes, until tender. Drain thoroughly.

To Serve Toss in melted butter.

Freezing Note *Blanch both types of bean for 2 minutes. Store up to a year. Cook from frozen for 5 to 10 minutes in boiling salted water.*

Beetroot
AVAILABLE All the year round
AMOUNT PER PERSON
4–6 oz/100–175 g

Appearance A dark red, edible root with long, green leaves veined with red.

To Cook Beetroots can be bought ready cooked. To cook them yourself, cut off the leaves 1 inch/2·5 cm above the root and cook the roots in boiling salted water until tender. The time will depend on their size and age, but it is usually about 2 hours. Drain and peel off the skins before use.

To Serve Serve cold with a salad, either diced or sliced in a little vinegar, or hot as a vegetable, coated with white sauce.

Freezing Note *Use only small whole beets. Cook as normal, peel, cool then freeze. Store for 6 months. Thaw, then serve tossed in vinegar.*

Broad Beans
AVAILABLE June and July
AMOUNT PER PERSON
8 oz/225 g unshelled weight

Appearance Bought in pods larger than garden peas. The beans inside are very pale green in colour and slightly flat.

To Cook Shell, then cook in boiling, salted water for 20 to 30 minutes, until tender.

To Serve Toss in melted butter or coat with a parsley sauce.

Freezing Note *Use only small young beans. Blanch for 3 minutes then store for 6 to 9 months. Cook from frozen for 5 to 10 minutes in boiling salted water.*

Broccoli
AVAILABLE February to April
AMOUNT PER PERSON
6–8 oz/175–225 g

Appearance From the same family as the cauliflower, broccoli comes in several varieties – White, Purple or Calabrese (green). It has a small flower head of either white, purple or green which is surrounded by green, fairly elongated leaves.

To Cook Discard the coarse leaves and stems. Cut off the flower heads with a stem of about 2 inches/5 cm and shred the rest of the leaves. Wash the broccoli then cook it in boiling, salted water for about 15 to 20 minutes, until tender. Drain thoroughly.

To Serve Toss in melted butter or serve with a Hollandaise sauce.

Freezing Note *Blanch for 2 to 3 minutes. Store for up to a year. Cook from frozen for 5 to 10 minutes in boiling salted water.*

Brussels Sprouts
AVAILABLE September to March
AMOUNT PER PERSON
4–6 oz/100–175 g

Appearance A small bud of the cabbage family, with green, densely packed leaves.

To Cook Wash, remove any damaged leaves and trim away stalks. Cut a cross in the base of the sprouts to help them cook to the centre. Cook in a pan of boiling, salted water, without a lid, for about 15 minutes, until tender. Drain thoroughly.

To Serve Toss in melted butter. Brussels Sprouts are delicious served with cooked chestnuts.

Freezing Note *Blanch for 2 to 3 minutes. Store for up to a year. Cook from frozen for 5 to 10 minutes in boiling salted water.*

Cabbage (Dutch, Savoy, Red)

AVAILABLE All the year round
AMOUNT PER PERSON
Approx. 4 oz/100 g

Appearance Round with dense leaves.
Dutch Leaves are smooth, almost white.
Savoy Leaves are green, sometimes tinged with purple and have an embossed appearance.
Red Smooth, dark red leaves.

To Cook Discard the coarse outer leaves, cut the cabbage into four and remove the centre stalk. Wash the cabbage well, then shred the leaves finely. Cook in boiling, salted water for 10 to 15 minutes. Drain well. (Add 1 tablespoon vinegar when cooking red cabbage.)

To Serve Toss in melted butter, with a little grated nutmeg. Dutch cabbage is also used for coleslaw.

Freezing Note *Not recommended for freezing.*

Carrots

AVAILABLE All the year round; new in the summer, old in the winter
AMOUNT PER PERSON
4–6 oz/100–175 g

Appearance An edible root, orange in colour with green, feathery leaves.

To Cook New Trim the leaves, then scrape the carrots with a knife. Cook them whole in boiling, salted water for about 15 minutes, until tender. Drain.
Old Peel thinly with a knife or potato peeler then cut into slices, dice or strips. Cook in boiling salted water for about 20 minutes and drain well.

To Serve Toss in melted butter with chopped parsley.

Freezing Note *Use only new carrots. Slice or dice to add to casseroles. To serve whole, blanch for 3 to 4 minutes then cook whole from frozen in boiling salted water for 5 to 10 minutes. They will store frozen for up to a year.*

Cauliflower

AVAILABLE Almost all the year round, but cheaper between June and October
AMOUNT PER PERSON
A medium cauliflower will serve four

Appearance A close white head surrounded by green leaves.

To Cook Trim the stalk, remove the outer coarse leaves, then cut a cross in the base of the stalk to enable the cauliflower to cook right through. Place it, stalk down, in a pan one-quarter full of boiling, salted water and cook, uncovered, for 20 to 30 minutes, depending on size. Drain well. The flower can be divided into florets before cooking, when they will take only 10 to 15 minutes.

To Serve Coat with white or cheese sauce, or sprinkle with breadcrumbs fried in butter.

Freezing Note *Blanch in florets with lemon juice added to the water, for 3 minutes. Store for up to 6 months. Cook from frozen in boiling salted water for 5 to 7 minutes.*

Celery

AVAILABLE Almost all the year round
AMOUNT PER PERSON
2–3 sticks, or ½ head, if small

Appearance A vegetable with long, whitish or green stalks and green leaves, on a central base.

To Cook Trim, then wash and scrub thoroughly. Cut the sticks into even lengths and cook in boiling salted water for 30 to 40 minutes, until tender. Drain well. Celery can also be braised: prepare as for boiling, cook for 5 minutes in boiling salted water, drain and place in an ovenproof dish. Season, dot with butter and bake, covered, for 1 to 1½ hours at gas mark 4 or 350°F/180°C.

To Serve Coat boiled celery with white, cheese or parsley sauce.

Freezing Note *Once frozen, it is only suitable to add to casseroles or soups. Prepare, cut into 1-inch/2·5-cm lengths and blanch for 3 minutes. Store for up to a year. Simmer in boiling salted water for 10 minutes or braise in a little stock.*

Chicory (Known in France and U.S.A. as Endive)

AVAILABLE Almost all the year round
AMOUNT PER PERSON
1–2 heads when cooked; less when raw

Appearance A very pale, almost white, closely-packed bud about 4 inches/10 cm long.

To Cook Trim off the end and, with a sharp knife, remove the core. Discard any damaged leaves and wash thoroughly. Cook in boiling, salted water with a little lemon juice for about 20 minutes. Drain thoroughly.

To Serve Toss in butter or coat with a white or cheese sauce.

Freezing Note *Only suitable, once frozen, as a hot vegetable dish. Blanch for 2 minutes with lemon juice added to the water. Drain well. Store for up to 6 months. Cook from frozen in stock or braise with butter.*

Courgettes (Zucchini)

AVAILABLE Almost all the year round
AMOUNT PER PERSON
Approx. 4 oz/100 g

Appearance Resembles a baby marrow, about 4 inches/10 cm long and 1 inch/2·5 cm in diameter. Green with paler markings.

To Cook Trim off the stalks and wash the vegetables then leave unpeeled and cook either whole or cut into slices. Place the courgettes in an ovenproof dish greased with butter, sprinkle with seasoning and dot with a little extra butter. Cover and cook at gas mark 4 or 350°F/180°C, for 30 to 40 minutes, until tender.

To Serve Serve from the dish, using any excess liquid as a sauce. Courgettes can also be served whole and stuffed as a first course.

Freezing Note *Freeze as for aubergines.*

Cucumber

AVAILABLE All the year round though cheaper in the summer months
AMOUNT PER PERSON
Approx. 4 oz/100 g

Appearance Usually about 12 inches/30 cm long and 2 inches/5 cm in diameter with a brilliant green, fairly shiny surface which is faintly ribbed.

To Cook Cucumber is normally served cold in a salad, but it can be eaten hot as an accompanying vegetable. Peel and cut the cucumber into fairly large dice. Melt 1 oz/25 g butter in a pan, add the cucumber, cover the pan, then cook gently for about 20 minutes, until tender. Season after cooking.

To Serve With the butter in which it was cooked, or coated with a white sauce.

Freezing Note *Not recommended.*

Greens (Spring)

AVAILABLE February to June
AMOUNT PER PERSON
6–8 oz/175–225 g

Appearance A very open cabbage of a dark green colour.

To Cook Cut off the base and separate the leaves. Remove any coarse stems, wash then shred the greens and cook in boiling salted water, uncovered, for 10 to 15 minutes. Drain thoroughly.

To Serve Toss in melted butter with a little grated nutmeg.

Freezing Note *Not recommended for freezing.*

Leeks

AVAILABLE August to May
AMOUNT PER PERSON
8–12 oz/225–350 g

Appearance A thick white stem blending into a green top. It is a member of the onion family.

To Cook Trim off the roots, outer leaves and as much of the green tops as necessary. Split from the top to within 1 inch/2·5 cm of the base and run cold water through to remove all the grit. Cook the leeks in boiling salted water for 20 to 30 minutes, until tender. Drain well. Leeks can also be braised in a moderate oven, gas mark 4 or 350°F/180°C, for about 1 to 1½ hours.

To Serve Coat with a white or cheese sauce.

Freezing Note *Cut into rings and blanch for 1 minute. Store for up to 3 months. Cook from frozen for 5 minutes in boiling salted water or add to soups and casseroles.*

Marrow

AVAILABLE July to September
AMOUNT PER PERSON
Approx. 6 oz/175 g

Appearance A long round vegetable at least 4 inches/10 cm in diameter. The skin is usually green and can have white markings.

To Cook Peel the marrow, cut it into even-sized pieces and remove the seeds. Cook in boiling salted water for 15 minutes, until just tender. Leave to drain.

To Serve Coat with a white or cheese sauce. Marrow can also be stuffed and baked either whole or in rings.

Freezing Note *Not recommended for freezing.*

Mushrooms

AVAILABLE All the year round
AMOUNT PER PERSON
Approx. 2 oz/50 g

Appearance An edible fungi, off-white in colour, with a darker brown inside cap.

To Cook Wipe the mushrooms and trim the stalks – there is no need to peel them unless they are field mushrooms, when they should be peeled and washed. Melt a little butter in a pan, add a squeeze of lemon juice and cook the mushrooms gently for about 10 minutes, until tender. Alternatively, they can be grilled or fried.

To Serve Normally eaten as an accompanying vegetable, but can be stuffed and served as a first course.

Freezing Note *Sauté in butter then drain. Store for up to 3 months. Add to casseroles or braise in butter.*

Onions

AVAILABLE – all the year round;
Spring Onions *– during the summer*
AMOUNT PER PERSON
4–6 oz/100–175 g

Appearance Varying in size from ½–4 inches/1–10 cm in diameter, they are generally round and bulbous in appearance, with light brown papery outer skin and white flesh.
Spring Onions Smaller and longer in shape than an onion, with a white bulbous case and green leaves.

To Cook Discard the outer skin, trim the root and slice or chop before frying in fat for 10 to 15 minutes, turning frequently. Alternatively, boil whole in salted water for 30 to 40 minutes and drain well.

To Serve If boiled, coat with a sauce. Spring onions are usually served in a salad.

Freezing Note *Use small onions for sauces, casseroles, etc. Blanch for 4 minutes, wrap well and store for 3 months. Reheat in a sauce or in casseroles. Large onions can be frozen, unblanched, for up to a month. Wrap well before freezing.*

Parsnips

AVAILABLE November to March
AMOUNT PER PERSON
Approx. 6 oz/175 g

Appearance Resembles a carrot in shape, but is much larger, with a light brown skin and off-white flesh.

To Cook Peel and cut into pieces. Cook in boiling salted water for 30 to 40 minutes, until tender, or place around a joint to be roasted.

To Serve Toss in butter with a little grated nutmeg.

Freezing Note *Freeze diced or sliced to add to casseroles or make into soup. Blanch for 3 minutes then store for up to a year. Cook in boiling salted water for 10 to 15 minutes.*

Peas

AVAILABLE June to August
AMOUNT PER PERSON
8 oz/225 g unshelled weight

Appearance Sold in pods, which are about 4 inches/10 cm long and fairly plump.

To Cook Shell, wash and cook the peas in boiling salted water for 20 minutes, until tender. Add a sprig of mint, if available. Drain well.

To Serve Toss in melted butter.

Freezing Note *Blanch for 1 minute, store for up to a year. Cook in boiling salted water for 3 to 5 minutes.*

Potatoes

AVAILABLE All the year round
AMOUNT PER PERSON
Approx. 6 oz/175 g

Appearance Round with a brown skin and off-white flesh.

To Cook Potatoes can be boiled, fried, creamed, roasted, baked in their jackets, and so on. To boil: peel and cut into pieces then cook in boiling salted water for about 30 minutes, until tender. Drain. New potatoes are scraped and boiled for 20 minutes in salted water. Drain.

To Serve Toss in melted butter with chopped parsley.

Freezing Note *As chips, blanch in fat for 2 to 3 minutes, store for up to a year. Brown carefully from frozen in hot fat. New potatoes freeze whole once cooked. Store for up to 6 months, then reheat from frozen at gas mark 6 or 400°F/200°C for 30 to 40 minutes, in a covered buttered casserole dish.*

Spinach

AVAILABLE October to July
AMOUNT PER PERSON
Approx. 8 oz/225 g

Appearance Fairly large, dark green leaves; sold loose.

To Cook Wash well to remove all the grit and sand. Remove the coarse stems before placing immediately in a pan, without adding any extra water. Heat the pan gently, turning the spinach occasionally and cook for about 10 to 15 minutes, until tender. Drain well.

To Serve Toss in melted butter with seasoning and a little grated nutmeg, or stir in a tablespoon of single cream instead of the butter.

Freezing Note *Blanch for 2 minutes then store for up to a year. Cook in a little boiling salted water for 5 minutes.*

Swedes

AVAILABLE October to March
AMOUNT PER PERSON
4–6 oz/100–175 g

Appearance Large and round in shape with yellow flesh and a pinkish skin.

To Cook Peel and cut into even-sized pieces. Cook in boiling salted water for about 30 to 40 minutes, until tender. Drain.

To Serve Mash and beat with butter, seasoning and grated nutmeg. Raw swede can also be added to casseroles, soups, etc.

Freezing Note *Freeze diced or sliced to add to casseroles or make into soup. Blanch for 3 minutes and store for up to a year. Cook from frozen in boiling salted water for 10 to 15 minutes.*

Sweet Peppers

AVAILABLE Almost all the year round
AMOUNT PER PERSON
4 oz/100 g or 1 medium pepper

Appearance They can be bought both red or green. The outside skin is usually shiny and the inside of the pepper has a small core with very hot seeds.

To Cook Cut the pepper in half and remove the core and seeds, then chop or slice the flesh, before adding to casseroles, etc. For a salad, blanch the pieces of pepper in boiling, salted water for 1 minute, then leave to cool.

To Serve Usually as an accompanying vegetable with other ingredients, e.g. onions, tomatoes, aubergines. Peppers can also be left whole and stuffed for a supper dish.

Freezing Note *Freeze only as part of a vegetable dish such as Ratatouille (see page 78). Store for up to 3 months then reheat over a moderate heat.*

Sweetcorn (Corn on the Cob)

AVAILABLE June to August
AMOUNT PER PERSON 1 cob

Appearance A large husk with many densely packed, pale yellow kernels (seeds). Usually bought in its outer casing of pale green leaves.

To Cook Remove the outer leaves and the thread-like strands inside. Cook the cobs in plenty of unsalted water, covered, for 15 to 30 minutes. Add salt to the water just before the sweetcorn is ready – if added earlier the corn will toughen.

To Serve Brush with melted butter and serve with extra butter. Corn skewers can be bought to hold the cobs while eating.

Freezing Note *Blanch for 4 to 8 minutes, depending on size. Store for up to a year. Thaw and cook for 10 minutes from frozen in boiling salted water.*

Tomatoes

AVAILABLE All the year round but cheaper in the summer
AMOUNT PER PERSON
Approx. 1 or 2

Appearance Brilliant red in colour; round, with numerous seeds inside.

To Cook Tomatoes may be grilled, fried, baked or eaten raw in salads. To bake: wipe, halve and place in an ovenproof dish. Dot with butter and sprinkle with salt and pepper. Cover with foil and bake the tomatoes for about 30 minutes at gas mark 4 or 350°F/180°C.

To Serve Sprinkle with freshly chopped herbs or parsley.

Freezing Note *Use only for cooking once frozen. Pack whole in polythene bags and store for up to 1 month. Thaw, peel then add to cooked dishes.*

Turnips

AVAILABLE October to March
AMOUNT PER PERSON
4–6 oz/100–175 g

Appearance Similar to a swede in shape, but the skin is white and pale green in colour, and the inside flesh white.

To Cook Peel, and cut into even-sized pieces, or, if small, leave the turnips whole. Cook in boiling, salted water for about 30 minutes, until tender. Drain well.

To Serve Toss in melted butter or coat with a white sauce. Cooked turnips can also be mashed with butter and a little nutmeg. Raw turnip can be chopped and added to casseroles and soups.

Freezing Note *Freeze diced or sliced to add to casseroles or make into soup. Blanch for 3 minutes and store for up to a year. Cook from frozen in boiling salted water for 3 to 5 minutes.*

Desserts-Hot and Cold

Although Britain is famous for its hot, steaming puddings, laden with dried fruit and dripping in syrup, there is also a host of less substantial desserts, both hot and cold, that are just as delicious and welcome after the main course of the meal.

Queen of Puddings

Serves 4–6

1 pint/600 ml milk
1 oz/25 g margarine
3 oz/75 g fresh white breadcrumbs
3 oz/75 g caster sugar
Finely grated rind of ½ orange
2 large eggs (size 2), separated
3 tablespoons raspberry jam
Caster sugar for sprinkling
A 2-pint/1·25-litre ovenproof dish

Put the milk and margarine into a saucepan over a low heat and melt the margarine. Sprinkle the bread-crumbs into a mixing bowl, pour over the heated milk, adding 1 oz/25 g of the measured sugar and the orange rind. Leave the mixture on one side to soak for 30 minutes.

Stir the yolks into the bread mixture, pour into the greased dish and bake in the centre of a moderate oven, gas mark 4 or 350°F/180°C, for 30 minutes or until it is just set. Warm the jam over a low heat and spread it over the cooked base.

Whisk the egg whites until they are stiff and stand in straight peaks, add 2 tablespoons of the remaining measured sugar and re-whisk the mixture until it returns to its original stiffness. Fold in the rest of the sugar and turn the meringue on to the pudding base. Spread it to the sides, leaving the surface rough. Sprinkle over a little extra caster sugar, then bake the pudding on the centre shelf of a moderately cool oven, gas mark 3 or 325°F/160°C, for about 10 minutes, until the meringue is tinged golden brown. Serve warm.

Orange Ginger Sponge

Serves 5–6

3 tablespoons golden syrup
2 medium oranges
4 oz/110 g margarine
4 oz/110 g light soft brown sugar
1 large egg (size 2), made up to ½ pint/300 ml with milk
6 oz/170 g self-raising flour
A pinch of salt
1½ teaspoons ground ginger
A 2½-pint/1·5-litre pudding basin, greased with an extra ½ oz/15 g margarine

Pour the syrup into the greased pudding basin. Cut each orange into six slices, put into a pan of cold water and bring to the boil. Boil the slices for 3 minutes to blanch them, then drain on absorbent paper. Arrange around the inside of the basin.

Beat the margarine to a soft cream, then beat in the sugar until light and fluffy in both colour and texture. Stir in the egg and milk with the sifted flour, salt and ground ginger and, when well blended, turn the mixture into the basin and hollow out the centre slightly.

Cover the basin with a piece of greased foil, forming a pleat down the centre. Place in a steamer (or a saucepan with a tight-fitting lid) and cook for 1½ hours, until the pudding feels springy. Replenish the steamer with boiling water when necessary.

Loosen the sponge from around the edges of the basin, turn on to a plate and serve hot with custard.

For a Baked Pudding

To bake instead of steam the pudding, cover the basin in the same way, then cook the sponge pudding on the centre shelf of a moderate oven, gas mark 4 or 350°F/180°C, for 1¼ hours, or until springy to touch.

Freezing Note *Store for up to 2 months, thaw then steam for about 45 minutes, until thoroughly hot.*

Orange Ginger Sponge

Steamed Chocolate Pudding

Serves 4–6

- 7 oz/200 g self-raising flour
- 1 oz/25 g cocoa powder
- A pinch of salt
- 3 oz/85 g margarine
- 3 oz/85 g granulated sugar
- 1 large egg (size 2), beaten and made up to ¼ pint/150 ml with milk

For the Sauce

- 2 tablespoons cornflour
- 1 tablespoon cocoa powder
- ¾ pint/450 ml milk
- 2 tablespoons granulated sugar

A 2-pint/1·25-litre fluted metal mould

Sift the flour, cocoa powder and salt into a mixing bowl. Add the margarine cut into small pieces and, using the fingertips only, rub the fat into the dry ingredients until it is evenly distributed and the mixture resembles fine breadcrumbs. Stir in the sugar. Add the beaten egg and milk and, using a wooden spoon, stir into the other ingredients to make a soft consistency.

Brush the mould with melted fat and turn the mixture into it. Cover the mould with a piece of greased foil, making a pleat down the centre to allow the pudding to rise, and secure it with string. Cook the pudding in a double steamer or in a saucepan with boiling water to come just halfway up the sides of the mould, for about 1½ hours. Add more boiling water when necessary.

Meanwhile make the sauce. Put the cornflour and cocoa powder into a pan and gradually blend in the milk. When the sauce is smooth, put the pan over the heat and, stirring all the time, bring the sauce to the boil. Cook it for a minute so that it thickens, then stir in the sugar.

Turn the pudding on to a plate, pour a little sauce over the top and serve the rest of the sauce separately.

Orange Sunflower Meringue

Serves 5–6

- 3½ oz/90 g margarine
- 2 egg yolks
- ¼ pint/150 ml water
- Grated rind and juice of 1 orange
- 6 oz/175 g caster sugar
- 4 oz/100 g fresh white breadcrumbs

For the Topping

- 1 orange
- 2 egg whites
- 4 oz/100 g caster sugar
- 2 oz/50 g desiccated coconut

A 2-pint/1·25-litre soufflé dish

Melt the margarine in a saucepan over a gentle heat, then brush a little over the base and sides of the soufflé dish.

Mix the egg yolks together, add the water, orange rind and juice, remaining melted margarine, sugar and breadcrumbs and, when they are all well mixed, turn into the greased soufflé dish and smooth over the surface. Bake in a moderate oven, gas mark 4 or 350°F/180°C, for 30 minutes. When cooked, the pudding should be firm to the touch but fairly moist in appearance.

Cut four slices of orange for the top and divide three of them in half. Whisk the egg whites until very stiff, so that they stand in straight peaks, then add 2 tablespoons of the caster sugar and whisk again until it regains its former stiff consistency. Using a metal spoon fold the remaining caster sugar and the desiccated coconut as lightly as possible into the whisked egg whites. Turn this meringue mixture on to the baked pudding base and spread it over with a knife, leaving the surface fairly rough. Arrange the orange slices on top, return the pudding to the oven and bake for a further 35 to 40 minutes. Serve immediately, while the topping is still crisp.

Freezing Note *Store the cooked pudding base only for up to a month. The egg whites will keep fresh in a covered container in the refrigerator. Thaw the pudding base for 4 hours then continue as in the recipe.*

Plum Dumpling

Serves 5

For the Suet Crust Pastry

- 8 oz/225 g self-raising flour
- A pinch of salt
- 3 oz/85 g prepared shredded suet

For the Filling

- 1½ lb/675 g ripe plums
- 4 oz/100 g light soft brown sugar

A 1½-pint/900 ml pudding basin

Sift the flour and salt into a mixing bowl, stir in the shredded suet, then mix in enough cold water to make a soft but not sticky dough. Cut off a quarter of the dough for a lid and roll the rest into a circle large enough to line the pudding basin. Brush the basin with melted fat and line it with the pastry to cover the sides and base evenly and come just above the rim.

Wipe the plums, halve them and remove the stones. Layer the halves into the lined basin, covering each layer with sugar. Roll out the piece of pastry for the lid, moisten the top of the crust in the basin with water and cover the dumpling with the lid, pressing the edges well together. Trim off any excess pastry with a pair of scissors.

Take a piece of foil large enough to loosely cover the top and tuck well down the sides, and make a pleat across it to allow for expansion of the pudding. Cover the pudding and tie the foil securely in position with a piece of string.

Cook the Plum Dumpling on the centre shelf of a moderate oven, gas mark 4 or 350°F/180°C, for about 2 hours. When ready, remove the string and foil, loosen the pudding

Plum Dumpling

around the sides of the basin and turn it out on to a heated serving plate. Serve immediately with custard.

Bread and Butter Pudding

Serves 4–6

¾ pint/450 ml milk
¼ teaspoon ground cinnamon
1½ oz/40 g granulated sugar
1 small bay leaf
6 thin slices white bread
2 oz/50 g butter
2 oz/50 g mixed dried fruit, cleaned
3 large eggs (size 2)
A 2-pint/1·25-litre ovenproof dish

Pour the milk into a saucepan, add the cinnamon, sugar and bay leaf, and bring it to just below boiling point over a low heat. Remove the pan from the heat and leave on one side for the flavours to infuse and for the milk to cool.

Meanwhile, spread the slices of bread with almost all the butter, and grease the dish with the rest. Trim off the crusts and cut each slice of bread into four triangles. Layer the triangles, butter side up, in the dish, sprinkling mixed fruit between each layer. Beat the eggs together, stir them into the milk, then strain into the dish over the bread slices, making sure that all the bread is evenly moistened with the milk.

Bake the Bread and Butter Pudding on the centre shelf of a moderate oven, gas mark 4 or 350°F/180°C, for about 1 hour, until well risen and golden brown. Serve immediately.

Swiss Apple Tart

Serves 6–8

For the Pastry
8 oz/225 g plain flour
A pinch of salt
2 oz/55 g margarine
2 oz/55 g lard
For the Filling
6 tart eating apples
Grated rind and juice of 1 orange
1 oz/25 g granulated sugar
½ teaspoon ground mixed spice
For the Topping
3 oz/75 g demerara sugar
3 oz/75 g plain flour
3 oz/75 g butter, softened
A 2-pint/1·25-litre shallow pie dish

Sift the flour and salt into a mixing bowl, add the fats cut into pieces and rub in with the fingertips until the mixture resembles fine breadcrumbs. Stir in sufficient cold water to make a fairly stiff dough and knead lightly until smooth.

Roll the dough into a large circle and use to line the pie dish; trim off any excess.

Peel, core and thickly slice the apples, then toss them in the orange juice and put into the pastry case. Mix the granulated sugar with the mixed spice and sprinkle over the apples.

Put the demerara sugar and flour into a mixing bowl with the orange rind, add the butter and, using a knife, cut it through into the dry ingredients until evenly distributed. Cover the apples with this topping and bake the tart on the centre shelf of a hot oven, gas mark 7 or 425°F/220°C, for 10 minutes, then reduce the heat to gas mark 4 or 350°F/180°C for a further 30 minutes, until golden. Serve hot with cream, if liked.

Freezing Note *Store the cooked and cooled tart for up to 3 months. Thaw, then heat through in a moderate oven, gas mark 4 or 350°F/180°C, for 20 to 30 minutes.*

Family Fruit Roll

Serves 6

For the Pastry
8 oz/225 g plain flour
A pinch of salt
1 tablespoon baking powder
4 oz/110 g margarine
2 oz/50 g porridge oats
About ¼ pint/150 ml milk

For the Filling and Topping
1 lb/450 g cooking apples, peeled, cored and sliced
4 oz/100 g currants, cleaned
7 oz/200 g caster sugar
1 teaspoon ground cinnamon
1 oz/25 g margarine
7½ fl oz/225 ml water
1 tablespoon lemon juice
A 2-pint/1·25-litre ovenproof dish

First make the pastry. Sift the flour, salt and baking powder into a mixing bowl, add the margarine and rub the fat into the flour so it is evenly distributed. Stir in the oats, then bind the ingredients together with enough milk to make a soft but not sticky dough. Turn the dough on to a lightly floured work surface and roll it into a 12 × 8-inch/30 × 20-cm rectangle. Trim the edges.

Mix the prepared apples with the currants, 1 oz/25 g sugar and the cinnamon. Melt the margarine, brush some of it over the pastry and cover it with the apple filling. Roll the dough up to make an 8-inch/20-cm length, then cut it into eight slices and lay them flat in the dish. Brush the surface of the slices with the rest of the melted margarine.

Put the remaining sugar into a pan with the water and dissolve over a low heat. Bring the syrup to the boil and boil it rapidly for 2 minutes. Remove the pan from the heat, stir in the lemon juice and pour the syrup over the slices.

Bake the pudding on the centre shelf of a fairly hot oven, gas mark 6 or 400°F/200°C, for 25 to 30 minutes, until the pastry is golden brown and cooked through.

Serve the Family Fruit Roll with cream or custard.

Freezing Note *Store cooked and cooled for up to 3 months, then reheat at gas mark 5 or 375°F/190°C for 30 minutes, or until hot.*

Baked Apples

Serves 4

4 medium cooking apples
3 tablespoons mincemeat
2 tablespoons golden syrup
A little lemon juice

Wash the apples and, keeping them whole, remove the cores. Using a sharp knife, score around the middle of the apples – this is to stop them bursting during cooking – and place in an ovenproof dish.

Mix together the mincemeat, syrup and lemon juice then spoon this filling into the centres of the apples. Cover the dish with foil and bake the apples in a moderately cool oven, gas mark 3 or 325°F/160°C, for 2 hours.

Serve the Baked Apples hot with custard.

Apple Charlotte

Serves 4–6

1½ lb/675 g cooking apples
6 oz/175 g fresh white breadcrumbs
Grated rind of 1 orange
6 oz/175 g demerara sugar
2 oz/50 g prepared shredded suet
2 oz/50 g butter
A 2-pint/1·25-litre ovenproof dish

Peel, core and slice the apples quite finely. Mix the breadcrumbs with the orange rind, sugar and suet.

Grease the ovenproof dish with a little of the butter, then pack it with alternate layers of sliced apple and crumb mixture, finishing with the crumbs – press each layer down really well as the pudding shrinks during cooking. Dot the top of the pudding with the rest of the butter, then cover it with a lid which has an air hole, or a piece of foil with a small hole made in it.

Cook the pudding on a baking tray on the centre shelf of a moderate oven, gas mark 4 or 350°F/180°C, for about 1 hour. The lid can be removed for the last 15 minutes to brown and crisp the top.

Freezing Note *Store the cooked and cooled pudding for up to 3 months. Thaw, then reheat at gas mark 4 or 350°F/180°C for about 30 minutes.*

French Apple Tart

Serves 6

For the Pastry
6 oz/170 g plain flour
3 oz/85 g butter, softened
3 oz/85 g caster sugar
1 egg yolk
1 tablespoon water

For the Filling
2 lb/1 kg cooking apples
2 oz/50 g caster sugar
3 tablespoons apricot jam, sieved
A 9-inch/23-cm fluted china flan dish

1 Sift the flour on to a work surface and form it into a circular 'wall'. Place the softened butter in the centre with the sugar, egg yolk and

water and combine them together with the fingertips only.

2 Flick in the flour from around the ring and work it in still using your fingertips. Knead the ingredients lightly to form a soft dough, then wrap in greaseproof paper and leave in a cool place for 30 minutes.

3 On a lightly floured work surface roll out the pastry to a circle at least 2 inches/5 cm larger than the flan dish. Fold it into three, lift into the centre of the dish then open it out and carefully press the dough into the base and sides.

4 Remove the surplus pastry by running a rolling pin across the top of the flan dish to neaten the edge. Peel and thinly slice the apples and place them in water with lemon juice, so that they do not discolour.

5 Overlap the slices in layers in the flan case, sprinkling each layer with sugar. Bake the tart on the centre shelf of a moderately hot oven, gas mark 5 or 375°F/190°C, for 35 to 40 minutes. Leave the tart to cool slightly.

6 Warm the sieved apricot jam in a small pan over a low heat and carefully brush the jam over the apples so they are well covered.

Serve the French Apple Tart either hot or cold with single cream.

Freezing Note *Store the cooled and cooked tart for up to 3 months. Thaw, then heat through at gas mark 4 or 350°F/180°C for 20 to 30 minutes.*

French Apple Tart

Rice Pudding

Serves 4–6

3 oz/75 g short-grain rice
3 oz/75 g caster sugar
1½ pints/900 ml milk
A little grated nutmeg
A 2-pint/1·25-litre ovenproof dish, greased with ½ oz/15 g butter

In the Oven
Tip the rice into the buttered dish and sprinkle with the sugar. Pour in the milk, then bake the rice pudding on the centre shelf of a cool oven, gas mark 2 or 300°F/150°C, for 2 hours.

On Top of the Cooker
Put the milk into a pan, slowly bring it to the boil then add the rice and sugar. Reduce the heat and simmer the pudding gently for about 30 minutes, uncovered, until the rice is tender. Stir the pudding occasionally so that it does not stick to the pan. When the rice is tender and creamy, turn into a heated serving dish and sprinkle with grated nutmeg.

Pears in Cider

Serves 6

6 firm ripe pears
¼ pint/150 ml cider
¼ pint/150 ml water
1 lemon
4 oz/100 g soft brown sugar
½ teaspoon ground cinnamon
1 teaspoon arrowroot

Using a potato peeler and working from the base of each pear, remove as much of the core as possible. Peel the pears but do not remove the stalks.

Pears in Cider

Pour the cider and water into a pan. Thinly pare the rind from the lemon using a potato peeler and add to the pan with the juice from the lemon, sugar and cinnamon; heat slowly to dissolve the sugar. Add the pears and poach them gently for about 30 minutes, until tender but still whole. Turn them several times in the syrup so they cook evenly.

Using a perforated spoon, transfer the pears to individual serving dishes. Remove the lemon rind from the pan, cut half of it into very fine strips and return to the syrup.

Blend the arrowroot to a smooth paste with a little of the syrup and stir into the rest. Bring the syrup to the boil, stirring all the time, and cook for 1 minute, until clear. Spoon the syrup over each pear.

Lemon Meringue Pie

Serves 6

For the Pastry
8 oz/225 g plain flour
A pinch of salt
2 oz/55 g margarine
2 oz/55 g lard
For the Filling
Grated rind and juice of 2 large lemons
¼ pint/150 ml water
2 oz/50 g cornflour
8 oz/225 g caster sugar
2 egg yolks
For the Meringue
2 egg whites
4 oz/100 g caster sugar
An 8½-inch/21-cm fluted flan ring

Sift the flour and salt into a mixing bowl. Add the fats, cut into small pieces, and, using the fingertips only, rub them in until evenly distributed. Stir in enough cold water to make a fairly firm dough, then turn on to a floured work surface and knead lightly.

Stand the flan ring on an upturned baking tray. Roll the pastry into a circle 2 inches/5 cm larger than the ring and lift it on a rolling pin into the ring. Using the back of the hand, press the pastry into the sides and base of the ring and remove any surplus pastry by rolling the pin first one way and then the other across the top of the flan ring. Cover the base of the flan with a piece of crumpled tissue paper and half-fill it with baking beans or dry crusts of bread, to maintain a good shape while cooking.

Bake the pastry flan case on the centre shelf of a moderately hot oven, gas mark 5 or 375°F/190°C, for 30 minutes. Remove the paper and beans and slip off the ring before baking the flan case for a further 10 minutes.

Meanwhile, make the filling. Put the lemon rind and juice into a pan with the water, cornflour and sugar. Stir over a very gentle heat until smooth, then bring the mixture to the boil and simmer for a few minutes. Take the pan off the heat and beat a little of the mixture into the egg yolks, then return this to the main bulk of filling and pour it all into the baked flan case.

Whisk the egg whites for the meringue until stiff and standing in straight peaks. Add 2 tablespoons from the measured sugar and re-whisk the mixture until it regains its original stiffness. Fold in the remaining sugar. Pile the meringue on top of the filling and spread it to the sides so that it is completely covered. Flick the meringue into peaks or swirl into a mound, and bake on the centre shelf of either a cool oven, gas mark 2 or 300°F/150°C, for about 30 minutes (to give a crisper meringue), or a fairly hot oven, gas mark 6 or 400°F/200°C, for 4 to 5 minutes, until the meringue is tinged golden brown. Serve hot or cold.

Freezing Note *Store the baked pastry case for up to 3 months. Thaw for 1 hour then continue as in the recipe.*

Lemon Meringue Pie, Meringue Mandarins

Meringue Mandarins

Serves 4

- 4 large oranges
- 2 tablespoons custard powder
- ½ pint/300 ml milk
- 2 oz/50 g caster sugar
- 1 egg yolk

For the Meringue

- 1 egg white
- 2 oz/50 g caster sugar

A large piping bag with No 8 large star pipe attached

Cut the tops from the oranges then, using a grapefruit knife, scoop out the fruit and chop it roughly.

In a pan, blend the custard powder with the milk then, over a gentle heat and stirring all the time, bring it to the boil and cook for a few minutes to thicken. Remove the pan from the heat, beat in the sugar and egg yolk, then return to the heat and, stirring all the time, bring the sauce back to the boil.

Leave the sauce to cool slightly. Drain the pieces of orange thoroughly, then gradually add them to the sauce, beating well between each addition to prevent curdling.

Stand the orange shells in a tin and divide the filling between them.

Whisk the egg white until stiff and standing in straight peaks. Add 1 tablespoon from the measured sugar and re-whisk the mixture until it regains its original stiffness. Fold in the remaining sugar. Fill the piping bag and pipe a swirl over the top of each orange to seal in the filling.

Place the oranges on the centre shelf of a moderate oven, gas mark 4 or 350°F/180°C, for 10 minutes, until the meringue is tinged golden brown. Serve at once.

Hot Lemon Soufflé

Serves 4

$\frac{3}{4}$ oz/20 g plain flour
$\frac{1}{2}$ pint/300 ml milk
2 oz/50 g caster sugar
$\frac{3}{4}$ oz/20 g butter
3 large eggs (size 2), separated
Grated rind and juice of $\frac{1}{2}$ lemon
A $2\frac{1}{2}$-pint/1·5-litre soufflé dish

Grease the soufflé dish with a little extra butter and dust it with extra caster sugar.

Blend the flour to a smooth paste with a little of the milk. Pour the rest of the milk into a pan and bring it to the boil. Remove from the heat and stir in the sugar and butter cut into pieces. When the butter has melted, pour the liquid on to the flour paste, stirring all the time, then return to the pan. Bring the sauce back to the boil, again stirring continuously, and cook it for 1 minute so that the sauce thickens. Cool for a few seconds then stir the egg yolks into the sauce.

Whisk the egg whites until they are quite stiff. Beat the lemon juice and rind into the sauce, then, using a metal spoon, very carefully fold in the egg whites. Do not over-mix at this stage as it will only knock air out of the mixture and the soufflé may fail to rise.

Turn the mixture quickly into the soufflé dish and bake on the centre shelf of a moderately hot oven, gas mark 5 or 375°F/190°C, for about 30 minutes, until the mixture is golden brown and risen.

Apricot Special
To make the soufflé really super, empty a can of drained apricot halves into the prepared dish, spoon the lemon soufflé mixture on top and bake as for Hot Lemon Soufflé.

Crêpes Suzette

Crêpes Suzette

Serves 4

For the Pancakes
4 oz/110 g plain flour
A pinch of salt
1 large egg (size 2)
$\frac{1}{2}$ pint/300 ml milk and water mixed
A little oil for frying
For the Filling and Sauce
2 oz/50 g sugar lumps
2 large oranges
3 oz/75 g butter, softened
A miniature bottle Grand Marnier
A 2-pint/1·25-litre shallow ovenproof dish

First make the pancakes. Sift the flour and salt into a bowl, make a well in the centre and break in the egg. Work in the flour, adding the liquid to make a batter.

Heat a little oil in a small frying pan, then drain off as much as possible. Pour a little batter into the pan, swirling it around to thinly coat the base. Cook the pancake on one side and, when it is golden brown, flick it over to cook the other side. As the pancakes are ready, stack them in a tea towel. Grease the pan after every third pancake.

Next, rub the sugar lumps over the oranges to remove the zest. Using a rolling pin, crush the saturated lumps and beat into the butter with 1 tablespoon each of Grand Marnier and squeezed orange juice.

Pour the remaining orange juice into the ovenproof dish. Spread each pancake with the orange butter then fold them in half and half again to make a triangle. Place in the dish and keep warm until required.

Just before serving, warm the remaining liqueur in a small pan, set light to it and pour the flaming liquid over the pancakes. Serve at once with cream.

Freezing Note *Store the pancakes unfilled for up to a month. Thaw overnight, covered, then continue as in the recipe.*

Cobweb Pudding

Serves 4–6

1 lb/450 g rhubarb
1 strawberry jelly
¼ pint/150 ml water
2 tablespoons strawberry jam
3 large eggs (size 2)
A few drops of pink food colouring

For the Topping
¼ pint/150 ml double cream
2 tablespoons redcurrant jelly, sieved
8 large strawberries
A greaseproof paper piping bag

Wash the rhubarb and cut it into ½-inch/1-cm lengths. Put into a pan without extra water and cook it slowly at first until the juice begins to flow, then more quickly until it is a soft pulp. Sieve the pulp or put it in a blender for a few seconds.

Break up the jelly square into sections and, using the same pan, dissolve the jelly in the water. Stir this into the rhubarb purée and add the jam to sweeten the mixture. Add a few drops of pink colouring to the rhubarb if necessary. Separate the egg whites from the yolks and beat the yolks into the rhubarb mixture. Whisk the whites stiffly and fold them in also. Pour the pudding into a glass bowl and leave it to set.

Whip the cream very lightly to thicken it slightly then spread over the surface of the pudding. Fill the piping bag with the sieved redcurrant jelly and pipe a spiral of jelly over the cream. Take a skewer and draw it from the centre to the outside of the dish in four sections, then from the outside to the centre dividing these sections and making the cobweb design.

Arrange the strawberries round the top – they often look nicer with the green stalks left on.

Freezing Note *The undecorated pudding will store for up to a month. Thaw overnight then decorate as in the recipe.*

Hazelnut Meringue Gâteau

Serves 6–8

For the Meringue
4 large egg whites (size 2)
8 oz/225 g caster sugar
2 oz/50 g hazelnuts
Caster sugar for sprinkling

For the Filling
4 tablespoons custard powder
1 pint/600 ml milk
6 oz/175 g butter
A few drops of rum essence
8 oz/225 g icing sugar, sifted
2 oz/50 g cocoa powder

For the Decoration
Sifted icing sugar for sprinkling
4 tablespoons double cream
6 whole hazelnuts
Two large piping bags with ⅝-inch/1·25-cm plain pipe and No 8 large star pipe attached

The meringue used in this recipe is made in a slightly different way from usual, giving a smooth and silky finish.

Whisk the egg whites and all the sugar for about 10 minutes in a bowl suspended over a pan of hot water, until the mixture becomes very stiff, white and glossy. (This meringue can also be made in a mixer, when the hot water will not be needed.)

Brown the hazelnuts under a preheated grill then, taking a few at a time, rub them in a cloth to remove the skins. Grind or very finely chop the nuts before folding them into the meringue with a metal spoon.

Cover two baking trays with a sheet of Bakewell paper. Fill the piping bag with the plain pipe attached and pipe on to the trays two circles of meringue, each 8 inches/20 cm in diameter. Sprinkle with a little extra caster sugar and bake them in a cool oven, gas mark 2 or 300°F/150°C, for 1 to 1½ hours, or until they are completely dry. Cool on a wire rack.

Meanwhile, blend the custard powder to a smooth paste in a pan with a little milk, then stir in the rest of the milk. Stirring all the time, bring the sauce to the boil over a gentle heat and cook it for a few minutes to thicken. Remove the pan from the heat, then gradually beat in the butter and rum essence. Leave the sauce to cool, stirring it occasionally to prevent a skin forming. Beat in the sifted icing sugar and cocoa powder.

Place one round of meringue on a large serving plate. Spread over the filling, top with the other round and dust the surface with icing sugar.

Whip the cream until it holds its shape, fill the piping bag with the star pipe and decorate the top with six swirls of cream and a hazelnut on each. Serve the gâteau within an hour of decoration.

Freezing Note *Not recommended for freezing but the meringue rounds, unfilled, will keep in an airtight tin for up to a month.*

Brandied Peaches

Serves 5–6

1 lb 13-oz/822-g can peach slices
2 tablespoons brandy
4 cloves
1-inch/2·5-cm length of cinnamon stick
Grated rind and juice of 1 orange

Turn the peaches and syrup into a pan, stir in the brandy, cloves, cinnamon stick and orange rind and juice. Cover and bring to the boil, then reduce the heat and simmer very gently for 20 to 25 minutes.

Turn the peaches into a dish and leave them to cool. Serve the Brandied Peaches chilled with cream.

Freezing Note *Store for up to 2 months, thaw then serve chilled.*

Cobweb Pudding

Baked Strawberry Alaska

Serves 5–6

A 5 × 7-inch/13 × 18-cm piece of sponge cake
2 tablespoons undiluted orange squash or fresh orange juice
½ lb/225 g strawberries
3 large egg whites (size 2)
6 oz/175 g caster sugar
17-fl oz/483-ml brick vanilla ice cream

Put the sponge on to an ovenproof plate and soak it with the orange squash. Hull and wipe the strawberries, then slice them and arrange on the sponge. Leave in a cool place.

Whisk the egg whites until they are really stiff and stand in straight peaks; add 3 tablespoonfuls of the sugar from the measured amount and re-whisk the whites until the same stiffness is achieved, then very carefully fold in the rest of the sugar. Put the brick of ice cream on to the fruit, then cover the whole pudding with the meringue, and – this is the secret of Baked Alaska – make sure the whole pudding is completely encased with the meringue, to act as a seal that prevents the heat penetrating through to the ice cream.

Immediately put the Baked Strawberry Alaska into a very hot oven, gas mark 8 or 450°F/230°C, for 3 minutes, until golden.

Fresh Fruit Trifle

Serves 6–8

1 packet trifle sponge cakes or stale sponge cake
4 tablespoons jam
2 tablespoons sweet sherry
1 pint/600 ml milk
3 bananas
½ lb/225 g black grapes
Juice of ½ lemon
2 tablespoons cornflour
1 oz/25 g caster sugar
2 large eggs
½ pint/300 ml double cream
A piping bag with No 8 large star pipe attached

Split the trifle sponge cakes in half lengthways and spread evenly with the jam. Put into the bottom of a glass serving dish and spoon over the sherry and 2 tablespoons of the milk. Keep 1 banana and 9 grapes aside for decoration. Peel and slice the bananas and toss in lemon juice to prevent discoloration. Pip the grapes using the curved end of a hair grip, then mix the fruit with the sponge cake.

Blend the cornflour, sugar, 1 egg plus 1 yolk to a smooth paste in a pan, and add the rest of the milk. Heat gently, stirring all the time, until the custard thickens. Pour it into the dish over the fruit and sponge mixture.

When the custard is quite cold, whip the cream until it is stiff enough to hold its own shape. Whisk the egg white to the same consistency and fold into the cream.

Carefully spread two-thirds of the cream over the custard. Put the rest into a piping bag and decorate the trifle with whirls of cream and the reserved banana and grapes.

Baked Strawberry Alaska

Lemon Chiffon Pie

Serves 5–6

For the Pie Case
6 oz / 175 g digestive biscuits
3 oz / 85 g butter
For the Filling
2 large eggs (size 2)
3 oz / 75 g caster sugar
Grated rind and juice of 1 large lemon
2 teaspoons powdered gelatine
2 tablespoons water
For the Decoration
3 crystallised orange slices
A plain 8-inch / 20-cm flan ring

Put the digestive biscuits into a polythene bag and crush them into fine crumbs with a rolling pin. Melt the butter over a gentle heat and stir in the biscuit crumbs. Stand the flan ring on a serving plate, turn the crumb mixture into it and, using the back of a spoon, spread it over the base and up the sides. Leave the flan case in a cool place to harden.

Separate the yolks and whites of the eggs into two bowls. Add the caster sugar and lemon rind and juice to the egg yolks, and stand the bowl over a pan of hot water. Whisk together until the mixture is light and fluffy in both colour and texture. Remove the bowl from the heat and continue whisking the mixture for a further few minutes.

Put the gelatine and water into a small saucepan over a very low heat, to dissolve the gelatine, but do not allow it to boil. When it is ready, mix the gelatine into the egg yolk mixture and leave in a cool place until it is just beginning to set.

Whisk the egg whites until they stand in straight peaks, then using a metal spoon, lightly fold them into the lemon mixture. Turn the Lemon Chiffon into the pie case and leave in a cool place to set.

To serve the Lemon Chiffon Pie, very carefully ease off the flan ring from around the pie case. Cut each orange slice into three pieces and arrange around the pie.

Freezing Note *Store undecorated for up to a month. Thaw overnight, remove from the flan ring then decorate before serving.*

Chocolate Pots

Chocolate Pots

Serves 4

4 oz / 100 g plain chocolate
2 tablespoons water
2 large eggs (size 2), separated
A few drops of vanilla essence
¼ pint / 150 ml double cream
For the Decoration
¼ pint / 150 ml double cream
8 blanched almonds
¼ lb / 100 g green grapes
1 egg white
Caster sugar for sprinkling
4 individual ¼-pint / 150-ml dishes
A large piping bag with star pipe attached

Break the chocolate into pieces and put into a pan with the water over a low heat. Stirring all the time, melt the chocolate but do not allow the mixture to overheat. Beat the egg yolks one at a time into the chocolate, add the vanilla essence and leave to cool slightly.

Whip the cream until it is stiff and just holds its shape and whisk the egg whites until they are really stiff and stand in straight peaks. Using a metal spoon, fold the cream and egg whites carefully and lightly into the chocolate. Divide the mixture between the four dishes and leave them in a cool place, preferably overnight, to set.

Next day, whip the cream for decoration, put it into the piping bag and pipe a swirl of cream on each Chocolate Pot. Cut the blanched almonds into slivers and brown under a preheated grill then stick them into the swirls of cream.

Divide the grapes into small clusters. Beat the egg white with a little water then, using a pastry brush, coat the grapes thoroughly with the egg white. Sprinkle them liberally with caster sugar.

Serve a cluster of frosted grapes with each Chocolate Pot.

Crème Caramel

Serves 4

For the Caramel
4 oz / 100 g granulated sugar
2 tablespoons water
For the Custard
4 large eggs (size 2)
1 pint / 600 ml milk
1½ oz / 40 g caster sugar
A 1½-pint / 900-ml ovenproof dish, lightly oiled

1 Put the granulated sugar and water into a pan and dissolve the sugar gently. When every grain has dissolved, and not before, boil rapidly, without stirring, until golden.

2 Take the pan off the heat and plunge the base into a bowl of cold water for a few seconds to check the heat and prevent the caramel from darkening any further.

3 Pour the caramel into the base of the dish. Beat the eggs together. Heat the milk and sugar in a pan and, when it is almost boiling, pour it over the eggs, stirring briskly.

4 Strain the custard into the caramel-lined dish, then stand the dish in a roasting tin filled with enough hot water to come halfway up the sides of the dish.

5 Bake the custard on the centre shelf of a moderately cool oven, gas mark 3 or 325°F / 160°C, for about 1 hour, or until just set and a knife pushed into the centre comes out clean.

6 Remove the dish from the roasting tin and leave in a cool place overnight before turning out. The caramel will have formed a sauce. Serve the dessert with fresh fruit.

Crème Caramel

Veiled Country Lass

Serves 4–5

3 oz / 85 g margarine
8 oz / 225 g stale brown bread crumbs
4 oz / 100 g caster sugar
2 oz / 50 g plain chocolate, grated
1½ lb / 675 g cooking apples, cooked, puréed and sweetened to taste
¼ pint / 150 ml double cream
Grated chocolate for sprinkling
A 2-pint / 1·25-litre glass soufflé dish

Melt the margarine in a pan and fry the breadcrumbs over a moderate heat for about 5 minutes. Stir in the sugar and chocolate and, when the chocolate has melted, place a third of this mixture in the bottom of the dish.

Spread over half the apple, half the remaining crumbs, the rest of the apple, then the remainder of the crumbs. Spread the top layer smooth and leave the pudding in a cool place for at least 2 hours.

To serve, whip the cream until it just holds its shape, then spread over the top of the pudding and sprinkle with grated chocolate.

Freezing Note *Not recommended for freezing although the pudding can be made the day before and left undecorated in a cool place. Decorate when required.*

Gooseberry Fool

Serves 4

1 lb/450 g gooseberries, topped and tailed
4–6 oz/100–175 g sugar
½ pint/300 ml cold custard (made with 2 dessertspoons each of custard powder and sugar and ½ pint/300 ml milk)
A few drops of green food colouring
To Serve
2 oz/50 g caster sugar
1 egg white

Put the gooseberries into a pan which has been rinsed in water. Cook the fruit over a low heat and, when tender, sieve it to make a purée. Stir in sugar to taste, then mix in the custard, sieved if necessary. Add colouring and chill.

Strawberry Fool, Blackcurrant Fool, Peach Fool, Gooseberry Fool, Cherry Fool, Blackberry and Apple Fool

Just before serving, put the caster sugar on to a plate. Beat the egg white with a teaspoon of water in a small bowl. Dip the rim of each serving glass first in the egg white and then into the sugar to frost them. Spoon in the Gooseberry Fool.

Blackcurrant Fool

Serves 4

- 1 lb/450 g unprepared or 10 oz/275 g prepared blackcurrants
- 4 oz/100 g caster sugar
- 5-fl oz/142-ml carton natural yogurt

If necessary, strip the blackcurrants from the stalks with a fork and wash them. Put the fruit into a pan with 1 tablespoon cold water and simmer gently until really soft. Stir in the sugar and, when every grain has dissolved, mash the fruit to a pulp with a potato masher or wooden spoon. Leave the fruit to cool.

Just before serving, layer the fruit and yogurt into individual serving glasses – spoon two layers alternately of each into the glasses ending with a layer of yogurt and a spoonful of fruit purée on top. Serve at once.

Cherry Fool

Serves 4

- 1 lb/450 g ripe cherries
- 4 oz/100 g caster sugar
- ¼ pint/150 ml cold custard (made with 1 dessertspoon each of custard powder and sugar and ¼ pint/150 ml milk)
- ¼ pint/150 ml single cream

Wash the cherries, remove the stalks and, using the tip of a potato peeler, take out the stones. Put the fruit into a pan and simmer until quite tender over a very low heat. Stir in the sugar and when it has dissolved, drain the cherries, reserving the syrup.

Put the cherries on to a board and chop them very finely. Alternatively blend in a liquidiser. Sieve the custard if necessary and stir in the cherries with the cream and syrup. Divide the fruit fool between four dishes and serve chilled.

Peach Fool

Serves 4

- 15-oz/425-g can peaches
- ¼ pint/150 ml double cream
- 1 teaspoon lemon juice
- A few drops of yellow food colouring

For the Decoration

- 4 tablespoons double cream
- 1 oz/25 g walnuts, chopped

If you have a blender, drain the fruit and purée it in the goblet. Alternatively, poach the fruit and syrup together in a pan over a gentle heat until the fruit is really soft. Strain off the juice and purée the fruit using a fork or potato masher.

Whip the cream for the fruit fool and the decoration together until stiff and just holding its shape. Using a metal spoon, fold two-thirds of the cream into the peach purée with the lemon juice and enough colouring to make it yellow. Chill well before serving.

Spoon the mixture into four glasses. Top with the remaining cream and the walnuts and serve at once.

Strawberry Fool

Serves 3

- ½ lb/225 g strawberries
- 4 oz/100 g caster sugar
- ¼ pint/150 ml double cream

Reserve 3 whole strawberries for decoration. Hull the remaining strawberries and purée them either in a blender or with a potato masher. (The purée should measure ½ pint/300 ml.) Stir in the sugar.

Whip the cream until it holds its shape and, using a metal spoon, fold into the purée. Divide the fruit fool between three glasses and chill.

Just before serving cut a slit in the side of each of the reserved strawberries and hook them over the rim of the glasses.

Blackberry and Apple Fool

Serves 4

- 1 lb/450 g eating apples
- 2 tablespoons water
- ½ lb/225 g blackberries
- 4 oz/100 g caster sugar
- ½ pint/300 ml cold custard (made with 2 dessertspoons each of custard powder and sugar and ½ pint/300 ml milk)

Wipe the apples, chop them roughly and put into a pan with the water and washed blackberries. Poach the fruit slowly until tender, then rub it through a sieve to make a purée. Stir in the sugar and, when it has melted, mix in the custard – sieved if it is lumpy.

Serve each fool chilled in individual glass goblets.

Rhubarb Fool

Serves 6

- 2 lb/1 kg rhubarb
- 8 oz/225 g caster sugar
- ¼ pint/150 ml double cream
- 5-fl oz/142-ml carton natural yogurt

For the Decoration

- ¼ pint/150 ml double cream
- ½ oz/15 g crystallised ginger, chopped

Wipe, trim and chop the rhubarb into pieces. Wash and place in a saucepan. Cook over a low heat until soft and pulpy then stir in the sugar until dissolved. The purée should now measure 1 pint/600 ml. Beat the fruit to a pulp and allow it to become completely cold.

Whip the cream and fold into the fruit pulp with the yogurt. Place in individual glasses. Whip the cream for decoration, pipe a swirl on top of each one and decorate with the crystallised ginger.

Cherry Cheesecake

Serves 6–8

For the Base
6 oz/175 g digestive biscuits
3 oz/85 g butter
2 egg yolks
For the Filling
8 oz/225 g cream cheese
3 oz/75 g icing sugar, sifted
2 teaspoons powdered gelatine
2 tablespoons water
1 oz/25 g blanched almonds, finely chopped
2 egg whites
For the Topping
1 lb/450 g fresh dark cherries
6 tablespoons redcurrant jelly
A few drops of red food colouring
Or
15-oz/425-g can black cherries
1 tablespoon arrowroot
An 8-inch/20-cm plain flan ring

Lightly oil a baking tray and stand the flan ring, also lightly oiled, on it.

Put the biscuits into a polythene bag and using a rolling pin, crush them to crumbs. Melt the butter in a pan, stir in the crumbs, then mix in the egg yolks. Turn the mixture into the flan ring and, using the back of a spoon, spread it to the sides, making the surface level.

Put the cream cheese into a bowl and beat in the icing sugar. Dissolve the gelatine in the water over a low heat and, when every grain has dissolved, stir the liquid into the cheese mixture with the almonds. Whisk the egg whites until they are stiff and stand in straight peaks then, using a metal spoon, fold them into the mixture lightly and quickly. Turn the filling on top of the biscuit base – it will form its own level – then leave the Cherry Cheesecake in a cool place to set, preferably overnight.

The following day, prepare the topping. If using fresh cherries, wipe, stalk and stone the fruit. (If you do not have a cherry stoner, use the end of a potato peeler.) Arrange the cherries on top of the cheesecake. Sieve the redcurrant jelly, beat in a little red food colouring if necessary, then spoon the jelly over the cherries before serving.

If using canned fruit, arrange the drained cherries over the cheesecake. In a pan, blend the arrowroot with a little of the fruit juice and, when it is smooth, stir in the rest of the juice. Put the pan over a low heat and, stirring all the time, bring the glaze to the boil, so that it clears and thickens. Carefully spoon the glaze over the cheesecake to coat the cherries.

Freezing Note *Store for up to 3 months without the topping. Thaw at room temperature for 4 to 5 hours then complete as in the recipe.*

Cherry Cheesecake

Lemon Cheesecake

Serves 6

For the Base and Top
3 oz/85 g butter
6 oz/175 g digestive biscuits, crushed
For the Filling
2 large eggs (size 2)
4 oz/100 g caster sugar
Grated rind and juice of 1 lemon
2 tablespoons cornflour
6 oz/175 g low fat cream cheese
¼ pint/150 ml double cream
A 7-inch/18-cm loose-bottomed round cake tin

Melt the butter and stir in the biscuit crumbs. Line the base of the cake tin with half this mixture.

Separate the eggs. Beat the egg yolks with the sugar until they are light in colour and thick in consistency. Add the lemon rind and juice and the cornflour. Beat the cream cheese until softened and add this to the mixture. Whip the cream until it just holds its shape, then, using a metal spoon, stir it into the mixture. Whisk the egg whites until they are stiff and stand in straight peaks. Using a metal spoon, carefully fold 1 tablespoon of egg white into the cheese mixture, then fold in the remainder.

Pour the mixture over the biscuit crumb base, then sprinkle the remainder of the biscuit crumbs on top. Bake the cheesecake on the centre shelf of a moderately cool oven, gas mark 3 or 325°F/160°C, for 1 to 1¼ hours, until firm.

When the cheesecake is cold, loosen the sides of the cake from the tin and push up the base to remove the cake.

Serve Lemon Cheesecake on a pretty plate and accompany it with single cream.

Freezing Note *Store for up to 2 months. Thaw overnight in a cool place.*

Mandarin Cheesecake

Serves 6–8

For the Base
3 oz/75 g plain flour
2 tablespoons caster sugar
A pinch of salt
2½ oz/65 g margarine
1 large egg yolk (size 2)
For the Filling
12 oz/350 g cream cheese
4 oz/100 g caster sugar
A few drops of vanilla essence
1 tablespoon flour
1 large egg white (size 2)
3 large eggs (size 2)
1 lb/450 g mandarin oranges
For the Topping
5-fl oz/142-ml carton soured cream
2 oz/50 g icing sugar, sifted
A few drops of vanilla essence
2 tablespoons chocolate spread
An 8-inch/20-cm springform tin

Brush the base and sides of the tin with melted butter or margarine. Sift the flour, sugar and salt for the base into a bowl. Add the margarine and rub it in so that the fat is evenly distributed. Stir in the egg yolk and bind the ingredients together.

On a lightly floured work surface, roll out the pastry to fit the base of the tin and then lift it into the tin. Bake the pastry base on the shelf above the centre of a moderate oven, gas mark 4 or 350°F/180°C, for 25 minutes, or until cooked. Remove the tin from the oven and reduce the temperature to moderately cool, gas mark 3 or 325°F/160°C.

Beat together the cream cheese, sugar, vanilla essence and flour. Beat the egg white with the whole eggs, then add it gradually to the other ingredients, beating well between each addition. The mixture should have the consistency of lightly whipped cream.

Peel the mandarins and remove any pips, then chop the fruit roughly and stir it into the cream cheese mixture. Pour this on to the cooked pastry base and bake the cheesecake on the centre shelf of the moderately cool oven for 1¼ hours, until the cake is a light golden brown and firm to the touch.

Mix the soured cream with the icing sugar and vanilla essence and spread it over the surface of the cake. Melt the chocolate spread then swirl it into the soured cream. Return the cheesecake to the oven and bake for a further 8 to 10 minutes until the topping sets. Remove the cake from the tin and leave it in a cool place overnight before serving.

Freezing Note *Store the cheesecake for up to 3 months. Thaw overnight.*

Mandarin Cheesecake

Lemon Cream Ice

Makes 2–2½ pints/1·15–1·4 litres

1 teaspoon powdered gelatine
¼ pint/150 ml water
Grated rind and juice of 3 lemons
1 large can sweetened condensed milk
2 large eggs (size 2)
A 3-pint/1·75-litre freezer container

Set the refrigerator dial to maximum freezing temperature.

Stir the gelatine in the water in a small pan, heating gently to dissolve. Leave to cool.

Make the lemon juice up to ½ pint/300 ml with water. Beat the lemon rind and juice, condensed milk and egg yolks together with a rotary whisk or wooden spoon, until well combined. Stir in the gelatine.

Pour the mixture into the container and put into the ice-making compartment of the refrigerator or freezer. Freeze until it is mushy. (Because of the sweetness of the condensed milk, this mixture will take at least 4 hours to freeze.)

Whisk the egg whites until stiff but not dry. Transfer the lemon mixture to a cold bowl and, with a rotary whisk, beat for about 30 seconds until the mixture is smooth but still very cold. Quickly and carefully fold the egg whites evenly through the lemon mixture then return it to the container and freeze until firm.

Once the ice cream has frozen, return the refrigerator dial to its normal setting.

Serve decorated with slices of lemon, if liked.

Freezing Note *Store for up to 3 months.*

Ice Cream with Nutty Chocolate Topping, Blackberry and Hazelnut Ice, Chocolate Ice Cream, Ice Cream with Tropical Topping, Fancy Ice Cake, Custard Ice Cream, Lemon Cream Ice, Rhubarb Sorbet, Ginger Cream Ice

Chocolate Ice Cream

Makes 2½–3 pints/1·4–1·75 litres

3 oz/75 g plain chocolate
½ pint/300 ml milk
2 large eggs (size 2), separated
4 oz/100 g caster sugar
1 large can evaporated milk, chilled
A 3½-pint/2-litre freezer container, or several smaller ones

Set the refrigerator dial to maximum freezing temperature.

Melt the chocolate in the milk over a low heat – it does not matter if the chocolate does not dissolve smoothly as chocolate bits in the ice cream make a pleasant contrast of textures.

Beat the egg yolks and sugar together in a basin until creamy. Gradually stir in the hot chocolate milk, return to the heat and, stirring all the time, cook over a low heat until the custard thickens – it should coat the back of a wooden spoon. Remove from the heat and leave to become cold, stirring occasionally to prevent a skin forming.

Whisk the evaporated milk for about 7 minutes until it is thick and leaves a trail when the whisk is lifted out. Fold in the chocolate custard, pour into the container and freeze until mushy in the ice-making compartment of the refrigerator.

Whisk the egg whites until stiff but not dry. Whisk the chocolate mush in the container to break up any large ice crystals. Fold in the egg whites until evenly mixed. Return the ice cream to the ice compartment and freeze until firm, then return the refrigerator dial to its normal setting.

Serve the ice cream topped with whole hazelnuts, grated chocolate or a chocolate mint cream.

Freezing Note *Store for up to 3 months.*

Custard Ice Cream

Makes 2½–3 pints/1·4–1·75 litres

- 1½ pints/900 ml milk
- 2 large eggs (size 2), separated
- 4 oz/100 g sugar
- 1 oz/25 g custard powder
- 1 teaspoon vanilla essence
- ¼ pint/150 ml single cream
- *A 3-pint/1·75-litre freezer container or three 1-pint/600-ml containers*

Set the refrigerator dial to maximum freezing temperature.

Heat 1¼ pints/750 ml milk. Mix the egg yolks, sugar and custard powder to a smooth cream with the remaining cold milk in a large bowl, then stir in the hot milk. Return the custard to the pan and gradually bring to the boil, stirring all the time, until it has thickened. Remove from the heat and stir in the vanilla essence. Wet a piece of greaseproof paper with water then press it down on to the surface of the custard – this prevents a skin from forming.

Leave the custard until it is quite cold. Whisk the egg whites until stiff but not dry. Fold the cream and egg whites into the cold custard.

Pour the ice cream mixture either into the large container or into the smaller ones. Freeze until firm in the ice-making compartment of the refrigerator and then return the refrigerator dial to its normal setting.

Serve in scoopfuls with fruit and wafers, or top with one of the following toppings.

Nutty Chocolate Topping

Serves 4–6

- 2 oz/50 g plain chocolate
- 3 tablespoons smooth or crunchy peanut butter
- 3 tablespoons milk
- 2 tablespoons icing sugar
- 1–2 tablespoons chopped mixed nuts

Stir all the ingredients together in a pan over a low heat until they are well mixed. Serve hot or cold over vanilla ice cream or home-made Custard Ice Cream.

Tropical Topping

Serves 4

- 3 tablespoons golden syrup
- 1 oz/25 g sultanas
- Grated rind and juice of ½ orange
- 4 glacé cherries, sliced
- ½ oz/15 g angelica, cut into diamonds
- ½ teaspoon rum essence

Heat the syrup, sultanas, orange rind and juice gently in a small pan for 2 to 3 minutes, to plump up the sultanas. Remove from the heat and stir in the cherries, angelica and rum essence.

Serve warm over vanilla ice cream or home-made Custard Ice Cream.

Ginger Cream Ice

Makes 1¼–1½ pints/750–900 ml

- 1 pint/600 ml milk
- 1 large egg (size 2), separated
- 2 oz/50 g caster sugar
- 1 tablespoon custard powder
- 1 teaspoon ground ginger
- 1½-oz/44-g packet Dream Topping
- *A 1½-pint/900-ml freezer container*

Set the refrigerator dial to maximum freezing temperature.

Heat ½ pint/300 ml milk. Mix the egg yolk, sugar, custard powder and ginger together in a bowl. Gradually blend in ¼ pint/150 ml cold milk to form a smooth cream. Stir in the hot milk then return the custard to the pan and gradually bring to the boil, stirring all the time, until the custard has thickened; remove from the heat.

Wet a piece of greaseproof paper with cold water then press it down on to the surface of the custard to prevent a skin forming. Leave to become quite cold.

Make up the Dream Topping with the remaining ¼ pint/150 ml milk, following the instructions on the packet. Whisk the egg white until stiff but not dry then fold it through the ginger custard together with the Dream Topping, until evenly mixed. Pour into the container and freeze until firm in the ice-making compartment or freezer. Once frozen, return the refrigerator dial to its normal setting.

Freezing Note *Store for up to 3 months.*

Blackberry and Hazelnut Ice

Makes 1¼–1½ pints/750–900 ml

- 1 lb/450 g blackberries
- 3 oz/75 g caster sugar
- ½ pint/300 ml plus 2 tablespoons water
- 1 teaspoon powdered gelatine
- 2 large eggs (size 2), separated
- 2 × 5-fl oz/142-ml cartons hazelnut yogurt
- *A 2-pint/1·25-litre freezer container, or several smaller ones*

Set the refrigerator dial to maximum freezing temperature.

Pick over the fruit then put it in a pan with the sugar and 1 tablespoon water. Cook over a low heat until some of the juice is extracted, then increase the heat slightly and simmer until the fruit is cooked – about 10 minutes. Press through a sieve.

Dissolve the gelatine in 1 tablespoon hot water, then stir it into the fruit purée with the egg yolks, the ½ pint/300 ml water and the yogurt. Pour into the container and freeze until mushy in the ice-making compartment or in the freezer.

Whisk the egg whites until stiff but not dry. Transfer the blackberry mush to a cold bowl and beat it quickly with a rotary whisk to break up any large ice crystals. Quickly but carefully fold the egg whites evenly through the mixture. Pour back into the container and freeze until firm, then return the refrigerator to its normal setting.

Freezing Note *Store for up to 3 months.*

Fancy Ice Cakes

Makes 6

- 6 wafer biscuits
- 4 tablespoons double cream
- 1 tablespoon drinking chocolate powder
- 17-fl oz/483-ml block cream or white ice cream
- *A piping bag with star pipe attached*

Cut 3 wafers in half, 1½ wafers into 6 triangles and the rest into 9 fingers.

Whip the cream and sifted chocolate powder together until thick, then spoon into the piping bag. Remove the ice cream from the freezing compartment of the refrigerator and cut it into six small blocks. Place each one on half a wafer. Working quickly, decorate the top of each one with rosettes of chocolate cream. Place wafer triangles and fingers in position and serve immediately.

Rhubarb Sorbet

Makes 1½–2 pints/750 ml–1·15 litres

- 1 lb/450 g rhubarb
- ½ pint/300 ml plus 1 tablespoon water
- 4 oz/100 g sugar
- 2 teaspoons lemon juice
- A few drops of pink food colouring (optional)
- 2 large egg whites (size 2)
- *A 2½-pint/1·5-litre freezer container*

Set the refrigerator dial to maximum freezing temperature.

Wash and trim the rhubarb. Cut into small chunks and simmer with the 1 tablespoon water until very

soft. Remove from the heat and purée in a blender or through a sieve.

Make a sugar syrup: dissolve the sugar in ½ pint/300 ml water in a small pan over a low heat then bring to the boil and boil gently for 10 minutes. Add the syrup to the rhubarb and stir in the lemon juice with a few drops of colouring, if required. Pour into the freezer container and freeze until mushy in the ice-making compartment or freezer.

Whisk the egg whites until stiff but not dry. Transfer the rhubarb mush to a cold bowl and beat it quickly with a rotary whisk to break up any large ice crystals. Quickly but carefully fold the egg whites evenly through the rhubarb then pour it back into the container and freeze until firm but still of a slightly soft texture. Return the refrigerator dial to its normal setting.

Rolled wafers make an excellent accompaniment to Rhubarb Sorbet.

Freezing Note *Store for up to a month.*

Gooseberry Ice Cream

Makes 1–1½ pints/600–900 ml

½ lb/225 g gooseberries
2 tablespoons water
3 oz/75 g caster sugar
1 tablespoon custard powder
2 eggs, separated
½ pint/300 ml milk
4 tablespoons double cream
A few drops of green food colouring
A 2-pint/1·25-litre metal container

Set the refrigerator dial to maximum freezing temperature.

Wash the gooseberries and cook gently in a small pan with the water until soft, then rub through a sieve.

In a pan, blend together the sugar, custard powder, egg yolks and a little of the milk. When this is smooth stir in the rest of the milk. Heat the custard over a moderate heat, stirring all the time and, as soon as it boils, remove from the heat and leave it to cool.

Stir the gooseberry purée into the cool custard. Whisk the egg whites until they are really stiff. Whip the cream until it is stiff and fold it into the gooseberry mixture with enough colouring to turn it pale green. Finally fold in the whisked egg whites. Turn the mixture into the container and freeze it in the ice-making compartment or freezer for about 35 to 40 minutes, until it is starting to set around the edges and is mushy.

Whisk the ice cream to break down the ice crystals then freeze it again until hard. Return the refrigerator dial to its normal setting.

Allow the ice cream to soften slightly for 15 minutes at room temperature before serving.

Freezing Note *Store for up to 3 months.*

Gooseberry Ice Cream

Entertaining

The secret of entertaining is to be organised. Never use your guests as guinea pigs and cook for them a dish you haven't tried before, and always arrange the table as attractively as possible, to help make the food look even more appealing. Most important of all, relax and enjoy yourself and you'll find your guests will follow suit.

Christmas Lunch

Serves 8

Menu

Roast Turkey
Sausages
Cranberry and Orange Baskets
Boiled Bacon
Creamy Brussels Sprouts
Roast Potatoes and Parsnips
Buttered Carrots
Bread Sauce

Christmas Pudding
Brandy Butter

Roast Turkey

Serves 8

1 turkey, fresh or oven ready
1 lb/450 g fat bacon, sliced
1 lb/450 g pork chipolata sausages
For the Stuffing
½ lb/225 g pork sausagemeat
5 oz/150 g fresh white breadcrumbs
1 oz/25 g blanched almonds, chopped
Grated rind of 1 lemon
2 oz/50 g stuffed green olives
Salt and pepper
1 large egg (size 2)
For the Cranberry and Orange Baskets
3 medium oranges
8-oz/227-g jar cranberry sauce

A frozen oven ready turkey will take at least 36 hours to thaw out completely, so do collect it from the shop in good time. Leave the bird at room temperature covered with a tea towel until it is completely soft.

Remove the giblets from the bird and use them to make stock for the gravy. Weigh the bird and calculate the cooking time allowing 20 minutes per pound/per half kilo plus an extra 20 minutes.

Mix the sausagemeat with the breadcrumbs, almonds, lemon rind and whole olives. Add plenty of seasoning, then bind the ingredients together with the egg to make a fairly soft consistency. Starting at the neck end of the turkey, gradually work your hand very carefully under the skin and over the breast until you have made a pocket about half the length of the breast. Insert the stuffing a little at a time into this pocket, pressing it well into the bird so that the breast meat is kept moist during cooking. Be very careful not to split the skin as this could result in the stuffing bursting out during cooking. Mould the stuffing to give the bird a well rounded appearance. Tuck the loose skin from the neck under the wings to keep the stuffing in place. (The turkey can be stuffed the night before as long as it is left in a cool place.)

Put the turkey into a large roasting tin and cover the legs and breast with the bacon, then cover the bird with kitchen foil. Cook the bird in a fairly hot oven, gas mark 6 or 400°F/200°C, for the first hour, then reduce to gas mark 4 or 350°F/180°C, and cook the turkey for the rest of the cooking time. (If the bird is really large – over 18 lb/8·25 kg – reduce the temperature after the first hour to gas mark 2 or 300°F/150°C.) Thirty minutes before the end of the cooking time, remove the foil and bacon from the bird and baste it with the fat. Put the sausages around the turkey and return the tin to the oven so the skin can brown and the sausages cook.

Meanwhile prepare the Cranberry and Orange Baskets. Using the point of a sharp knife, cut the oranges in half zig-zag fashion, making the points fairly large. Then, using a grapefruit knife, remove the flesh from each half, and cut the orange segments away from the

Christmas Lunch: Roast Turkey with Cranberry and Orange Baskets, Creamy Brussels Sprouts

membranes. Put the orange segments into a small bowl, keeping the juice for a refreshing drink, and mix in the cranberry sauce. Divide the mixture between the orange shells and put them into an ovenproof dish. Cover with foil and heat through for the last 10 minutes of the turkey's cooking time. Arrange around the turkey to serve.

Creamy Brussels Sprouts

Serves 6–8

2 lb/1 kg Brussels sprouts
Salt
¼ lb/100 g ham, sliced
5-fl oz/142-ml carton soured cream
A little grated nutmeg

Trim the sprouts, removing any damaged leaves, then cut a small cross in the base of each. Wash them well.

Cook the sprouts for 15 minutes in boiling salted water, and when they are tender drain them thoroughly. Cut the slices of ham into pieces and put them into the pan in which the sprouts were cooked. Add the sprouts with the soured cream. Cover the pan and toss it so that the vegetables are well coated. Turn them into a heated dish and sprinkle the surface with nutmeg.

Boiled Bacon

Serves 8

3½–4-lb/1·5–1·75-kg collar of green or smoked bacon
6 peppercorns
½ bay leaf
2 oz/50 g dried breadcrumbs, browned

Soak the bacon for about 4 hours, changing the water once.

Calculate the cooking time by allowing 20 minutes per pound/per half kilo plus an extra 20 minutes on top.

Put the bacon joint into fresh water to cover with the peppercorns and bay leaf. Place the pan over a low heat and bring to the boil, without the lid, then cover and simmer for the remainder of the calculated cooking time. Check the water occasionally to make sure it is not boiling too fast as this can cause the joint to toughen.

When the bacon is cooked, drain off the liquid and lift the joint out of the pan. Carefully peel off the skin before pressing the browned breadcrumbs all over the fat surface of the joint.

Serve the joint either hot or cold to accompany the Christmas turkey.

Bread Sauce

Serves 8

1 onion stuck with 8 cloves
¾ pint/450 ml milk
4 oz/100 g stale white bread, crusts removed
Salt and pepper
A pinch of grated nutmeg
½ oz/15 g butter

Put the onion into a pan with the milk and heat gently so that the flavour of the onion and cloves infuses into the milk, Meanwhile break the bread into small pieces and add to the warmed milk. Cover the pan and leave the bread sauce on one side to soak for about an hour, to allow the flavours to mingle.

Stir in the seasoning, nutmeg and butter and bring the sauce to the boil, stirring occasionally. Remove the onion and cloves and, using a fork, beat the sauce until it is smooth. Check for seasoning before serving it in a small dish.

Freezing Note *Store without the onion for up to 3 months. Thaw then reheat gently.*

Christmas Pudding

Serves 8–10

8 oz/225 g sultanas, cleaned
8 oz/225 g currants, cleaned
8 oz/225 g seedless raisins, cleaned
4 oz/100 g chopped mixed peel
8 oz/225 g dark soft brown sugar
6 oz/175 g prepared shredded suet
8 oz/225 g fresh white breadcrumbs
6 oz/175 g self-raising flour
½ teaspoon salt
1 teaspoon ground cinnamon
2 teaspoons ground mixed spice
½ lb/225 g cooking apples, peeled, cored and grated
2 tablespoons black treacle
2 large eggs (size 2), beaten
½ pint/300 ml stout or brown ale
One 3-pint/1·75-litre pudding basin or two 1½-pint/900-ml basins, lightly greased

Mix the sultanas, currants, raisins, peel, sugar, suet and breadcrumbs together in a large mixing bowl. Sift in the flour with the salt, cinnamon and mixed spice, then stir in the grated apple and treacle. Bind with the eggs and stout and beat well to make a fairly wet sticky consistency.

Turn the mixture into the basin, pressing it down with the back of a spoon. Cover the top with a doubled sheet of greased greaseproof paper, with a pleat down the centre to allow the pudding to rise, and fasten it with string.

Put the pudding into a steamer over a pan of simmering water, or into a large pan with sufficient boiling water to come halfway up the side of the basin. Cook the larger pudding for 7 hours and the smaller puddings for 5 hours. Replenish the pan with more boiling water when necessary.

When the puddings are cooked, remove from the pan and leave until cold. Recover with fresh greaseproof paper then store in a cool place until required – they will keep for up to 6 months.

To reheat, steam the large pudding for 3 hours and the smaller puddings for 1½ hours.

Brandy Butter

Serves 8

6 oz/175 g unsalted butter
¼ teaspoon grated nutmeg
12 oz/350 g icing sugar, sifted
1½ tablespoons brandy

Beat the butter until soft, then beat in the grated nutmeg. Gradually add the sifted icing sugar with the brandy, beating well between each addition.

Turn into small dishes and leave in a cool place until required.

Freezing Note *Store for up to a month. Thaw at room temperature then beat until soft.*

A Celebration Finger Buffet

Serves 25

Menu

Sandwiches
Piccalilli Ham
Cheese Nectar
Sea Food

Vol-au-Vents
Chicken and Mushroom
Shrimp and Tomato

Cheese Triangles
Sausage Rolls
Stuffed Eggs

Fork Fruit Salad
Chocolate Alpine Meringue
Caribbean Mousse

Sandwiches

There are about 22 slices in a thin sliced white or brown sandwich loaf.

You will need a large sliced loaf of both white and brown bread. The fillings for the white loaf are sufficient for five complete rounds of Piccalilli Ham and six complete rounds of Cheese Nectar, and the bread needs no buttering. The Sea Food filling for the brown will be enough for the whole loaf – 8 oz/225 g softened butter is needed for this.

The sandwiches can be made a few hours before they are required. Wrap them in cling film or kitchen foil and leave in a cool place.

Alternatively the sandwiches can be stored in the freezer for up to a month. Thaw overnight in a cool place then cut off the crusts and cut each round into four.

Piccalilli Ham

Makes 5 rounds

¼ lb/100 g ham, sliced or in a piece
3 dessertspoons piccalilli
2 oz/50 g butter, melted
Salt and pepper

Mince the ham and piccalilli together, stir in the melted butter and season if necessary, being careful not to add too much salt.

Sea Food

Makes 11 rounds

2-oz/56-g can anchovy fillets
15-oz/425-g can pilchards in tomato sauce
7-oz/198-g can tuna fish
Pepper

Chop the anchovy fillets, then mash all the fish together to a paste. Season with a little pepper.

Cheese Nectar

Makes 6 rounds

6 oz/175 g cream cheese
1 dessertspoon clear honey
2 oz/50 g walnuts, very finely chopped

Beat the cream cheese and honey together until smooth and soft; mix in the chopped nuts.

Vol-au-Vents

Makes 36

You will require 36 vol-au-vent cases – buy them ready cooked from your baker or frozen but uncooked, or make them yourself. They can be made and filled several hours before the buffet is to be served. Put them on a baking tray, cover with a piece of kitchen foil, then 15 minutes before they are required, heat through in a moderately cool oven, gas mark 3 or 325°F/160°C.

Alternatively, they can be filled and stored in a freezer for up to 2 months. Thaw, cover loosely with foil and reheat at gas mark 3 or 325°F/160°C.

Basic White Sauce

Sufficient for both recipes

3 oz/75 g margarine
3 oz/75 g plain flour
1½ pints/900 ml milk
Salt and pepper

Melt the margarine in a pan over a gentle heat, stir in the flour, remove the pan from the heat and gradually blend in the milk. When the sauce is smooth return it to the gentle heat and, stirring all the time, bring it to the boil. Boil for a few minutes to thicken then check it for seasoning.

Chicken and Mushroom

Fills 24 vol-au-vent cases

1 oz/25 g butter
¼ lb/100 g mushrooms, wiped, trimmed and sliced
8 oz/225 g cooked chicken, diced
1 pint/600 ml basic white sauce
Salt and pepper

Melt the butter in a pan, add the sliced mushrooms, then cover the pan and cook them gently for about 10 minutes, shaking the pan occasionally so they do not stick. By the end of this time the butter should be absorbed.

Stir the diced chicken and the mushrooms into the white sauce, check the filling for seasoning then divide it between the vol-au-vent cases.

Shrimp and Tomato

Fills 12 vol-au-vent cases

4-oz/113-g can peeled shrimps
½ pint/300 ml basic white sauce
2 large tomatoes
Salt and pepper

Drain the liquid from the shrimps, reserve 12 shrimps for decoration, chop the rest and stir them into the sauce. Plunge the tomatoes into boiling water for a count of 20, then remove from the water and peel off their skins. Chop them roughly and add to the sauce. Mix the ingredients well together, check the filling for seasoning, then divide it between the cases.

Heat the vol-au-vents if required, then just before serving garnish each one with a shrimp.

Cheese Triangles

Makes 20

13-oz/368-g packet frozen puff pastry, thawed
Beaten egg for glaze
For the Filling
8 oz/225 g Lancashire cheese
1 large egg (size 2), beaten
2 tablespoons milk
1 small onion, grated
¼ teaspoon grated nutmeg
Salt and pepper

Crumble the cheese into a mixing bowl. Add the beaten egg with the milk, grated onion, nutmeg and seasoning and blend well together.

On a lightly floured work surface roll the pastry out to a 12 × 15-inch/30 × 37·5-cm rectangle. Cut the pastry into 3-inch/7·5-cm squares. Put a little filling into the centre of each square, damp the edges with

Quantity of Food Required

Food	50 people	75 people	100 people
Sandwiches	2 white and 2 brown loaves	3 white and 3 brown loaves	4 white and 4 brown loaves
Vol-au-vents	36 chicken 24 shrimp	48 chicken 36 shrimp	60 chicken 48 shrimp
Cheese Triangles	2 batches	3 batches	4 batches
Sausage Rolls	2 batches	3 batches	4 batches
Stuffed Eggs	2 quantities	3 quantities	4 quantities
Fork Fruit Salad	2 quantities	3 quantities	4 quantities
Chocolate Alpine Meringue	1 quantity	1 quantity	2 quantities
Caribbean Mousse	1 quantity	2 quantities	2 quantities

Tea 2–3 oz/50–75 g tea is enough for 8 pints/4·5 litres of boiling water, depending on the strength required. This will make 36 cups and require 2 pints/1·15 litres milk.
Coffee Use a rounded dessertspoonful of instant coffee for every 1 pint/600 ml boiling water, with a third of the quantity of hot milk for white coffee.
Note When calculating quantities, don't forget to allow for second cups.

Finger Buffet: Sausage Rolls, Stuffed Eggs, Vol-au-Vents, Cheese Triangles, Assorted Sandwiches, Fork Fruit Salad with shortbread fingers, Chocolate Alpine Meringue, Caribbean Mousse

a little water and fold them diagonally in half to form a triangle. Seal the edges well together.

Put the triangles on to baking trays and lightly brush them all with beaten egg. Make a hole in the top of each with a skewer and leave in a cool place for about 10 minutes.

Bake the Cheese Triangles on the centre shelf of a fairly hot oven, gas mark 6 or 400°F/200°C, for 20 minutes, until the pastry is golden brown.

Freezing Note *Store cooked for up to 2 months. Thaw then reheat at gas mark 4 or 350°F/180°C for 15 to 20 minutes.*

Sausage Rolls

Makes 32

For the Quick Flaky Pastry
10 oz/275 g plain flour
A generous pinch of salt
8 oz/225 g margarine (in a hard block straight from the refrigerator)
Beaten egg for glaze
For the Filling
1 lb/450 g sausagemeat

Sift the flour and salt into a bowl. Grate the margarine into the flour using a coarse grater, then mix it in lightly with a knife. Add just enough cold water to make a dough a little softer than for shortcrust pastry, then put the dough aside in a cool place for at least 30 minutes.

Roll out the pastry into a 18 × 14-inch/45 × 35-cm rectangle. Cut it lengthways into four strips. Divide the sausagemeat into four and, using a little flour to prevent it from sticking, shape it into four 18-inch/45-cm rolls. Lay the rolls of sausagemeat on the strips of pastry, moisten one long edge, then fold the other side over the sausagemeat and press the edges firmly together. Brush the rolls with beaten egg. Assemble the four rolls side by side and, using a sharp knife, cut them in half and then divide each half into four to make 32 rolls in all. Make a snip in the top of each with a pair of scissors, if liked.

Leave the sausage rolls in a cool place for 10 minutes before cooking them. Bake in a fairly hot oven, gas mark 6 or 400°F/200°C, for 10 minutes, then reduce the heat to gas mark 5 or 375°F/190°C, for a further 15 minutes.

Serve the Sausage Rolls hot or cold.

Freezing Note *Store cooked for up to 2 months. Thaw then reheat at gas mark 4 or 350°F/180°C for 15 to 20 minutes.*

Stuffed Eggs

Makes 24

12 hard-boiled eggs
Salt and pepper
1 tomato
Parsley
Neptune Filling
$4\frac{1}{4}$-oz/120-g can sardines in oil
3 tablespoons mayonnaise
Indian Filling
2 oz/50 g butter
$1\frac{1}{2}$ teaspoons curry powder
A piping bag with star pipe attached

Shell the eggs and cut them in half across the width. Scoop out the yolks with a teaspoon and divide them between two bowls. If the egg white cases do not stand firmly, shave a little off the bases.

Neptune Filling
Mash the sardines with one half of the egg yolks until smooth, then mix in the mayonnaise and check for seasoning. Put the filling into the

piping bag and pipe whirls into half the egg whites.

Indian Filling

Melt the butter in a pan, then stir in the curry powder and cook for 2 minutes – this brings out the flavour of the curry. Mash the remaining egg yolks with a fork and stir in the curry powder, checking the mixture for seasoning. Put the mixture into the cleaned piping bag and pipe whirls into the remaining egg whites.

Arrange the Stuffed Eggs on a serving plate and decorate the Neptune ones with a small piece of sliced tomato, and the Indian ones with a small sprig of parsley.

Fork Fruit Salad

Choose a selection of canned fruits that can be filled with a little cream and are easy to eat with a fork. We chose pineapple rings and peach, pear and apricot halves. For 25 servings you will need:

15-oz/425-g can pineapple rings
1 lb 13-oz/825-g can peach halves
1 lb 13-oz/825-g can pear halves
15-oz/425-g can apricot halves
½ pint/300 ml double cream
¼ pint/150 ml single cream
Glacé cherries
Angelica diamonds
A piping bag with star pipe attached

Drain the fruits well and arrange them in rows on a large serving dish – or a tray covered with kitchen foil looks rather nice for this.

Mix the two creams together and whip them until they just hold their shape. Fill the piping bag with the cream and pipe whirls in the centre of each fruit, then decorate them alternately with a piece of cherry and a diamond of angelica.

The fruits can be prepared several hours before they are required as long as they are kept in a cool place.

Serve the Fork Fruit Salad with shortbread fingers.

Chocolate Alpine Meringue

For the Meringue
6 large egg whites (size 2)
12 oz/350 g caster sugar
For the Buttercream
8 oz/225 g unsalted butter
8 oz/225 g caster sugar
¼ pint/150 ml water
4 large egg yolks (size 2)
7 oz/200 g plain chocolate
A piping bag with star pipe attached
A double bow of white ribbon

Brush two baking trays with tasteless salad oil and dust them lightly with flour.

Put the egg whites into a large mixing bowl and whisk very stiffly until they stand up in straight peaks. Add 6 tablespoons of the measured caster sugar and whisk the whites again until the original stiff consistency is regained. Using a metal spoon very lightly fold in the remaining sugar. Fill the piping bag with the meringue mixture and pipe individual whirls of it on the baking tray.

Bake the meringues in a very cool oven, gas mark ¼ or 225°F/110°C, for about 4 hours.

When the meringues are ready they will lift off the trays very easily. Cool them and store in an airtight tin until required.

Meanwhile, prepare the buttercream. Beat the butter until very soft then leave to stand at room temperature.

Put the sugar into a pan with the water and dissolve it over a gentle heat, stirring occasionally – *do not let it boil at this stage.* When every grain of sugar has dissolved, boil the syrup rapidly until the short thread stage is reached. To test for this, lift a little syrup with a spoon, touch the surface with the first finger, press it to the thumb, then separate the finger and thumb quickly. If the syrup is ready it should form a short thread between the fingers before breaking.

Put the egg yolks into a bowl, stand it on a damp cloth to prevent slipping, then beat the egg yolks well with a whisk or electric mixer. Very gradually pour on the syrup, whisking all the time; as the mixture cools it should become thick and creamy. While it is still slightly warm, beat it into the creamed butter, adding a little at a time.

Break the chocolate into pieces and melt in a basin over a pan of hot water. Beat the melted chocolate into the buttercream mixture and leave to cool.

To assemble the sweet, preferably the day before it is required, form the meringues into a pyramid, sticking them to each other with a little soft buttercream. Top the meringue pyramid with a bow.

Advance Preparation The unfilled meringues will keep successfully in an airtight tin for several weeks.

The buttercream will also keep for up to 2 weeks in a covered container in a cool place.

Caribbean Mousse

1 lime jelly
¼ pint/150 ml water
Grated rind of 1 lemon
Juice of 2 lemons
4 large eggs (size 2), separated
6 oz/175 g caster sugar
For the Decoration
3 candied lemon slices
1 glacé cherry
Angelica
A 3-pint/1·75-litre glass dish

Break the jelly into pieces and put into a pan with the water. Dissolve the jelly over gentle heat then remove from the heat and stir in the lemon rind and juice. Leave the jelly to cool slightly.

Beat the egg yolks with the caster sugar until creamy in colour and texture, then stir in the cooled jelly and leave until almost set.

Whisk the egg whites until very stiff and standing in straight peaks. Fold them into the setting jelly mixture with a metal spoon as lightly but evenly as possible.

Turn the mousse into the glass dish and leave in a cool place to set.

Cut each lemon slice into segments, cut the cherry in half and the angelica into two long thin strips and three diamonds. When the pudding is set, arrange these into a spray of flowers on top and serve immediately.

Freezing Note *Store undecorated for up to 2 months. Thaw slowly overnight before decorating.*

A Dinner Party for Four

Menu

Festive Egg Starters

Honey Roast Duck with Orange
Duchesse Potatoes
Garden Peas

Mocha Russe

Festive Egg Starters

Serves 4

2 large hard-boiled eggs (size 2)
¼ lb/100 g ham
1 oz/25 g margarine
1 oz/25 g plain flour
¾ pint/450 ml milk
Salt and pepper
1 tomato
4 individual ovenproof dishes

Shell and slice the eggs, and roughly chop the ham; divide them between the dishes and leave on one side.

Melt the margarine in a pan over a low heat then remove from the heat, stir in the flour and gradually blend in the milk. When the sauce is smooth, bring it to the boil over a medium heat, stirring all the time, and boil it for a few minutes until it thickens. Check the sauce for seasoning then pour it into the dishes, filling them almost to the top. Cut the tomato into four slices and put a slice in the centre of each dish.

The starters can now be left on one side. Just before they are to be served, place them under a preheated grill for a few minutes until they are tinged golden brown then serve immediately.

Honey Roast Duck with Orange

Serves 4

1 large roasting duck (about 4½ lb/2 kg trussed weight)
Salt and pepper
1 bay leaf
1 tablespoon plain flour
¾ pint/450 ml stock (see method)
For the Stuffing
1 lb/450 g pork sausagemeat
2 oz/50 g fresh white breadcrumbs
1 oz/25 g walnuts, chopped
A pinch of dried mixed herbs
For the Glaze
1 tablespoon clear honey
For the Decoration
2 oranges
3 slices cucumber
3 stuffed olives
1 bunch watercress
A large skewer

Remove the giblets from the carcass of the duck and put into a pan of cold water. Add plenty of salt and pepper and the bay leaf and boil into stock for the gravy.

Mix together the sausagemeat, breadcrumbs, walnuts, herbs and seasoning and form this stuffing into a barrel shape. Season the inside of the duck and pack the stuffing into the carcass from the tail end; push the parson's nose under the loose skin above to keep the stuffing in place, or re-truss the bird.

Put the duck into a roasting tin, prick the surface all over with a fork, then rub salt into the skin. Roast the bird on the centre shelf of a fairly hot oven, gas mark 6 or 400°F/200°C, for 30 minutes, then reduce to gas mark 4 or 350°F/180°C, for a further 1 to 1¼ hours. Ten minutes before the end of the cooking time, take the bird out of the oven and smear it with the honey. Return the duck to the oven to finish cooking. To test if the duck is cooked, gently pull one of the legs from the carcass and, if the joint feels loose, the duck is ready. Whilst the duck is cooking, prepare the decoration.

Using a sharp, stainless steel knife cut the peel from the oranges. To do this, cut off one end, then holding the orange in one hand cut just beneath the white pith using a sawing action and working spirally round the orange until all the skin and white pith have been removed. Cut off the other end. Keep one of the lengths of peel for decoration and cut the oranges into slices.

Spear the skewer through one end of the peel, then through the cucumber slices, with a stuffed olive on top of each. Space them out and twist the orange peel carefully between them as shown in the photograph overleaf.

When the duck is cooked, carefully lift it on to a serving plate. Insert the skewer in one end of the duck and curl the end of the orange peel over the breast. Garnish it with a bunch of watercress and arrange Duchesse potatoes and orange slices around the bird.

Strain almost all the fat from the roasting tin into a small bowl, leaving only about a tablespoonful; stir into this the flour, then blend in the strained ¾ pint/450 ml stock. Put the tin over a gentle heat and, stirring all the time, bring the gravy to the boil, then pour it into a gravy boat.

Mocha Russe

Serves 4

3 tablespoons cornflour
1 tablespoon instant coffee powder
3 oz/75 g caster sugar
1¼ pints/750 ml milk
4 oz/100 g plain chocolate
1 oz/25 g powdered gelatine
4 tablespoons water
2 large eggs (size 2), separated
A thin 6½-inch/16-cm sponge cake or 3 trifle sponge cakes
24 sponge finger biscuits
1 tablespoon sherry or milk

For the Decoration

4 tablespoons double cream
1 oz/25 g plain chocolate, grated
A 7½-inch/19-cm loose-bottomed cake tin
A large piping bag with No 8 star pipe attached
1 metre of 3-cm wide ribbon

Put the cornflour, coffee powder and sugar into a pan, blend in some of the milk and when the mixture is smooth stir in the rest of the milk. Put the pan over the heat and, stirring all the time, bring the sauce to the boil. Boil for a few minutes to thicken the sauce and cook the flour, stirring constantly. Remove the pan from the heat, break the chocolate into small pieces and stir it into the sauce until melted.

Put the gelatine in a small pan with the water and dissolve it over a low heat – do not allow the liquid to boil. When the sauce is slightly cool, stir in the egg yolks and the gelatine. Stand the pan in a sink of cold water and, stirring occasionally, leave it till nearly set.

Meanwhile arrange the sponge or sponge cakes in the base of the tin, and stand the sponge fingers round the edge, trimming them where necessary so they fit tightly. Soak the sponge base with the sherry or milk.

As soon as the sauce is on the point of setting, whisk the egg whites until they are stiff and stand in straight peaks and, using a metal spoon, fold them into the mocha sauce. Pour the filling into the sponge-lined tin and leave in a cool place for at least 4 hours to set firmly.

When the pudding is set, remove it from the tin. The easiest way to do this is to rest the tin on another, smaller tin. Carefully push the sides of the cake tin downwards, leaving the pudding standing on the loose base of the cake tin on the smaller tin. Transfer it to a glass cake stand or plate, and tie the ribbon around the sponge fingers.

Whip the cream until it just holds its shape, fill the piping bag and pipe five whirls on top of the pudding. Scatter a little grated chocolate over them.

Keep the Mocha Russe in a cool place until required.

Dinner Party for 4: Honey Roast Duck with Orange, Festive Egg Starters, Mocha Russe

A Dinner Party for Six

Menu

Paradise Salad

Potters Pork Chops
Roast Potatoes
Broccoli
Buttered Carrots

Austrian Torte
Citrus Whip

Paradise Salad

Serves 6

½ lb/225 g tomatoes
½ cucumber
2 ripe avocado pears
For the Dressing
2 tablespoons corn oil
1 tablespoon vinegar
A pinch of caster sugar
A little made French mustard
Salt and pepper
6 individual dishes

Plunge the tomatoes into boiling water for the count of 20, then transfer them to cold water and peel off their skins. Cut the tomatoes into quarters and remove the seeds. Put the tomato pieces into a bowl. Peel the cucumber, using a potato peeler, then cut into 1-inch/2·5-cm strips and add to the tomatoes.

Put the oil, vinegar, sugar, mustard and seasoning into a small screw-topped jar and, with the lid on tightly, shake the ingredients so that they combine.

Half an hour before the meal is served, cut the avocado pears into quarters, remove the stones and peel and cut the flesh into cubes. Mix the pear pieces with the tomato and cucumber and toss them in the dressing. Divide the salad between the dishes and serve with thin brown bread and butter.

Potters Pork Chops

Serves 6

6 pork chops
1 large egg (size 2)
Salt and pepper
4 oz/100 g fresh white breadcrumbs
1 teaspoon dried sage
½ oz/15 g butter
7½-oz/213-g can peach halves
Just under ¼ pint/150 ml dry cider
2 tablespoons redcurrant jelly
A few sprigs of watercress for garnish
A large shallow ovenproof dish

Using a sharp knife, trim the excess fat from the chops. Beat the egg with a little salt and pour it on to a plate. Mix the breadcrumbs with the sage and seasoning and put on another plate. Coat the chops thoroughly, first in the egg and then in the breadcrumbs. Grease the dish with the butter and arrange the chops in it.

Drain the peaches and make the juice up to ¼ pint/150 ml with cider. Blend in the redcurrant jelly then pour over the chops.

Cook the chops on the centre shelf of a moderately hot oven, gas mark 5 or 375°F/190°C, for about 1 hour, until golden brown and tender.

Serve each chop topped with a peach half and garnish the dish with watercress.

Austrian Torte

Serves 6

2 teaspoons instant coffee powder
¼ pint/150 ml hot water
6 oz/175 g butter
6 oz/175 g icing sugar, sifted
1 large egg (size 2)
1 oz/25 g chopped mixed peel
3 oz/75 g plain chocolate
28 sponge finger biscuits
For the Decoration
¼ pint/150 ml double cream
1 oz/25 g plain chocolate, grated
A 2-lb/1-kg loaf tin

Dissolve the coffee powder in the hot water and leave on one side to cool.

Cut a piece of greaseproof paper to fit the base of the loaf tin and slip it in place.

Beat the butter until soft, then gradually beat in the icing sugar. Add the egg, beating well so that the mixture does not curdle, then mix in the chopped peel. Break the chocolate into pieces and melt in a basin over a pan of hot water. Stir into the mixture.

Dip the biscuits into the coffee so that they soak up some of the liquid – be careful they do not become too saturated – then place a layer in the base of the tin, cutting them to fit if necessary. Spread half the chocolate cream mixture on top, then add another layer of soaked biscuits, the rest of the chocolate mixture and complete the dessert with a final layer of soaked biscuits. Leave the dessert in a cool place for 2 to 3 hours so that it sets.

Just before serving, run a knife around the inside of the tin and turn the torte on to a serving plate. Whip the cream until it is thick enough to hold its shape, then spread it over the dessert. Finally sprinkle with grated chocolate.

Freezing Note *Store in the tin for up to a month. Thaw overnight then serve as in the recipe.*

Citrus Whip

Serves 6

1 lemon jelly
¼ pint/150 ml water
Grated rind of 1 lemon
Juice of 2 lemons
3 large eggs (size 2)
6 oz/175 g caster sugar
4 slices lemon for decoration
A 3-pint/1·75-litre serving dish

Dissolve the jelly in the water over a moderate heat. Stir in the lemon rind and juice and leave it on one side.

Separate the eggs, putting the whites and yolks into separate bowls. Mix the sugar and yolks and beat them until light in colour and creamy in consistency. Stir in the melted jelly. Whisk the egg whites until they are stiff and just stand in straight peaks, then, using a metal spoon, fold them into the lemon mixture. Turn the dessert into the serving dish and leave it to set overnight in a cool place.

For the decoration, cut the lemon slices just to the centre, twist one end one way and the other end in the opposite direction, so that the slices stand up, and arrange them down the centre of the dish.

Freezing Note *Store undecorated for up to 2 months. Thaw slowly overnight then decorate before serving.*

Dinner Party for 6: Paradise Salad, Potters Pork Chops, Austrian Torte, Citrus Whip

1973
GV
GILBEY VINTNERS
LONDON
BOURGOGNE
PASSE-TOUT-GRA
RED BURGUNDY
Appellation Contrôlée

A Fondue Party

Fondue Bourguignonne

Serves 4–6

Allow 6–8 oz/175–225 g rump steak per person. Your guests will help themselves to pieces of raw meat on a fondue fork or skewer and cook it in hot oil. While the food is cooking, everyone helps themselves to the various accompaniments and, when the meat is cooked to their taste, it is eaten with the accompaniments while more food is being cooked.

We have given you a selection of accompaniments and sauces and suggest you choose six or seven, completing the meal with French bread and a green salad.

It is advisable to limit the number of guests to five or six per fondue set, otherwise the food will take a long time to cook.

The Preparation
Trim the fat from the meat and cut it into 1-inch/2·5-cm pieces. Half-fill the fondue pan with oil then add a knob of butter to help prevent the liquid spitting when it is used. Heat the oil on the cooker then transfer it to the fondue burner.

Sauces

Serves 4–6

- 2 large eggs (size 2)
- ½ pint/300 ml cooking oil
- 1 teaspoon made French mustard
- A pinch of sugar
- Salt and pepper
- 3 dessertspoons white vinegar

By Hand
The eggs and oil should be at room temperature. Mix just the egg yolks with the mustard, sugar, pepper and a good pinch of salt. Measure the oil into a jug and add it, a drop at a time, to the yolks, beating all the time with a wooden spoon. When the mayonnaise starts to thicken, *but not before*, the oil can be added a little more quickly. When it is really thick, add a little vinegar to thin it and keep it to the right consistency.

Fondue Bourguignonne with Sauces and Accompaniments

Blender Method
Put the whole eggs into the blender goblet with the mustard, sugar, salt and pepper and blend them together for a second. Add the oil in a steady stream, and when it suddenly thickens, add a little vinegar, then continue to add the oil.

Keep the mayonnaise in a covered container in a cool place.

Tomato Sauce
Stir 1 dessertspoon tomato purée into a quarter of the mayonnaise.

Parsley Sauce
Stir 2 tablespoons chopped parsley into a quarter of the mayonnaise.

Mustard Sauce
Stir 1 dessertspoon French mustard into a quarter of the mayonnaise.

Tartare Sauce
Chop together 1 dessertspoon capers and a gherkin, then stir them into a quarter of the mayonnaise.

Curry Sauce
Peel and chop a small onion and fry it in ½ oz/15 g butter. Add 1 dessertspoon curry powder and fry for a minute. Stir in 1 teaspoon apricot jam and, when cool, stir into a quarter of the mayonnaise.

Accompaniments

Tomatoes
Wipe the tomatoes, cut them into thin slices and arrange overlapping in a small serving dish.

Bananas
Just before serving the fondue, peel and slice the bananas and toss them in a little lemon juice to prevent discoloration; turn them into a small serving dish.

Chutney
Serve your favourite chutney in a small dish.

Olives
Choose Spanish stuffed green olives and arrange them in a small serving dish.

Mushroom Marinade

¼ lb/100 g button mushrooms
For the Marinade
1 teaspoon malt vinegar
1 teaspoon oil
1 teaspoon lemon juice
A drop of Worcestershire sauce
1 dessertspoon tomato ketchup
1 dessertspoon water
1 teaspoon chopped parsley
1 small onion, peeled and grated
Salt and pepper

Put the vinegar, oil, lemon juice, Worcestershire sauce, tomato ketchup, water, parsley, onion and seasoning into a screw-topped jar and shake until combined. Wipe and slice the mushrooms and add them to the jar, replace the lid and shake again so the mushroom slices are coated.

Stand the jar in a cool place for about 24 hours, shaking it occasionally until the mushrooms are soft and impregnated with marinade. Turn the mushrooms into a small serving dish.

Cheese Fondue

Serves 4–6

1 small clove garlic
¼ pint/150 ml dry white wine or cider
1 teaspoon lemon juice
14 oz/400 g Edam cheese, grated
1 tablespoon cornflour
1 tablespoon gin or water
A pinch of grated nutmeg
A pinch of pepper
1 French loaf, cut into cubes

Peel the garlic, then cut it and rub the cut edges around the inside of the fondue pan.

Chop the rest of the garlic clove finely and put it into the fondue pan with the wine or cider and lemon juice. Bring the liquid nearly to the boil over the fondue burner, then gradually add the grated cheese, stirring it all the time with a fork. As the cheese melts, add more cheese so that you have a completely smooth mixture. Mix the cornflour to a smooth paste with the gin or water and stir it in with the nutmeg and seasoning. Bring the fondue to the boil and cook for a minute so that it thickens. It is then ready to serve.

Guests then spear a cube of bread on to a fondue fork and dip it into the cheese fondue.

Serve the fondue with a coleslaw salad.

Cheese Fondue

A Barbecue Party

Menu

Sunset Kebabs
Sausage Porkies
Barbecue Sauce
Minted Cutlets
Green Salad

Strawberry Dip
Fresh Fruit

Before the Party
Build the barbecue of two staggered rows of bricks, two bricks high, and suspend two wire cake racks across the top. A barbecue two feet long will be large enough to cook sufficient food for 12 people. If you have invited more, either increase the length of your barbecue or build another one in a different part of the garden to encourage your guests to circulate. There are also many ready-made barbecue sets on the market, but it is advisable to look at several before making your choice.

Light the fire at least an hour before your guests are expected – it will probably take longer than you anticipate to get the fire hot and the open air is a great stimulator of appetites so don't leave your guests too long a wait for the party fare. Use paper and twigs initially then gradually add charcoal until a really good glow is obtained; restoke with more charcoal as necessary.

It is always a good idea to begin the evening meal with a mug of hot soup while the first round of cooking gets under way.

Sunset Kebabs

Makes 18

9 dried prunes
9 lambs' kidneys
¾ lb/350 g pie pork
1 large green pepper
18 small tomatoes
18 long bread rolls
18 skewers (wooden are best as they don't overheat)

Soak the prunes in cold water overnight.

Next day, peel the skins off the kidneys, halve them, cut out the core and cut each half in two. Cut the pork into 36 cubes. Drain the prunes, cut each in half and remove the stones. Halve the pepper with a sharp knife, cut out the core and remove all the seeds. Cut the flesh into at least 18 1-inch/2·5-cm pieces. Wipe the tomatoes.

Thread the ingredients on to the skewers, using two pieces of both pork and kidney on each and one piece of everything else – the tomatoes remain whole. Keep the kebabs in a cool place until required, then brush them with barbecue sauce (see below) and cook over the fire, turning frequently until tender.

To serve the kebabs, split a long roll and butter it; place the kebab in the centre, close the roll around it and pull out the skewer.

Sausage Porkies

Makes 16

1 lb/450 g pork chipolata sausages
½ lb/225 g streaky bacon rashers
1 long French loaf

Separate the sausages. Using a pair of scissors, remove the rind and any small bones from the rashers of bacon, then with the back of a knife, stretch each rasher and cut it into two. Wrap one half around the centre of each sausage and keep them in a cool place until required.

Cut the loaf into rounds, allowing one slice per sausage, and make a fairly large hole through the centre of each. Cook the sausages over the barbecue – brushing them with barbecue sauce if liked – until they are well done and golden brown. Serve the sausages pushed through the holes in the slices of bread.

Minted Cutlets

Makes 18

18 lamb chops
For the Marinade
1 tablespoon chopped mint
2 tablespoons malt vinegar
1 tablespoon caster sugar
½ pint/300 ml cider
A pinch of garlic salt
Salt and pepper

The day before the barbecue, trim the chops, removing any excess fat and discarding the milky white spinal cord that runs along the back bone. Lay the chops in a large shallow dish.

Mix the mint, vinegar, sugar and cider together, add the garlic salt and seasoning, then pour this marinade over the chops. Cover the dish and leave overnight in a cool place.

Next day, drain the chops and cook them over the barbecue, turning frequently with a pair of tongs, until tender – they will take from 20 to 30 minutes.

Serve the Minted Cutlets in paper napkins.

Barbecue Party: Sunset Kebabs, Minted Cutlets, Sausage Porkies

Barbecue Sauce

12 oz/350 g plum jam
6 tablespoons tomato ketchup
3 dessertspoons Worcestershire sauce
Salt and pepper

Turn the jam into a small bowl, stir in the tomato ketchup and Worcestershire sauce and add plenty of seasoning. Brush the sauce over the kebabs and sausages when needed.

The sauce will keep well in a cool place so it can be made up to 5 days before it is required.

Strawberry Dip

Serves 6–8

1 lime jelly
1 large can evaporated milk, chilled
1 lb/450 g ripe strawberries

Break the jelly into squares in a bowl, pour over ¼ pint/150 ml boiling water and stir until the jelly has dissolved. To set the jelly really quickly, now stir in sufficient ice cubes to raise the level of the liquid to ½ pint/300 ml and leave the jelly on one side until nearly set; if you have no ice cubes, add ¼ pint/150 ml cold water and leave the jelly in a cool place.

When the jelly is nearly set, whip the chilled evaporated milk in a large bowl until it has doubled in bulk and is thick and creamy, and the whisk leaves a trail when lifted from the mixture. Hull and wipe all but eight strawberries (these are left for decoration), and using a fork, crush the rest to a pulp. Stir the jelly and the strawberries lightly and quickly into the evaporated milk and turn the pudding into a serving dish.

Leave the Strawberry Dip in a cool place until required, then decorate it with the strawberries and serve accompanied by sweet biscuits.

Entertaining Chinese Style

Serves 8

Combine all the following Chinese recipes together and you could entertain eight friends in true Chinese style. However, if the party is smaller, say four in number, I suggest you serve half the quantity of soup, then choose two of the main courses, accompanying them with plain boiled rice and fried rice; complete the meal with a fruit salad using a selection of Chinese fruits and finally of course, Jasmine Tea.

Menu

Mushroom Soup
Barbecued Spare Ribs
Sweet and Sour Pork
Chicken Chow Mein
Spring Rolls
Boiled and Fried Rice

A Selection of Chinese Fruit

Jasmine Tea

Mushroom Soup

Serves 8

3 pints/1·75 litres good clear stock
6 oz/175 g button mushrooms
1 bunch spring onions
A pinch of ground ginger
1 tablespoon sherry
Salt and pepper

Pour the stock into a large pan. Wipe and trim the mushrooms, slice thinly and add to the pan. Wipe the spring onions and trim the stalk and roots, removing any damaged leaves at the same time. Cut the onions into thin rings and add them to the pan with the pinch of ginger.

Bring the stock to the boil, then reduce the heat and simmer it for 15 to 20 minutes. Stir in the sherry at the last minute and season to taste.

Barbecued Spare Ribs

Serves 4

2½–3 lb/1·25–1·5 kg spare ribs of pork
2 tablespoons malt vinegar
For the Sauce
2 tablespoons soy sauce
2 tablespoons clear honey
1 tablespoon white vinegar
1 teaspoon Worcestershire sauce
2 tablespoons plum jam
1 teaspoon dry mustard
A squeeze of lemon juice
1 teaspoon tomato ketchup

Remove the skin and excess fat from the meat, then cut it into chops between the bones. Put the chops into a pan of boiling water with the vinegar and simmer for 15 minutes.

Mix the soy sauce, honey, white vinegar, Worcestershire sauce, plum jam, mustard, lemon juice and tomato ketchup together in a pan and heat them slowly.

Drain the meat and arrange the chops in a roasting tin, pour over the sauce, then cook the spare ribs on the centre shelf of a moderate oven, gas mark 4 or 350°F/180°C, for 30 minutes, basting the meat twice during this time. Increase the heat to gas mark 6 or 400°F/200°C, for a further 20 minutes, or until the chops are cooked. Serve in a dish with any sauce poured over them.

Freezing Note *Store for up to a month. Thaw then reheat and crisp in a fairly hot oven for 20 to 30 minutes.*

Entertaining Chinese Style: Spring Rolls, Chicken Chow Mein, Mushroom Soup, Sweet and Sour Pork, Barbecued Spare Ribs

Sweet and Sour Pork

Serves 4

- 1 lb/450 g lean pork
- 1 teaspoon demerara sugar
- 1½ tablespoons soy sauce
- ½ teaspoon salt
- ½ teaspoon monosodium glutamate (see Note)
- 1 teaspoon sherry

For the Batter

- 3 oz/75 g self-raising flour
- A pinch of salt
- 1 large egg (size 2), separated
- 3 teaspoons cooking oil
- 6 tablespoons cold water

For the Sauce

- 8-oz/226-g can pineapple tidbits
- 1 small green pepper, deseeded and thinly sliced
- 1 small onion, peeled and sliced
- 1 small carrot, peeled and sliced
- 2 sticks celery, chopped
- ¼ pint/150 ml vinegar
- 3 tablespoons demerara sugar
- A pinch of salt
- 2 tablespoons tomato ketchup
- 1 tablespoon cornflour
- Cooking oil for deep frying

Cut the pork into ½-inch/1-cm pieces. Put into a bowl with the sugar, soy sauce, salt, monosodium glutamate and sherry and stir together. Cover the bowl and leave in a cool place for at least 15 minutes to marinate the meat.

Sift the flour and salt into a mixing bowl, make a well in the centre, add the egg yolk and cooking oil and work them into the flour, gradually adding the cold water.

Heat a deep fat fryer half-filled with cooking oil. Whisk the egg white and carefully fold it into the batter. Dip a few pieces of the pork at a time into the batter and then fry them for about 7 minutes, or until they are golden brown. Reheat the oil between each batch. Drain the pork on absorbent paper and keep warm while making the sauce.

Drain the pineapple and make the juice up to 7½ fl oz/225 ml with water. Cook the pepper, onion, carrot and celery in a pan of boiling salted water for 5 minutes. Drain them well and leave on one side.

Put the vinegar, sugar, salt, tomato ketchup and drained pineapple pieces into a pan. Blend the cornflour to a smooth paste with a little of the pineapple juice, then stir the rest of the juice into the pan and heat the ingredients to boiling point. Stir 3–4 tablespoons of the hot liquid into the cornflour then mix it into the sauce. Return the pan to the heat and, stirring all the time, bring to the boil and cook for a few minutes to thicken the sauce.

Stir the vegetables into the sauce, pour over the pork and serve with boiled or fried rice.

Note Monosodium glutamate is available from most leading stores. It is a white powder, sometimes called 'Accent', and is used extensively by the Chinese as a seasoning to help stimulate the taste buds.

Chicken Chow Mein

Serves 4

- 2 tablespoons cooking oil
- 1 large onion, peeled and chopped
- 3 sticks celery, chopped
- ¼ lb/100 g button mushrooms
- 1 pint/600 ml chicken stock
- 6 oz/175 g Chinese dried egg noodles
- 5-oz/142-g can bamboo shoots, cut into strips
- 9½-oz/270-g can bean sprouts, drained
- 2 tablespoons cornflour
- 2 tablespoons soy sauce
- Salt and pepper
- A pinch of monosodium glutamate
- 12 oz/350 g cooked chicken, shredded

Heat the oil in a frying pan, add the onion and celery and fry them for a few minutes until they start to soften. Wipe the mushrooms, trim the stalks, then slice them and add to the pan with the stock. Bring to the boil and simmer for 5 minutes.

Meanwhile, cook the noodles in boiling salted water for 8 to 10 minutes, until tender, stirring them occasionally to prevent sticking. Drain well, run hot water through the strands then turn them on to a serving dish and keep warm.

Add the bamboo shoots and bean sprouts to the stock. Mix the cornflour with the soy sauce and stir in 2 tablespoons of the hot stock. Return this to the pan, sprinkle with salt and pepper and monosodium glutamate and, stirring all the time, bring to the boil. Finally, stir in the chicken pieces and simmer for 2 to 3 minutes.

Turn the Chow Mein into the centre of the noodles and serve immediately.

Spring Rolls

Makes 18

For the Dough

- 8 oz/225 g plain flour
- A pinch of salt
- 1 large egg (size 2)
- 3 tablespoons cold water

For the Filling

- ½ lb/225 g freshly minced beef
- 2 oz/50 g peeled prawns
- 2 oz/50 g bean sprouts
- ½ bunch spring onions
- 2 oz/50 g mushrooms
- Salt and pepper
- Fat or oil for deep frying

Sift the flour and salt into a mixing bowl. Beat the egg with the water, add it to the flour and mix to form a stiff dough. Turn the dough on to a lightly floured work surface and knead it for about 5 minutes or until it feels soft and smooth. Wrap in greaseproof paper and leave in a cool

Sweet and Sour Pork

place for about 20 minutes to rest.

Meanwhile, make the filling. Put the minced beef into a bowl, chop the prawns and add them to the beef with the bean sprouts. Trim off the roots and tops of the spring onions then wash them and cut into rings. Wipe the mushrooms – there is no need to peel them – trim the stalks, then chop the mushrooms finely. Add the spring onions and mushrooms to the other filling ingredients, season with plenty of salt and pepper, and leave on one side.

Cut the dough in half. Roll one half into a square as thinly as possible. Slip your hands underneath the dough and, working from the centre to the edges, stretch the dough on the back of your hands until it is so thin that you could read through it. Do this very carefully to avoid splitting the dough. When the dough is ready it should measure about 15 inches/37·5 cm square. Trim the edges then cut into nine 5-inch/12·5-cm squares.

Taking a little of the filling at a time, roll it into a sausage shape and place it diagonally across one corner of a square of dough. Dampen the edges, then fold the top corner over the filling and roll up the parcel towards you, making sure all the edges are well sealed. Form the other squares into rolls in the same way, then repeat the whole process using the remaining dough.

Half-fill a deep fat fryer with fat or cooking oil and heat it to 340°F/175°C. Fry the rolls, six at a time, for about 6 minutes, or until golden brown. Drain the rolls on absorbent paper and keep them warm while cooking the other batches.

Serve the Spring Rolls hot.

Fried Rice

Serves 4

1 small onion
2 large eggs (size 2)
1 oz/25 g butter
6 oz/175 g long-grain rice, cooked
$1\frac{1}{2}$ tablespoons soy sauce
1 teaspoon monosodium glutamate
4-oz/113-g can peeled shrimps
Salt and pepper

Peel and finely chop the onion and cut into thin rings. Beat the eggs thoroughly.

Melt the butter in a frying pan, add the eggs and start to scramble them; whilst still half liquid stir in the cooked rice and quickly coat the grains with the egg. As the mixture dries, stir in the onion and sprinkle over the soy sauce and monosodium glutamate. Fry for a further 3 to 4 minutes, then stir in the shrimps and season to taste before turning into a bowl to serve.

Boiled Rice

Allow 2 oz/50 g rice per person. Wash the grains, then put them into a pan of salted water – it must cover the grains by at least 2 inches/5 cm. Bring the water to the boil, then reduce the heat, cover the pan and simmer the rice for 12 minutes.

To test if it is ready, rub a grain between the thumb and first finger. If it still has a hard core, cook the rice for a few more minutes, but if it is tender, drain the rice and run hot water through the grains to separate them and remove any excess starch.

Turn the rice into a bowl to serve.

Cakes, Traybakes and Biscuits

Whoever is coming to tea, here is a cake, bake or biscuit to cook for the occasion. There are cakes both large and small, plain or fancy, bakes that are quick and easy to make and biscuits that are difficult to resist. All the recipes ensure the cake tin will never be empty – at least until the family discover you've been baking!

Half Pound Cake

- ½ lb/225 g butter
- ½ lb/225 g caster sugar
- 2 large eggs (size 2)
- ½ lb/225 g mixed dried fruit, cleaned
- ½ lb/225 g self-raising flour
- *A 7-inch/18-cm square cake tin*

Brush the tin with melted fat and line the base with a piece of greaseproof paper cut to fit; grease this also.

Cream the butter until it is soft, then add the sugar and continue beating until light in colour and texture. Beat the eggs then add them gradually to the creamed mixture, beating well between each addition. Stir in the fruit with the flour and turn the cake mixture into the tin. Spread it to the sides and hollow out the centre slightly so that the cake rises evenly.

Bake the cake on the centre shelf of a moderate oven, gas mark 4 or 350°F/180°C, for 2 to 2¼ hours, or until the cake is slightly shrinking away from the sides of the tin, and a warmed skewer pushed into the centre comes out clean.

Cool the cake on a wire rack and store it in an airtight tin.

Freezing Note *Store for up to 3 months. Thaw overnight.*

Dundee Cake

- 6 oz/175 g butter
- 6 oz/175 g light soft brown sugar
- 3 large eggs (size 2)
- 8 oz/225 g plain flour
- 1 teaspoon baking powder
- 1 teaspoon ground mixed spice
- 8 oz/225 g currants, cleaned
- 8 oz/225 g sultanas, cleaned
- 2 oz/50 g chopped mixed peel
- 1 tablespoon milk
- 1 oz/25 g blanched almonds, halved
- *A 7-inch/18-cm round cake tin*

Brush the tin with melted fat. Cut two circles of greaseproof paper to fit the base of the tin, place one in position and brush it with melted fat. Cut a doubled strip of greaseproof paper 2 inches/5 cm deeper than the tin and long enough to go round the inside and slightly overlap. Turn the folded edge up 1 inch/2·5 cm, then make slanting cuts to the crease about 1 inch/2·5 cm apart. Fit the strip into place with the slits neatly overlapping in the base and cover it with the second circle of greaseproof paper. Brush the entire lining with melted fat.

Cream the butter and sugar together until light and fluffy in both colour and texture. Beat the eggs together, then gradually add them to the creamed mixture, beating well between each addition.

Sift together the flour, baking powder and mixed spice. Combine the fruit and chopped peel in a bowl and stir a tablespoon of the flour into the mixture.

Using a metal spoon, fold the flour and milk into the creamed mixture, then stir in the fruit. Turn the cake mixture into the prepared tin, spread it to the sides and hollow out the centre slightly. Arrange the almonds evenly on top of the cake in circles.

Bake the Dundee Cake on the centre shelf of a moderate oven, gas mark 4 or 350°F/180°C, for 1 hour, then reduce to gas mark 2 or 300°F/150°C for a further 1¼ to 1½ hours, until a warmed skewer inserted into the cake comes out clean. Leave the cake to cool in the tin for 10 minutes, then turn it on to a wire rack to cool completely.

Freezing Note *Store for up to 3 months, thaw overnight.*

Dundee Cake

Victoria Sandwich

Basic Recipe

Ingredients	*Two 6½-inch/16-cm sandwich tins*	*Two 7½-inch/19-cm sandwich tins*	*Two 8½-inch/21-cm sandwich tins*
Margarine	4 oz/110 g	6 oz/175 g	8 oz/225 g
Caster sugar	4 oz/110 g	6 oz/175 g	8 oz/225 g
Large eggs (size 2)	2	3	4
Self-raising flour	4 oz/110 g	6 oz/175 g	8 oz/225 g
Salt	Pinch	Pinch	Pinch
Baking times – gas mark 5 or 375°F/190°C	20–25 mins.	25–30 mins.	30–35 mins.
Flavourings			
Orange, grated rind and juice	½ orange	1 small orange	1 medium orange
Walnuts, finely chopped	2 oz/50 g	2½ oz/65 g	3 oz/75 g
Coconut, desiccated	1 oz/25 g (omit 1 oz/25 g flour)	2 oz/50 g (omit 2 oz/50 g flour)	3 oz/75 g (omit 3 oz/75 g flour)
Ground mixed spice	½ teaspoon	1 teaspoon	1½ teaspoons
Liquid coffee	1 teaspoon	1 dessertspoon	1 tablespoon
Cocoa powder	½ oz/15 g (omit ½ oz/15 g flour)	1 oz/25 g (omit 1 oz/25 g flour)	1½ oz/40 g (omit 1½ oz/40 g flour)
Decoration and Filling			
Double cream	4 tablespoons	¼ pint/150 ml	¼ pint/150 ml
Single cream			4 tablespoons
Jam	2 tablespoons	3 tablespoons	4 tablespoons
Icing sugar	2 tablespoons	3 tablespoons	4 tablespoons
Little Cakes			
Basic ingredients will make	16 buns	24 buns	32 buns
Icing sugar	6 oz/175 g	9 oz/250 g	12 oz/350 g

Bake all the little cakes at gas mark 5 or 375°F/190°C for 20 minutes.

Basic Method
Brush the sandwich tins with melted fat, then line the base of each with a circle of greaseproof paper cut to fit and grease this too.

Beat the margarine to a soft cream with a wooden spoon, then add the caster sugar and cream them together until light and fluffy in colour and texture. Beat the eggs and add them gradually to the creamed mixture, beating well between each addition. (If the eggs are added too quickly the mixture is likely to curdle; if this happens beat in a little of the measured flour to bring the mixture back to its original consistency.)

Sift the flour and salt together then, using a metal spoon, fold them very carefully into the creamed mixture. Divide it between the two prepared tins and spread it to the sides, hollowing out the centres slightly so that the cakes rise evenly.

Bake the cakes on the centre shelf of a moderately hot oven, gas mark 5 or 375°F/190°C, for the required time (see chart). The cake is ready when it has shrunk slightly from the sides of the tin and feels springy to the touch. Remove from the oven, carefully run a knife around the inside of the tins and turn the cakes on to wire racks. Remove the greaseproof paper and leave to cool.

Addition of Flavourings
Orange Beat in the rind and juice with the last addition of beaten egg.
Walnut Stir in the chopped nuts with the sifted dry ingredients.
Coconut As for walnut.
Mixed spice Sift the spice with the flour and salt.
Liquid coffee As for walnut.
Cocoa powder As for mixed spice.

Decoration and Filling
Spread the jam over one of the cakes. Whip the cream until thick, then spread it over the jam. Place the other cake on top and sift the icing sugar over the surface.

Little Cakes
Make as for Victoria Sandwich, then divide the mixture between paper cake cases arranged on baking trays or set into little bun tins. (The latter help to keep the buns in a good shape.)

Bake the buns on the centre shelf of a moderately hot oven, gas mark 5 or 375°F/190°C, for the required time.

Leave the cakes to cool on a wire rack. Sift the icing sugar into a mixing bowl and stir in enough cold water to make an icing that just

forms its own level. Spoon a little on the top of each cake and decorate them as liked, with glacé cherries, chocolate vermicelli or coloured strands.

Freezing Note *Store the unfilled cakes in a polythene bag. The large cakes will keep for up to 6 months, the little cakes for 3 months. Thaw for 3 hours.*

Butter Cakes, Rock Buns, Victoria Sandwich

Butter Cakes

Basic Recipe

Ingredients	*6-inch/15-cm round cake tin*	*7-inch/18-cm round cake tin*	*8-inch/20-cm round cake tin*
Butter	6 oz/175 g	8 oz/225 g	10 oz/275 g
Caster sugar	6 oz/175 g	8 oz/225 g	10 oz/275 g
Large eggs (size 2)	3	4	5
Plain flour	8 oz/225 g	10 oz/275 g	12 oz/350 g
Baking powder	1 teaspoon	1½ teaspoons	2 teaspoons
Salt	Pinch	Pinch	Pinch
Milk	2–3 tablespoons	3 tablespoons	3–4 tablespoons
Flavourings			
Madeira	Grated rind of ½ lemon 2 teaspoons lemon juice (omit 2 teaspoons milk) 1 slice citron peel	Grated rind of 1 lemon 2½ teaspoons lemon juice (omit 2½ teaspoons milk) 1 slice citron peel	Grated rind of 1 lemon 1 tablespoon lemon juice (omit 1 tablespoon milk) 1 slice citron peel
Chocolate	3 tablespoons cocoa powder (omit 3 tablespoons flour)	4 tablespoons cocoa powder (omit 4 tablespoons flour)	5 tablespoons cocoa powder (omit 5 tablespoons flour)
Caraway	Grated rind of ½ orange ½ teaspoon caraway seed 2 teaspoons orange juice (omit 2 teaspoons milk)	Grated rind of 1 orange 1 teaspoon caraway seed 2½ teaspoons orange juice (omit 2½ teaspoons milk)	Grated rind of 1 orange 1½ teaspoons caraway seed 1 tablespoon orange juice (omit 1 tablespoon milk)
Walnuts, chopped	2 oz/50 g	3 oz/75 g	4 oz/100 g
Coconut	3 oz/75 g desiccated 1 tablespoon extra milk 1 drop of vanilla essence	4 oz/100 g desiccated 1½ tablespoons extra milk 2 drops of vanilla essence	5 oz/150 g desiccated 2 tablespoons extra milk 3 drops of vanilla essence
Cherries, glacé	6 oz/175 g	8 oz/225 g	10 oz/275 g
Sultana	3 oz/75 g, cleaned	4 oz/100 g, cleaned	5 oz/150 g, cleaned
Baking Times – cook all the cakes gas mark 4 or 350°F/180°C			
Madeira	1 hr. 25–30 mins.	1 hr. 35–40 mins.	1 hr. 45–50 mins.
Chocolate	1 hr. 35–40 mins.	1 hr. 45–50 mins.	2 hrs.
Caraway	1 hr. 25–30 mins.	1 hr. 35–40 mins.	1 hr. 45–50 mins.
Walnut	1 hr. 35 mins.	1 hr. 45 mins.	1 hr. 55 mins.
Coconut	1 hr. 40 mins.	1 hr. 50 mins.	2 hrs.
Cherry	1 hr. 35–40 mins.	1 hr. 45–50 mins.	1 hr. 55 mins. to 2 hrs.
Sultana	1 hr. 35–40 mins.	1 hr. 45–50 mins.	1 hr. 55 mins. to 2 hrs.

Basic Method

First line the tin with greaseproof paper as follows: place the tin on a doubled sheet of greaseproof paper and mark around the base, then cut out two circles; brush the tin with melted fat, place one circle in the base and grease it also. Cut a doubled strip of paper long enough to go round the inside of the tin and slightly overlap, and wide enough to extend at least 2 inches/5 cm above the top. Turn the folded edge up 1 inch/2·5 cm, then make slanting cuts to the crease about 1 inch/2·5 cm apart. Fit the strip into place with the slits neatly overlapping in the base. Lastly, place the other circle of greaseproof paper into the base and brush the entire lining with melted fat.

Beat the butter to a soft cream, add the caster sugar and beat them together until light and fluffy. Beat the eggs and add them gradually to the creamed mixture, beating well between each addition.

Sift together the flour, baking powder and salt then, using a metal spoon, carefully stir them into the creamed mixture, alternating with the milk. Turn the mixture into the prepared tin, smooth the surface then hollow out the centre slightly with the back of the spoon so that the cake will rise evenly.

Bake the cake on the centre shelf of a moderate oven, gas mark 4 or 350°F/180°C, for the length of time required (see chart). To test if the cake is cooked, push a warm skewer into the centre; if it comes out clean and the cake is 'silent' it is ready, but if any mixture adheres to the skewer and the cake still sounds as though it is cooking, return the tin to the oven until both tests are satisfactory.

Leave the cake to cool in the tin for 15 minutes, then turn it on to a wire rack; remove the greaseproof paper and cool the cake completely.

The cake will keep in an airtight tin for at least 1 week.

Addition of Flavourings

Madeira Beat in the lemon rind with the eggs and stir in the lemon juice with the milk. Cook the cake for 40 minutes then, very carefully, slip the citron peel on top of the cake without removing it from the oven.

Chocolate Sift the cocoa powder with the dry ingredients.

Caraway Beat in the orange rind with the eggs, then stir in the orange juice and caraway seeds with the flour.

Walnut Stir in the chopped nuts with the dry ingredients.

Coconut As for walnut, adding the vanilla essence with the milk.

Cherry Wash cherries thoroughly to remove all the syrup, dry them well and coat in a little of the measured flour. Stir them in with the dry ingredients.

Sultana As for cherry.

Freezing Note *Store for up to 6 months. Thaw overnight.*

Battenburg

4 oz/110 g butter
4 oz/110 g caster sugar
2 large eggs (size 2)
4 oz/110 g self-rasing flour
A few drops of rose pink food colouring
4 tablespoons apricot jam, sieved
Caster sugar for sprinkling

For the Almond Paste

6 oz/175 g ground almonds
3 oz/75 g caster sugar
3 oz/75 g icing sugar, sifted
1 large egg yolk (size 2)
A little lemon juice
A 7-inch/18-cm square cake tin

1 Brush the tin with fat, line the base with a piece of greaseproof paper cut to fit, then grease this also. Divide the tin into two with four thicknesses of foil the depth of the tin; secure the foil with paper clips.

2 Put the butter, sugar, eggs and flour into a mixing bowl, mix them slowly together, then beat for a minute to incorporate air. (Use the same method if making the mixture with a wooden spoon.)

Battenburg

3 Spread half the mixture into one side of the tin, hollowing out the centre. Colour the rest of the mixture pink and turn it into the other side of the tin. Bake in a moderately hot oven, gas mark 5 or 375°F/190°C, for 25 to 30 minutes.

4 Leave the cakes to cool, then trim each piece level and sandwich them together with warmed apricot jam. Cut them in half down the centre, brush one cut side with jam and put the other half on top to alternate the colours.

5 Mix the ground almonds, caster and icing sugar together, then work in enough egg yolk and lemon juice to make a stiff mixture. Roll this almond paste into a rectangle 7 inches/18 cm wide. Brush with jam and wrap round the cake.

6 Smooth the joins together with a palette knife and trim the ends of the cake. Crimp the top edges with the fingers, then using the back of the knife mark a diamond design on top. Sprinkle the cake with caster sugar.

Freezing Note *Store the sponge cakes before assembly for up to 3 months. Thaw for 4 hours then continue as in the recipe.*

Honey Parkin

4 oz/110 g margarine
8 tablespoons honey
4 oz/110 g dark soft brown sugar
4 oz/110 g self-raising flour
1 teaspoon ground ginger
1 teaspoon ground mixed spice
4 oz/110 g porridge oats
1 large egg (size 2)
6 tablespoons milk
A 6½-inch/16·5-cm square tin

Grease the tin and line the base with a piece of greaseproof paper cut to fit; grease the paper lining also.

Melt together the margarine, honey and sugar in a pan over a low heat, then leave on one side for the mixture to cool slightly.

Sift the flour, ginger and mixed spice into a bowl and stir in the porridge oats. When the melted mixture is ready, stir it into the dry ingredients with the well-beaten egg and the milk. Pour the mixture into the tin, then bake on the centre shelf of a moderately cool oven, gas mark 3 or 325°F/160°C, for about 1¼ hours, until the cake feels springy to the touch and is shrinking away from the sides of the tin.

Turn on to a wire rack to cool, then keep it in an airtight tin for at least a day before serving.

Roundabout Ring, Honey Parkin, Apple and Raisin Cake, Date and Orange Cake, Californian Chocolate Cake

Californian Chocolate Cake

4 oz/110 g lard
8 oz/225 g caster sugar
2 large eggs (size 2)
8 oz/225 g plain flour
3 oz/85 g cocoa powder
½ teaspoon baking powder
A pinch of salt
½ teaspoon bicarbonate of soda
¼ pint/150 ml plus 3 tablespoons cold water
A few drops of vanilla essence

For the Filling and Icing

4 oz/100 g margarine
2 tablespoons golden syrup
1 oz/25 g cocoa powder
2 oz/50 g icing sugar, sifted
Two 7½-inch/19-cm sandwich tins

Grease the tins and line each base with a circle of greaseproof paper cut to fit; grease the paper lining also.

Cream the lard until soft then add the caster sugar and cream the mixture again. Beat the eggs and add them gradually to the creamed mixture, beating well between each addition. Sift the flour, cocoa powder, baking powder, salt and bicarbonate of soda together, then stir them into the creamed mixture with the water and vanilla essence. Pour the cake mixture evenly into both the tins.

Bake the cakes on the centre shelf of a moderate oven, gas mark 4 or 350°F/180°C, for 30 to 35 minutes or until they are shrinking away from the sides of the tin. Leave the cakes to cool slightly, then carefully turn them on to a wire rack to cool completely.

Blend the margarine with the syrup and sifted cocoa powder in a pan over a gentle heat. Leave on one side until the mixture cools and starts to set, then gradually beat in the icing sugar to make a soft glossy mixture. Divide this filling between the two cakes, then sandwich them together and decorate the top.

Freezing Note *Store before filling and decorating for up to 3 months. Thaw for 3 hours then continue as in the recipe.*

Roundabout Ring

4 oz/110 g butter
4 oz/110 g light soft brown sugar
2 large eggs (size 2), beaten
8 oz/225 g self-raising flour
A pinch of salt
3 oz/75 g glacé cherries, washed and chopped
2 oz/50 g chocolate Polka Dots
2–3 tablespoons milk
Icing sugar for sprinkling
A 7-inch/18-cm ring mould of 1½ pint/900 ml capacity, greased

Beat the butter until it is soft, then add the sugar and cream them together until light and fluffy in texture. Add the eggs gradually, beating the mixture well between each addition, then finally sift in the flour and salt. Add the cherries and chocolate Polka Dots, then, using a metal spoon, fold these ingredients into the creamed mixture, adding sufficient milk to make a soft, dropping consistency.

Turn the cake mixture into the prepared tin and spread the surface level. Bake on the centre shelf of a moderate oven, gas mark 4 or 350°F/180°C, for 50 minutes to 1 hour, or until the cake feels springy to the touch and is starting to shrink away from the sides of the tin. Cool the cake in the tin for 10 minutes, then turn it on to a wire rack to cool completely.

Serve the cake dusted with icing sugar and cut into slices.

Freezing Note *Store the cake before dusting with icing sugar for up to 2 months. Thaw for 4 hours and dust with icing sugar before serving.*

Date and Orange Cake

4 oz/110 g margarine
3 oz/75 g soft brown sugar
3 tablespoons golden syrup
2 large eggs (size 2), beaten
8 oz/225 g wholemeal flour
1½ teaspoons baking powder
A pinch of salt
8 oz/225 g cooking dates, chopped
Grated rind and juice of 1 orange
1 tablespoon demerara sugar
A 7-inch/18-cm round cake tin

Brush the tin with melted fat and line the base with a circle of greaseproof paper cut to fit; grease the paper lining also.

Cream the margarine until soft, then add the soft brown sugar and beat together until light and creamy in texture. Beat in the golden syrup, then gradually add the eggs, beating the mixture well between each addition.

Stir in the flour with the baking powder, salt, 6 oz/175 g of the dates, half the orange rind and about 6 tablespoons orange juice – use water to make up the liquid if necessary. Turn the mixture into the tin and spread the surface level. Mix the remaining dates with the rest of the orange rind and the demerara sugar and sprinkle over the surface of the cake so that it is evenly covered all over.

Bake the cake on the centre shelf of a moderately cool oven, gas mark 3 or 325°F/160°C, for about 1¼ to 1½ hours. To test if the cake is cooked, push a warmed skewer into the centre; if any mixture adheres to it, cook the cake for a little longer until the skewer comes out quite clean. Cool the cake in the tin for 10 minutes, then turn it on to a wire rack to cool completely.

Freezing Note *Store for up to 3 months, thaw overnight.*

Apple and Raisin Cake

12 oz/350 g plain flour
A pinch of salt
$1\frac{1}{2}$ teaspoons bicarbonate of soda
1 teaspoon ground cinnamon
6 oz/175 g margarine
6 oz/175 g caster sugar
2 oz/50 g walnuts, chopped
6 oz/175 g seedless raisins, cleaned
1 lb/450 g cooking apples, cooked to make $\frac{1}{2}$ pint/300 ml apple pureé
$\frac{1}{4}$ pint/150 ml milk
1 oz/25 g demerara sugar
A 7 × $9\frac{1}{2}$-inch/18 × 24-cm roasting tin

Lightly grease the tin and line the base with a piece of greaseproof paper cut to fit; grease the paper lining also.

Sift the flour, salt, bicarbonate of soda and cinnamon into a bowl. Add the margarine cut into small pieces and, using the fingertips only, rub it into the flour until evenly distributed. Stir in the sugar, walnuts and raisins, then bind the ingredients together with the apple purée and milk to make a stiff consistency.

Turn the mixture into the prepared tin and level the surface, then sprinkle over the demerara sugar. Bake the cake on the centre shelf of a moderate oven, gas mark 4 or 350°F/180°C, for $1\frac{1}{4}$ hours, or until the mixture feels springy to the touch and is starting to shrink away from the sides of the tin.

Cool the cake on a wire rack, then store in an airtight tin for at least a day before serving cut into slices.

Note The cake will store in an airtight tin for at least 2 weeks and becomes even more delicious with keeping.

Freezing Note *Store for up to 3 months, thaw overnight at room temperature.*

Gingerbread Ring

Gingerbread Ring

4 oz/110 g margarine
4 oz/110 g dark soft brown sugar
4 oz/110 g black treacle
6 oz/170 g plain flour
1 dessertspoon ground ginger
$1\frac{1}{2}$ dessertspoons ground cinnamon
1 large egg (size 2)
$\frac{1}{4}$ pint/150 ml milk
1 teaspoon bicarbonate of soda
A 3-pint/1·75 litre ring mould

Brush the ring mould with melted fat and dust it completely with flour.

Put the margarine, sugar and treacle into a pan and melt them over a low heat, but do not allow to boil. Sift together the flour, ground ginger and cinnamon, then stir into the melted mixture with the egg. Warm the milk to blood heat – that is when it feels neither hot nor cold to the touch. Pour the milk on to the bicarbonate of soda, stir it well then mix into the other ingredients to form a smooth batter-like consistency. Pour into the prepared tin.

Bake the Gingerbread Ring on the centre shelf of a cool oven, gas mark 2 or 300°F/150°C, for $1\frac{3}{4}$ hours, or until it feels springy to the touch and is slightly shrinking away from the sides of the tin. Carefully turn the cake on to a wire rack to cool.

Serve the gingerbread with about 12 butter balls piled up in the centre of the ring.

Freezing Note *Store for up to 3 months, thaw for 4 hours.*

Angel Cake

2½ oz/65 g plain flour
4 oz/100 g caster sugar
5 large egg whites (size 2)
½ teaspoon cream of tartar
A pinch of salt
2 oz/50 g caster sugar
A few drops of vanilla essence
For the Buttercream
3 oz/75 g caster sugar
¼ pint/150 ml water
3 large egg yolks (size 2)
6 oz/175 g unsalted butter
2 tablespoons cocoa powder
An angel cake tin 8 inches/20 cm in diameter or a plain 8-inch/20-cm round cake tin

If you do not have an angel cake tin, you can contrive one in the following way.

Cut a 3-inch/7·5-cm length from the cardboard centre of a roll of kitchen paper or foil and cover it with foil. Stand the tube in the centre of an 8-inch/20-cm cake tin. Do not grease the tin.

Heat the oven to gas mark 5 or 375°F/190°C. Sift the flour with the 4 oz/100 g sugar three times (the secret of success with this cake is to work in as much air as possible). Put the egg whites into a mixing bowl with the cream of tartar and salt, and whisk them until foamy. Gradually whisk in the 2 oz/50 g sugar, a tablespoon at a time. Continue whisking until the egg whites are really stiff and stand in straight peaks, then sift in the flour and sugar mixture, add the vanilla essence and, using a metal spoon, fold in as lightly and quickly as possible.

Spoon the mixture into the ungreased tin and, using a knife, gently cut through it to release any large air bubbles.

Bake the cake for 35 to 40 minutes, until the cake springs back when the surface is lightly pressed. Invert the cake tin on the neck of a milk bottle or funnel and leave the cake like this until quite cold. Loosen it carefully from the edges of the tin, then turn it out.

Dissolve the sugar in the water over a low heat. When every grain has dissolved, and not before, bring the syrup to the boil and boil it rapidly for about 10 minutes. To test if it is ready, lift a little syrup on a wooden spoon, dip a fingertip into it, then press the tip against your thumb; as you part finger and thumb, a short thread should form before breaking.

Pour the syrup slowly on to the egg yolks and whisk continuously until the mixture is very thick and creamy, and the whisk leaves a definite trail when lifted out of the bowl. Beat the butter to a soft cream, then gradually beat in the syrup until a buttercream is formed. Stir in the sifted cocoa powder and leave the buttercream in a cool place to stiffen.

Split the Angel Cake into three layers, and sandwich them together again with a little buttercream. Turn the rest of the buttercream on top and coat the whole cake, leaving the surface rough.

Freezing Note *Store the cake either plain or iced. Keep the plain cake for up to 3 months. Thaw at room temperature for 2 hours before filling and decorating.*

It is best to freeze the iced cake uncovered then wrap and seal when solid. Store for up to a month and thaw slowly overnight.

German Apple Cake

For the Cake
4 oz/110 g butter
4 oz/110 g caster sugar
1 large egg (size 2), beaten
8 oz/225 g self-raising flour
A pinch of salt
For the Filling
¾ lb/350 g cooking apples, peeled, cored and chopped
2 oz/50 g sultanas, cleaned
1 oz/25 g walnuts, chopped
½ teaspoon ground cinnamon
2 oz/50 g demerara sugar
A deep 7-inch/18-cm round cake tin

Brush the tin with melted fat and line the base with a circle of greaseproof paper cut to fit; grease the paper lining also.

Melt the butter in a pan over a low heat. Remove the pan from the heat and mix in the caster sugar, beaten egg and sifted flour and salt to make a fairly stiff consistency. Turn two-thirds of the mixture into the tin and spread it to the sides, making the surface level.

Mix the apples, sultanas, walnuts and cinnamon together and scatter this over the cake base, then sprinkle over the demerara sugar. Dot the remaining cake mixture over the filling – it will not cover it completely. Bake the cake on the centre shelf of a moderate oven, gas mark 4 or 350°F/180°C, for 50 to 60 minutes, or until the cake is cooked and a light golden brown colour. Leave the cake in the tin for 10 minutes to cool, then turn it out and serve either slightly warm with custard for a dessert or as a cake for tea.

Freezing Note *Store for up to 2 months. Thaw overnight.*

Jam Swiss Roll

2 large eggs (size 2)
2 oz/55 g caster sugar
A few drops of vanilla essence
2 oz/55 g self-raising flour, sifted
For the Filling
6 tablespoons raspberry jam
A 12 × 8-inch/30 × 20-cm Swiss roll tin

Brush the tin with melted fat. Cut a piece of greaseproof paper 1 inch/2·5 cm larger than the tin all round, make a 1-inch/2·5-cm diagonal cut from each corner and fit the lining into the tin; grease the paper lining also.

Break the eggs into a mixing bowl, add the caster sugar and vanilla essence and place the bowl over a pan of hot water. Whisk the ingredients together using a rotary or wire whisk.

When they are thick and creamy and leave a clear trail when the whisk is lifted out, fold in the sifted flour using a metal spoon. Turn the mixture into the tin and spread it to the sides.

Bake the sponge on the centre shelf of a moderately hot oven, gas mark 5 or 375°F/190°C, for 12 minutes, then quickly turn it out on to greaseproof paper thickly dusted with caster sugar.

Remove the lining paper and spread the jam over the sponge. Using a sharp knife, trim off all the edges – this helps it to roll more easily. Mark a line 1 inch/2·5 cm in from one of the shorter sides.

Using the sugared paper as a guide, and starting at the marked end, roll the sponge up tightly. Keep it wrapped in the paper for about 10 minutes before leaving it to cool.

Lemon and Orange Swiss Roll Add the finely grated rind of an orange before turning the mixture into the tin. When cooked, spread with lemon curd and roll up as described for Jam Swiss Roll.

Individual Swiss Rolls Make the sponge mixture as described for Jam Swiss Roll but divide the sugared paper into four before turning the cooked Swiss roll on to it. Spread the sponge with jam and trim the edges. Divide it into four and using a piece of paper for each, roll them up separately to make four small rolls.

Neapolitan Swiss Roll Make the mixture as described for Jam Swiss Roll. Before turning it into the tin, put a third of the mixture into another bowl and colour it with green food colouring. Dot spoonfuls of half the remaining mixture into the tin. Colour the rest pink, then dot spoonfuls of both the pink and the green mixtures into the tin between the plain mixture. Spread the mixture very carefully to the sides of the tin, then follow the recipe for the Jam Swiss Roll.

Freezing Note *Store for up to 2 months. Thaw for 4 hours.*

Chocolate Swiss Roll, Neapolitan Swiss Roll, Lemon and Orange Swiss Roll, Jam Swiss Rolls

Chocolate Swiss Roll

2 large eggs (size 2)
2 oz/55 g caster sugar
1½ oz/40 g self-raising flour
½ oz/15 g cocoa powder
A few drops of vanilla essence
Caster sugar for sprinkling
For the Filling
4 oz/100 g butter
4 oz/100 g icing sugar, sifted
1 dessertspoon cocoa powder
A 12 × 8-inch/30 × 20-cm Swiss roll tin

Make and bake the Swiss roll as for the Jam Swiss Roll recipe (see above), sifting the cocoa powder in with the flour. When it is cooked, turn it on to a sugared sheet of greaseproof paper. Remove the lining and trim the edges. Place another sheet of paper on top and roll it up inside the Swiss roll, guiding it with the sugared paper. Leave to cool.

Meanwhile make the buttercream. Beat the butter to a soft cream with the sifted icing sugar and cocoa powder. Unroll the sponge, remove the paper and spread the buttercream over the surface, then reroll the sponge and dredge with a little extra caster sugar before serving.

Freezing Note *Store for up to 2 months. Thaw for 4 hours.*

Golden Cheesecakes

Makes 14

For the Pastry
6 oz / 170 g plain flour
A pinch of salt
$1\frac{1}{2}$ oz / 40 g margarine
$1\frac{1}{2}$ oz / 40 g lard
For the Filling
2 oz / 50 g soft margarine
2 oz / 50 g caster sugar
1 large egg (size 2)
2 oz / 50 g self-raising flour, sifted
Finely grated rind of $\frac{1}{2}$ lemon
1 dessertspoon milk
About 4 oz / 100 g raspberry jam
4 glacé cherries, quartered
A $2\frac{1}{2}$-inch / 6-cm plain cutter
14 tartlet tins

First make the pastry. Sift the flour and salt into a mixing bowl. Add the fats cut into small pieces and, using the fingertips only, rub them in until evenly distributed. Add just enough cold water to make a fairly stiff dough, then roll it out thinly and cut out 14 rounds. Press them into the base of each tartlet tin and reserve the pastry trimmings.

Put the margarine, sugar, egg, sifted flour, lemon rind and milk into a mixing bowl. Using a wooden spoon, mix the ingredients together, then beat them well for a minute to incorporate some air.

Put a teaspoon of jam into the base of each tart and spread a spoonful of the sponge mixture on top.

Cut the pastry trimmings into thin strips and lay a twist of pastry on top of each tart. Place a cherry quarter on each twist, and bake the tartlets on the centre shelf of a moderately hot oven, gas mark 5 or 375°F / 190°C, for 20 to 25 minutes, until golden brown and well risen.

Freezing Note *Store for up to 3 months then thaw for 4 hours.*

Chocolate Choux Buns

Chocolate Choux Buns

Makes about 10

For the Choux Pastry
$2\frac{1}{2}$ oz / 70 g plain flour
2 oz / 55 g margarine
$\frac{1}{4}$ pint / 150 ml water
2 large eggs (size 2)
For the Filling
$\frac{1}{4}$ pint / 150 ml double cream
2 teaspoons caster sugar
For the Icing
4 oz / 100 g plain chocolate
1 oz / 25 g caster sugar
1 teaspoon cooking oil
2 tablespoons water
A large piping bag with $\frac{3}{4}$-inch / 1·5-cm plain pipe attached

Sift the flour on to a piece of paper. Melt the margarine in a pan over a low heat, then add the water and bring the mixture to the boil. Take the pan off the heat and immediately shoot in all the flour. Using a wooden spoon, beat the mixture vigorously until it is smooth and leaves the sides of the pan. Beat the eggs, then gradually add them to the mixture, beating well between each addition; when all the egg has been added, the mixture should be smooth and glossy.

Fill the piping bag with the choux pastry and pipe the buns on to lightly greased baking trays, making each one about $1\frac{1}{2}$ inches / 3·5 cm in diameter and spacing them fairly well apart.

Bake the buns on the centre shelf of a hot oven, gas mark 7 or 425°F / 220°C, for 15 to 20 minutes until they are well risen, golden brown and crisp. As soon as the buns are removed from the oven, slit them to allow the steam to escape and keep them crisp. The buns should be cooked to the centre but if there is any moistness remaining inside, scrape it out with a teaspoon. Leave the buns on a wire rack to cool.

Whip the cream until it holds its

shape, then mix in the caster sugar. Fill the cooled buns with the cream – it is often easier to pipe this into each bun.

Put all the ingredients for the icing into a pan over a very low heat and, stirring occasionally, melt the chocolate and mix the ingredients to a smooth consistency. Pour a small spoonful of icing over the top of each bun and leave on one side to set.

The recipe can easily be adapted for chocolate éclairs; the mixture is the same but it is piped into 3-inch/7·5-cm finger lengths and then baked as for the choux buns. Fill with cream and ice with chocolate icing.

Freezing Note *Store the buns unfilled for up to a month. Thaw for 2 hours then re-crisp in a moderate oven, gas mark 4 or 350°F/180°C, for 10 to 15 minutes. Cool then continue as in the recipe.*

Custard Tarts

Makes 12

For the Pastry
5 oz/140 g plain flour
A pinch of salt
1 oz/30 g margarine
1½ oz/40 g lard
For the Filling
2 large eggs (size 2)
1½ oz/40 g granulated sugar
1 tablespoon plain flour
¼ pint/150 ml plus 4 tablespoons milk
½ oz/15 g margarine, melted
A little grated nutmeg
12 tartlet tins
3½-inch/8·5-cm fluted cutter

Sift the flour and salt into a mixing bowl, add the fats cut into small pieces and, using the fingertips only, rub them in until the mixture resembles fine breadcrumbs. Stir in enough cold water to make a fairly stiff dough.

Roll out the pastry on a lightly floured work surface to about ⅛ inch/3 mm thick, then cut out 12 rounds – you may have to gather up the scraps and reroll the pastry to get out the last few rounds. Line the tartlet tins with the rounds, then leave them in a cool place while making the filling.

Beat the eggs with the sugar, then beat in the flour before adding the milk and margarine. Divide the filling between the tartlets, almost to the top of each, then sprinkle the surfaces with a little grated nutmeg.

Bake the tartlets on the centre shelf of a moderately hot oven, gas mark 5 or 375°F/190°C, for about 25 minutes, or until the pastry is cooked and the filling well risen. Transfer to a wire rack to cool.

Walnut and Coffee Cake

3 oz/75 g butter
8 oz/225 g caster sugar
½ teaspoon vanilla essence
2 large eggs (size 2)
3 oz/75 g walnut halves
7 oz/200 g plain flour
2½ teaspoons baking powder
Just under ¼ pint/150 ml milk
For the Decoration
6 oz/175 g icing sugar, sifted
2 teaspoons coffee essence
A 7-inch/18-cm square cake tin

Brush the tin with melted fat. Line the base and sides with greaseproof paper; brush the paper lining also.

Beat the butter until it is soft, then beat in the caster sugar and vanilla essence. Separate the eggs and add the yolks one at a time, beating well between each addition. Reserve 9 walnut halves for decoration, chop the rest and stir them into the mixture. Sift the flour and baking powder together, then fold alternately into the mixture with the milk. Lastly whisk the egg whites until stiff and fold them in lightly and quickly. Turn the mixture into the tin, smooth over the surface and hollow out the centre slightly.

Bake the cake on the centre shelf of a moderately hot oven, gas mark 5 or 375°F/190°C, for 45 to 50 minutes, when it should be golden brown in colour and slightly shrinking from the sides of the tin. Turn the cake on to a wire rack to cool and remove the greaseproof paper.

When the cake is cold, mix the icing sugar with the coffee essence and sufficient cold water to make an icing thick enough to coat the back of a wooden spoon. Turn the icing on to the top of the cake and guide it to the sides so that it starts to trickle down them. Arrange the reserved walnut halves on top of the cake.

Freezing Note *Store the cake uniced for up to 2 months, thaw for 4 hours then decorate as in the recipe.*

Walnut and Coffee Cake

Orange Honey Sponge

3 large eggs (size 2)
3 oz/75 g caster sugar
3 oz/75 g plain flour
2 teaspoons glycerine (optional)
Grated rind of 1 orange and 1 tablespoon juice

For the Filling and Icing

3 oz/75 g butter or margarine
3 tablespoons clear honey
1 lb/450 g icing sugar, sifted
2 oz/50 g digestive biscuits, crushed
Orange juice to mix

An 8-inch/20-cm round tin, base lined and greased

A small greaseproof paper icing bag

Whisk the eggs with the sugar in a basin over a pan of hot but not boiling water, until the mixture is thick and pale in colour and holds the trail of the whisk for 5 seconds.

Remove from the heat and continue whisking until the mixture is cool. Sift half the flour over the egg mixture, then fold it in lightly and quickly. Repeat with the rest of the flour; add the glycerine, orange rind and juice.

Turn into the prepared tin. Bake in a moderately hot oven, gas mark 5 or 375°F/190°C, for about 30 minutes, until firm and springy to the touch. Cool on a wire rack.

Cream the butter or margarine and honey together. Add half the icing sugar and beat well. Split the cake in half and sandwich it together again with most of this filling. Mask the sides with the rest of the filling and firmly press the biscuit crumbs on to it.

Mix enough orange juice into the remaining icing sugar to give a stiffish consistency – one that will coat the back of a spoon. Spread most of the icing over the top of the cake, and leave for a few minutes to dry.

Spoon the rest of the icing into the greaseproof icing bag, snip off the end and pipe in a pattern over the top of the cake.

Freezing Note *Store the sponge unfilled and undecorated for up to 3 months. Thaw for 4 hours then continue as in the recipe.*

Upside-Down Ginger Cake

For the Topping

8-oz/227-g can pineapple rings
2 oz/50 g butter or margarine
2 oz/50 g demerara sugar

For the Cake

8 oz/225 g plain flour
½ teaspoon salt
1 teaspoon ground cinnamon
2 teaspoons ground ginger
1 teaspoon bicarbonate of soda
4 oz/110 g margarine
4 oz/110 g soft brown sugar
4 oz/110 g golden syrup
2–3 tablespoons pineapple juice
1 large egg (size 2)

A solid-based 7-inch/18-cm square tin

Line the base of the cake tin with greaseproof paper; grease this and the sides of tin. Drain the juice from the pineapple rings and reserve 2–3 tablespoons for the cake.

First prepare the topping. Melt the butter or margarine, remove from the heat and stir in the demerara sugar, then spread the mixture over the base of the tin. Arrange the pineapple rings on top.

Sift the flour, salt, cinnamon, ginger and bicarbonate of soda into a mixing bowl.

Gently heat together the margarine, sugar, syrup and pineapple juice, making sure they do not boil. When melted, stir into the flour, add the eggs and beat well. Pour this mixture carefully over the pineapple topping.

Bake in the centre of a moderately cool oven, gas mark 3 or 325°F/160°C, for 1¼ to 1½ hours, until well risen and springy to the touch. Turn out and cool on a plate with the pineapple side uppermost.

Freezing Note *Remove from the tin, cool, wrap in polythene then store for up to 3 months. Thaw for 4 hours.*

Coffee Marble Ring

6 oz/175 g butter
6 oz/175 g caster sugar
3 large eggs (size 2)
6 oz/175 g self-raising flour
2 tablespoons coffee essence
Icing sugar for sprinkling

A 2½–3-pint/1·5–1·75-litre ring mould

Beat the butter until soft but not oily; add the sugar and cream together until light and fluffy. Add the eggs one at a time, beating well after each addition. Fold in the sifted flour.

Divide the mixture into two, and add the coffee essence to one half only, stirring until well mixed. Place spoonfuls of the plain and coffee mixtures alternately into the prepared mould. Level the surface. To achieve a marbled effect, draw a skewer through the mixture with a few bold, swift strokes.

Bake in the centre of a moderate oven, gas mark 4 or 350°F/180°C, for about 45 minutes, until well risen and springy to the touch. Turn out on to a wire rack to cool.

When cold, dust with sifted icing sugar.

Freezing Note *Store before dusting with icing sugar for up to 3 months. Thaw for 4 hours then dust with sugar before serving.*

Orange Honey Sponge, Upside-Down Ginger Cake, Coffee Marble Ring

Date Crumble Squares, Vienna Tray Bake, Mincemeat Slices, Chocolate Shorties

Mincemeat Slices

Makes 16

10 oz/275 g plain flour
A pinch of salt
8 oz/225 g margarine (in a hard block straight from the refrigerator)
1 teaspoon lemon juice
1 lb/450 g mincemeat
1 tablespoon caster sugar
A 13 × 9-inch/33 × 23-cm Swiss roll tin

Sift the flour and salt into a mixing bowl. Coarsely grate the margarine and, using a knife, stir it through the flour so that it is evenly distributed. Mix in the lemon juice with enough cold water to make a soft but not sticky dough. Wrap the pastry in greaseproof paper and leave it in a cool place for about 10 minutes to rest.

Roll out half the dough on a

lightly floured work surface and line the base and sides of the tin. Turn the mincemeat into the centre and spread it to the sides. Roll out the other piece of pastry to the size of the tin. Brush the edges with a little water, then lift the lid in place and press the edges together well. Brush the surface with water, then using the back of a knife mark the top into diamonds. Sprinkle it with caster sugar and mark a few holes in the top to release the air as it cooks.

Bake on the centre shelf of a fairly hot oven, gas mark 6 or 400°F/200°C, for about 45 minutes, or until the pastry is golden brown.

Leave the tray bake to cool slightly, then cut it carefully into 16 slices. Transfer them to a wire rack to cool completely.

Freezing Note *Store the cooked bake, still in the tin, for up to 3 months. Thaw for 4 hours.*

Date Crumble Squares

Makes 15

7 oz/200 g self-raising flour
6 oz/175 g butter
6 oz/175 g caster sugar
4 oz/100 g porridge oats
For the Filling
6 oz/175 g cooking dates, chopped
4 tablespoons cold water
1 oz/25 g caster sugar
1 teaspoon vanilla essence
An 11 × 7-inch/28 × 18-cm shallow tin

Brush the tin with melted fat.

First make the filling. Put the chopped dates into a pan with the water and sugar, then stir them over a low heat until they are thick and well combined. Mix in the vanilla essence and leave the filling on one side to cool.

Sift the flour into a mixing bowl, add the butter cut into small pieces and, using the fingertips only, rub the fat into the flour so that it is evenly distributed. Stir in the sugar and oats, then turn half the mixture into the tin and press it evenly into the base. Spread the cooled date filling on top and sprinkle over the remaining oat mixture.

Bake the tray bake on the centre shelf of a moderate oven, gas mark 4 or 350°F/180°C, for about 45 minutes, until the mixture is a light golden brown colour.

Cut the Date Crumble Squares into 15 pieces while still hot, then leave to cool slightly in the tin. Lift out the pieces on to a wire rack to cool completely.

Freezing Note *Store the bake still in the tin for up to 3 months, thaw for 4 hours.*

Vienna Tray Bake

Makes 16

6 oz/170 g butter
2 oz/55 g icing sugar, sifted
4 oz/110 g self-raising flour
2 oz/55 g cornflour
A pinch of salt
A few drops of vanilla essence
For the Topping
1 tablespoon caster sugar
1 oz/25 g flaked almonds
An 11 × 7-inch/28 × 18-cm shallow tin

Cream the butter until it is really soft, then stir in the sifted icing sugar, flour and cornflour, salt and vanilla essence to form a stiff dough. Turn the mixture into the tin and spread it evenly to the sides. Sprinkle over the caster sugar and flaked almonds.

Bake the Vienna Tray Bake on the centre shelf of a moderate oven, gas mark 4 or 350°F/180°C, for 20 to 25 minutes, until light golden brown in colour.

Cut the tray bake into 16 pieces while still warm, then transfer the pieces to a wire rack to cool completely.

Freezing Note *Store the bake either still in the tin or in a rigid container for up to 3 months. Thaw for 3 hours.*

Chocolate Shorties

Makes 24

2½ oz/70 g butter
2½ oz/70 g lard
2 oz/55 g caster sugar
6 oz/175 g plain flour
1 oz/25 g cocoa powder
1½ oz/40 g digestive biscuits, crushed
For the Icing
12 oz/350 g icing sugar, sifted
1 oz/25 g cocoa powder
A 12 × 8-inch/30 × 20-cm Swiss roll tin

Brush the tin with melted fat.

Beat the butter and lard together, then add the caster sugar and cream the ingredients until light and fluffy in both colour and texture. Sift the flour and cocoa powder, then gradually work into the creamed mixture with the biscuit crumbs.

Turn the mixture into the tin and spread it over the base so that the surface is level. Bake on the centre shelf of a moderate oven, gas mark 4 or 350°F/180°C, for about 25 minutes. As soon as the tray bake comes out of the oven, cut it into 12 squares then cut them across into triangles. Leave them in the tin to cool completely.

Sift the icing sugar and cocoa powder into a bowl. Stir in enough cold water to make a coating consistency. Turn the icing on to the tray bake and spread it over the surface, then very carefully lift the triangles on to a wire rack for the icing to set.

Freezing Note *Store the cooled uniced bake still in the tin for up to 4 months. Thaw for 4 hours then ice as in the recipe.*

Flapjacks

Makes 16

6 oz/175 g margarine
4 oz/100 g caster sugar
6 oz/175 g porridge oats
2 oz/50 g self-raising flour, sifted
A pinch of salt
A 12 × 8-inch/30 × 20-cm Swiss roll tin

Brush the tin with a little melted fat.

Melt the margarine in a pan over a low heat, stir in the sugar and, when it is well mixed, stir in the oats, sifted flour and salt. Turn the mixture into the tin and spread it level.

Bake the Flapjacks on the centre shelf of a moderately hot oven, gas mark 5 or 375°F/190°C, for about 20 minutes, until they are a very light brown colour.

Cut into 16 finger-shaped pieces and leave them in the tin to cool slightly, then carefully transfer to a wire rack to cool completely.

Store the Flapjacks in a tin – they keep well as there is no syrup in the recipe.

Freezing Note *Store cooked for up to 3 months, thaw for 3 hours.*

Rock Buns

Makes 14

8 oz/225 g plain flour
A pinch of salt
2 teaspoons baking powder
¼ teaspoon grated nutmeg
2½ oz/65 g margarine
2½ oz/65 g caster sugar
3 oz/75 g mixed dried fruit
1 large egg (size 2)
Milk

Sift the flour, salt, baking powder and nutmeg into a bowl. Add the fat, cut into small pieces, then using the fingertips only, rub it in until the ingredients resemble breadcrumbs. Stir in the sugar and dried fruit.

Beat the egg then add sufficient milk to make up to ¼ pint/150 ml liquid; mix it into the dry ingredients with a fork to make a soft, sticky dough.

Grease a baking tray with a little melted fat and put 14 spoonfuls of the mixture on to it. Bake the buns in a fairly hot oven, gas mark 6 or 400°F/200°C, for about 15 minutes.

Freezing Note *Store the buns for up to 3 months. Thaw for 3 hours.*

Half Pound Cake, Golden Cheesecake, Shortbread, Midas Macaroon, Flapjack, Fruit Scone (see recipe page 176).

Wellington Squares

Makes 16

For the Shortbread Base
5 oz/140 g plain flour
A pinch of salt
2 oz/55 g caster sugar
4 oz/110 g butter
For the Filling
4 oz/100 g butter
4 oz/100 g soft brown sugar
2 tablespoons golden syrup
1 small can sweetened condensed milk
A few drops of vanilla essence

For the Topping

6 oz/175 g plain chocolate

A 7½-inch/19-cm square tin

Grease the tin. Sift the flour and salt into a mixing bowl and stir in the caster sugar. Add the butter, cut into small pieces. Using the fingertips only, rub in the butter until it is evenly distributed, then knead the mixture to a dough. Press it into the base of the tin, levelling the surface as much as possible. Bake on the centre shelf of a moderate oven, gas mark 4 or 350°F/180°C, for 25 minutes. Leave in the tin to cool.

Put the butter, sugar, syrup and condensed milk into a pan and stir over a low heat until the sugar has dissolved. Bring the mixture to the boil and, stirring continuously, boil gently for 7 minutes. Add the vanilla essence, beat the mixture well, then pour it on to the shortbread base. Leave the filling to cool and set.

Break the chocolate into pieces and melt in a basin over a pan of hot water. Pour it on to the set filling and spread over the surface evenly. Leave to set then cut into 16 pieces.

Butterscotch Squares

Makes 16

2 oz/55 g butter

5 oz/140 g light soft brown sugar

1 large egg (size 2)

3 oz/85 g self-raising flour

1 teaspoon vanilla essence

1 oz/25 g walnuts, chopped

A 7½-inch/19-cm square tin

Melt the butter and sugar in a saucepan; the mixture will turn a darker brown when it is ready, but do not allow it to boil. Leave to cool then beat in the egg. Sift the flour and fold into the mixture with the vanilla essence and chopped nuts.

Grease the tin and turn the mixture into it, spreading evenly. Bake on the centre shelf of a moderate oven, gas mark 4 or 350°F/180°C, for 25 to 30 minutes, or until the mixture shrinks from the sides of the tin. Immediately it comes out of the oven, cut into 16 squares. Leave to cool in the tin and then store in an airtight container.

Freezing Note *Store for up to 4 months. Thaw for 2 hours.*

Almond Squares

Makes 24

For the Pastry

6 oz/170 g plain flour

A pinch of salt

1½ oz/40 g margarine

1½ oz/40 g lard

For the Filling

2 large egg whites (size 2)

4 oz/100 g ground almonds

2 oz/50 g ground rice

6 oz/175 g caster sugar

4 tablespoons cold water

4 oz/100 g raspberry jam

2 oz/50 g flaked almonds

A 12 × 8-inch/30 × 20-cm Swiss roll tin

Sift the flour and salt into a mixing bowl and add the fats, cut into small pieces. Using the fingertips only, rub them in until the mixture resembles fine breadcrumbs. Stir in enough cold water to make a fairly soft dough. On a lightly floured work surface roll out the dough into an oblong a little larger than the tin. Lift the pastry over the rolling pin into the tin and line the sides and base carefully. Trim the edges and leave the tin in a cool place.

Put the egg whites into a bowl and break them up with a fork. Add the ground almonds, ground rice and caster sugar and mix these ingredients to a smooth paste with the water. Spread the jam over the pastry base in the tin and cover it with the almond mixture. Sprinkle flaked almonds over the top.

Bake on the centre shelf of a moderately hot oven, gas mark 5 or 375°F/190°C, for 30 to 35 minutes.

Cut the tray bake into 24 squares, and cool on a wire rack.

Freezing Note *Store in the tin for up to 3 months. Thaw for 4 hours.*

Ginger Bites

Makes 25

4 oz/110 g self-raising flour

2 teaspoons ground ginger

4 oz/110 g porridge oats

4 oz/110 g margarine

4 oz/110 g dark soft brown sugar

1 large egg (size 2)

2 tablespoons golden syrup

For the Icing

2 oz/50 g butter

6 oz/175 g icing sugar, sifted

1 tablespoon milk

A few drops of vanilla essence

A 7-inch/18-cm square tin

Lightly grease the tin with melted fat.

Sift the flour and ginger into a bowl, stir in the oats, then rub in the margarine. When it is evenly distributed, add the sugar, then bind the ingredients together with the egg and syrup, warmed if necessary.

Turn the mixture into the tin and spread it to the sides, then bake on the centre shelf of a moderate oven, gas mark 4 or 350°F/180°C, for about 25 minutes, until springy to the touch. Leave to cool in the tin.

Gently melt the butter, then remove from the heat and gradually beat in the icing sugar and milk to make a smooth but soft consistency. Stir in the vanilla essence, then turn the icing on to the cake base, ease it to the sides and leave until it has cooled and stiffened. Finally, decorate the top using the prongs of a fork and cut the bake into 25 small pieces; ease them out of the tin, and store in an airtight container.

Freezing Note *Store in the tin for up to 2 months. Thaw overnight.*

Shortbread

Makes 6 pieces

- 6 oz/170 g plain flour
- A pinch of salt
- 1 oz/25 g caster sugar
- 4 oz/110 g butter
- Caster sugar for sprinkling

Sift the flour and salt into a mixing bowl with the caster sugar. Cut the butter into pieces and rub it into the flour so that it is evenly distributed, then knead the ingredients together to make a dough.

On a lightly floured work surface, roll the dough into a 7–8-inch/18–20-cm round and slip the round on to a baking tray. Decorate the edge by pinching it together with the thumb and first finger of one hand and the first finger of the other to make a scallop edge. Mark the surface into six portions using the back of a knife, then prick the top with a skewer or fork.

Sprinkle a little extra sugar over the Shortbread and bake it on the centre shelf of a moderately cool oven, gas mark 3 or 325°F/160°C, for about 40 minutes, until it is just beginning to turn a pale golden colour. Cool on a wire rack.

Freezing Note *Store for up to 3 months. Thaw for 3 hours.*

Shrewsbury Biscuits

Makes 24

- 4 oz/110 g margarine
- 4 oz/110 g caster sugar
- Grated rind of 1 lemon
- 8 oz/225 g plain flour, sifted
- 1 small egg (size 4), beaten
- Caster sugar for sprinkling

Beat the margarine until soft, then add the caster sugar and beat together until light and fluffy in colour and texture. Add the lemon rind and sifted flour and bind the ingredients with the well beaten egg to form a fairly soft dough, similar to shortcrust pastry.

On a lightly floured work surface, roll the dough into a 12×9-inch/30×23-cm rectangle and trim the edges with a sharp knife. Cut the dough into three lengthways, then cut across to make 24 pieces in all. Place them fairly close together on baking trays which have been brushed with melted fat and dusted with flour. Make more biscuits out of the scraps if possible, before baking on the centre shelf of a fairly hot oven, gas mark 6 or 400°F/200°C, for about 12 minutes, or until golden brown.

Transfer the biscuits to a wire rack, dust with sugar and cool.

Freezing Note *Store for up to 3 months, thaw for 3 hours.*

Ginger Snaps

Makes 24

- 4 oz/100 g plain flour
- 1½ teaspoons baking powder
- 1½ teaspoons ground ginger
- Finely grated rind of ½ lemon and 2 teaspoons juice
- 3 oz/75 g golden syrup
- 2 oz/50 g caster sugar
- 1 oz/25 g margarine

Sift the flour, baking powder and ground ginger together, then stir in the lemon rind.

Next weigh the syrup – the easiest method is to weigh the empty pan and spoon which you are going to use. Then spoon the syrup into the pan and deduct the weight of the pan and spoon from the total.

Add the caster sugar, lemon juice and margarine to the syrup and melt over a gentle heat before stirring into the dry ingredients. Leave to cool slightly, when it will stiffen, then roll it into small balls and place them on greased baking trays. Space out the biscuits, as they spread during cooking.

Bake the Ginger Snaps on the centre shelf of a moderately cool oven, gas mark 3 or 325°F/160°C, for 15 to 20 minutes, until golden brown. Cool slightly to allow them to firm a little then lift with a palette knife on to a wire rack.

Freezing Note *Store for up to 2 months. Thaw for 3 hours.*

Cinnamon Pinwheels

Makes 24

- 4 oz/110 g butter
- 4 oz/110 g caster sugar
- 8 oz/225 g plain flour, sifted
- 1 small egg (size 4), beaten
- 1 teaspoon ground cinnamon

Beat the butter until it is soft, then add the caster sugar and beat until light and fluffy. Add the sifted flour, then bind the ingredients together with the egg to form a dough similar in consistency to shortcrust pastry. Divide the dough in half and knead the cinnamon into one portion so the spice is evenly distributed.

On a lightly floured work surface, roll each piece of dough into a 12×8-inch/30×20-cm rectangle and trim the edges. Place the cinnamon dough on top of the plain dough and roll them together across the width to make a 12-inch/30-cm length. Cut the roll into 24 slices and place the rounds, cut side down, on greased baking trays. Bake in a fairly hot oven, gas mark 6 or 400°F/200°C, for 10 to 15 minutes.

Cool on a wire rack then store in a tin until required. They will keep for 2 weeks.

Chocolate Melting Moments, Ginger Snaps, Almond Squares, Shrewsbury Biscuits

Midas Macaroons

Makes 18

- 2 oz/50 g ground almonds
- 2 oz/50 g cake crumbs
- 2 oz/50 g ground rice
- 6 oz/175 g caster sugar
- 2 large egg whites (size 2)
- A few drops of almond essence
- 18 pieces flaked almond
- *Rice paper*

Put the ground almonds, cake crumbs, ground rice and caster sugar into a mixing bowl and stir them together until they are well blended. Whisk the egg whites a little until slightly frothy, then stir into the dry ingredients with the almond essence.

Put the rice paper on to baking trays. Divide the mixture into 18 pieces and roll each one into a ball about the size of a walnut. Space the macaroons on the baking trays, then put a piece of flaked almond on each, flattening them slightly.

Bake the macaroons on the centre shelf of a moderate oven, gas mark 4 or 350°F/180°C, for 15 to 20 minutes, until a pale brown in colour. Remove the macaroons from the baking tray and tear off any excess rice paper. Leave to cool completely then store the macaroons in an airtight tin until required.

Freezing Note *Store cooked for up to 2 months. Thaw for 3 hours.*

Speculaas

Makes 20–24

These delicious biscuits are traditional St. Nicholas Day fare for the children in Holland. They can be cut into all kinds of shapes.

- 6 oz/175 g unsalted butter
- 5 oz/150 g light soft brown sugar
- 8 oz/225 g self-raising flour
- ½ teaspoon ground mixed spice
- 1 teaspoon ground cinnamon
- Grated rind of ½ lemon
- 2 oz/50 g blanched almonds, chopped
- 1 oz/25 g digestive biscuits, crushed
- *Biscuit cutters*

Cream the butter and sugar together until light and fluffy. Sift in the flour, mixed spice and cinnamon, then add the lemon rind, almonds and biscuit crumbs and bind the ingredients together to make a stiff dough.

On a lightly floured work surface, roll out the dough to ⅜ inch/8 mm thick, then cut out the biscuits, using various cutters.

Place the biscuits on baking trays and cook on the centre shelf of a moderate oven, gas mark 4 or 350°F/180°C, for 15 to 20 minutes, until golden brown. Transfer the biscuits to a wire rack to cool.

If liked, the biscuits can be decorated with a little glacé icing and some silver balls.

Freezing Note *Store the biscuits undecorated for up to 2 months. Thaw for 2 hours then decorate if desired.*

Chocolate Melting Moments

Makes about 20

- 3 oz/85 g margarine
- 3 oz/85 g lard
- 5 oz/150 g caster sugar
- ½ teaspoon vanilla essence
- 1 large egg (size 2)
- 9 oz/250 g self-raising flour, sifted
- 1 oz/25 g cocoa powder

For the Buttercream

- 5 oz/150 g butter
- 9 oz/250 g icing sugar, sifted
- ½ oz/15 g cocoa powder

Beat the margarine and lard together until light and fluffy; add the sugar and vanilla essence and beat again until the same consistency is reached. Beat the egg and add it to the creamed mixture with the sifted flour and cocoa powder, stirring until a fairly firm dough is formed.

Grease several baking trays with melted fat. Take small pieces of the biscuit mixture and roll them into balls about the size of a walnut. Place the biscuits on the baking trays, making sure they are well spaced out as they will spread during cooking. Flatten each slightly with a fork, then bake them on the centre shelf of a moderate oven, gas mark 4 or 350°F/180°C, for about 20 minutes, until they are cooked. Cool the biscuits on a wire rack.

Beat the butter until soft and fluffy, then gradually beat in the sifted icing sugar and cocoa powder.

When the biscuits have cooled, sandwich them in pairs with the buttercream.

Freezing Note *Store the biscuits already sandwiched together with buttercream for up to a month. Thaw overnight.*

Strawberry and Mint Shortcake

Makes 5

For the Shortcakes

- 6 oz/170 g plain flour
- A pinch of salt
- 4 oz/110 g butter
- 2 oz/55 g caster sugar

For the Filling and Decoration

- ½ pint/300 ml double cream
- 1 oz/25 g caster sugar
- ½ lb/225 g strawberries
- A few sprigs of mint
- *A 3½-inch/8·5-cm fluted cutter*

Sift the flour and salt into a mixing bowl. Rub in the butter, cut into small pieces, until the mixture re-

sembles fine breadcrumbs. Add half the sugar and knead the dough into a ball. Roll out to about ⅜ inch/8 mm thick and cut out five rounds with the cutter. Place the rounds on baking trays, sprinkle them with the remaining sugar and bake for about 25 minutes in a moderately cool oven, gas mark 3 or 325°F/160°C. Leave on a wire rack to cool.

Whip the cream until it just holds its shape, then lightly fold in the sugar. Reserve five strawberries for decoration and slice the remainder. Fold all but a few slices into the whipped cream. Pile the mixture on the shortcakes and stand each one on a plate. Decorate each shortcake with one whole strawberry, some strawberry slices and mint sprigs.

Strawberry and Mint Shortcakes

Freezing Note *Store the shortcakes for up to 3 months. Thaw for 2 hours then fill and decorate as in the recipe.*

Celebration Cakes and Gâteaux

A special occasion calls for a special cake, whether there is a wedding in the family, a children's party or it is Christmas time again. If the cake is based on a rich fruit mixture it is best made 3 months in advance, so the flavours have time to mellow.

Christmas Cake

12 oz/350 g mixed dried fruit, cleaned
4 oz/100 g seedless raisins, cleaned
4 oz/100 g glacé cherries, washed, dried and quartered
2 oz/50 g walnuts, chopped
2 oz/50 g ground almonds
Grated rind of 2 lemons
8 oz/225 g butter
8 oz/225 g soft brown sugar
3 large eggs (size 2)
3 dessertspoons black treacle
10 oz/275 g plain flour
A pinch of salt
2 teaspoons ground mixed spice
A 7-inch/18-cm square cake tin

Grease the tin. Cut out two lengths of doubled greaseproof paper, the width of the tin and depth of two sides, plus 2 inches/5 cm. Press in one strip, grease it, cross over the other strip, then grease all the lining.

Mix the dried fruit with the raisins, cherries, walnuts, almonds and grated lemon rind. Beat the butter and, when it is soft, add the sugar. Cream together until they are light and fluffy in colour and texture. Add the eggs, one at a time, beating well between each addition, so the mixture does not curdle. Next beat in the black treacle. Sift the flour with the salt and mixed spice and stir a third of the flour into the fruit mixture. Using a metal spoon, stir in the fruit alternately with the dry ingredients to make a mixture that just falls from the spoon with a gentle tap. Turn the mixture into the prepared tin and spread it to the sides. Hollow out the centre quite deeply so the cake will rise evenly.

Bake the cake in a moderate oven, gas mark 4 or 350°F/180°C, for 30 minutes, then reduce the heat to gas mark 2 or 300°F/150°C for a further 2¾ hours. The cake is cooked when a warm skewer inserted into the centre comes out clean; if any mixture adheres, continue to cook. Remove from the tin and when cold, wrap the cake first in greaseproof paper then in foil and store for up to 3 months. The flavours mellow and improve during this time.

Note The same mixture can be cooked in an 8-inch/20-cm round tin. Cook this cake at gas mark 4 or 350°F/180°C, for 30 minutes, then gas mark 2 or 300°F/150°C, for a further 2½ hours. Test with a warmed skewer, as above.

Freezing Note *Rich fruit cakes can be stored in the freezer for up to 6 months. Thaw overnight then decorate as required.*

Icing and Decoration

This is sufficient icing for either a 7-inch/18-cm square or an 8-inch/20-cm round cake.

Almond Paste
10 oz/275 g ground almonds
5 oz/150 g icing sugar, sifted
5 oz/150 g caster sugar
2 large egg yolks (size 2)
Juice of ½ lemon
A dusting of cornflour
Apricot jam
Royal Icing
3 large egg whites (size 2)
2 teaspoons lemon juice
About 1½ lb/675 g icing sugar, sifted
1 teaspoon glycerine
A 9-inch/23-cm square cake board
4 greaseproof paper icing bags
No 2 writing pipe and No 6 star pipe
Candle and holly leaves for decoration

Mix the ground almonds with the sifted icing sugar and the caster sugar. Beat the egg yolks together and add them to the sugars with

Christmas Cake, Festive Fruit Loaf, Mr Snowmen

enough lemon juice to make a stiff dough a little softer than the consistency of shortcrust pastry. Keep the almond paste covered or it will form a hard crust. The cake, when covered with this almond paste, must be left in a cool place for 1 week to dry before it is coated with royal icing.

Make the royal icing the day before it is needed, to allow the bubbles to rise to the surface. Beat the egg whites and lemon juice together in a large bowl, then gradually blend in the icing sugar to make a fairly thick consistency. Beat the icing really well until it is glossy and will coat the back of a wooden spoon thickly but smoothly. Cover the icing with a piece of polythene and leave overnight. An electric mixer is ideal for making this icing, but always use the slowest speed.

1 Lightly dust your work surface with cornflour and roll out half the almond paste into a square; using the cake tin as a guide, cut round it for the exact size. The base of the cake becomes the top, so brush this with the warmed jam and place it on the almond paste.

2 Add the trimmings to the remaining almond paste, divide it in four and roll each piece out to fit the sides, using the tin as a guide. Brush the cake sides with jam and lift the almond paste into place. If necessary cover and leave the cake to dry on a wire rack in a cool place for 1 week.

3 Take a 1-pint/600-ml bowlful out of the royal icing to use for the decoration, and stir the glycerine into the rest. Pour enough of this remaining icing over the cake to cover the top and start flowing down the sides, guiding it with a palette knife. Prick out the bubbles with a skewer, then leave the cake to set.

4 When the icing is dry, loosen the cake from the rack, smear a little icing on the cake board and lift the cake on to it. Beat extra icing sugar into the icing in the bowl to make a piping consistency. Divide the top of the cake into nine squares, marking two lines in each direction with a skewer.

5 Snip the tip off an icing bag and drop in the No 2 pipe; fill the bag two-thirds full with icing and pipe the trellis. The bottom layer is parallel lines from the centre to the edges and the top lines cross over them. Cut the tip off another icing bag and drop in the star pipe.

6 Fill the bag two-thirds full with icing and pipe a shell edge all round the trellis, then down the corners and round the top and base of the cake. Stick the candle to the centre of the cake with a little icing and pipe a shell edge around the base, then finish the cake with the holly leaf decorations.

How to Make a Paper Icing Bag

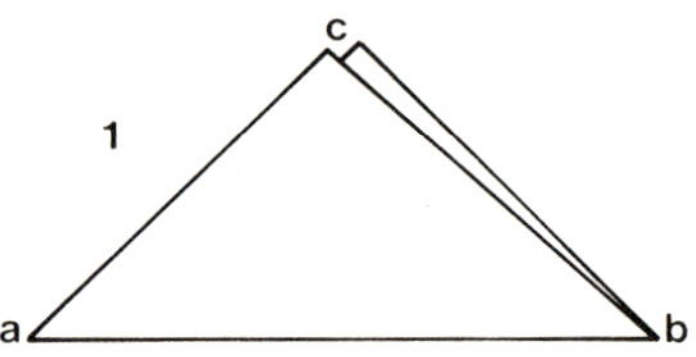

1 Fold a 10-inch/25-cm square of greaseproof paper in half diagonally. With a sharp knife make a small slit in the exact centre of the folded side.

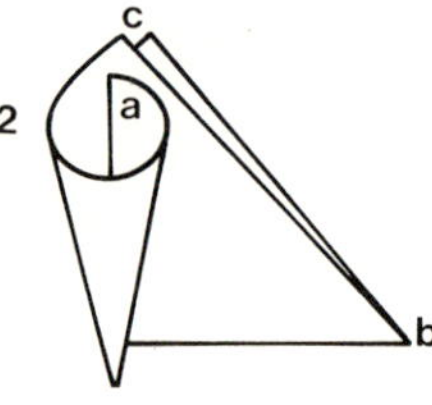

2 Roll point **a** to come in front of point **c**.

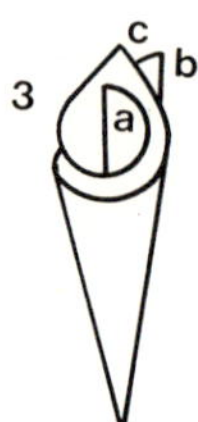

3 Roll point **b** to come behind **c**.

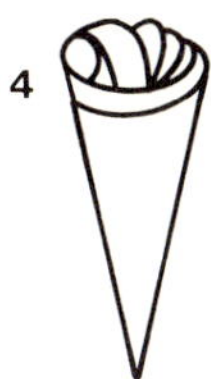

4 Fold down all points to secure the bag. Cut off tip straight across to insert a piping nozzle if needed.

Mr Snowmen

Makes 2

For the Cake
2 oz/55 g soft margarine
2 oz/55 g caster sugar
1 large egg (size 2)
2 oz/55 g self-raising flour

For the Almond Paste
2 tablespoons ground almonds
1 tablespoon caster sugar
1 tablespoon sifted icing sugar
1 teaspoon lemon juice

For the Icing and Decoration
1 large egg white (size 2)
1 teaspoon lemon juice
A few drops of glycerine
10 oz/275 g icing sugar, sifted
A selection of sweets for buttons, hats and faces
Two 8-fl oz/250-ml teacups
Two thin 4-inch/10-cm cake boards
A little thin ribbon for scarves

First make the cakes. Put the margarine, sugar, egg and sifted flour into a mixing bowl and, using a wooden spoon, stir them together, then beat for a minute to incorporate some air. Brush the teacups with melted fat and divide the mixture between them. Bake the cakes on the centre shelf of a moderate oven, gas mark 4 or 350°F/180°C, for about 30 minutes, or until the mixture feels springy to the touch. Cool the cakes on a wire rack.

Meanwhile, make the almond paste for the heads. Mix the ground almonds, caster and icing sugar together, then bind the ingredients to a stiff paste with the lemon juice. Divide this almond paste in half and roll each piece into a ball for the heads of the snowmen.

Beat the egg white, lemon juice and glycerine together, then stir in the sifted icing sugar to make a fairly stiff consistency. Beat the icing really well until very white.

Dust your hands with icing sugar, then place a little of the icing on them and roll the almond paste balls in the icing so they are covered and the surface is smooth. Put the heads in position on the cake bodies, then cover the remainder of the snowmen with a roughened surface of icing. Decorate them with the sweets, as illustrated, and tie a length of ribbon around the neck of each one to complete the snowmen.

Freezing Note *Freeze the cake bodies for up to 3 months. Thaw for 4 hours, continue as above.*

Festive Fruit Loaf

This is sufficient to decorate a fruit cake cooked in a 2-lb/1-kg loaf tin

For the Decoration
6 dried apricots, soaked overnight
4 dried prunes, soaked overnight
4–5 tablespoons sieved apricot jam
1 tablespoon water
4 glacé cherries, halved
½ oz/15 g blanched almonds

Drain the soaked fruit and cut the apricots in half. Remove the stones from the prunes and cut in half. Heat the jam and water together then brush a little over the surface of the cake. Arrange the prune halves, side by side, down the centre of the loaf, with a row of apricot halves on either side. Place the cherry halves on top. Split each almond in half and arrange them in a row on either side of the prunes. Carefully spoon the apricot jam over the entire decoration, allowing it to run down the sides in places.

Wedding Cake

For the Decoration
4 large egg whites (size 2)
About 3 lb/1·5 kg icing sugar, sifted
Brown and yellow food colouring
9-inch/23-cm, 12-inch/30-cm and 15-inch/38-round cake boards
1·5 metres gold wrapping paper
3 metres of 12-mm wide cream velvet ribbon
12 greaseproof paper icing bags
No 8 star pipe and No 2 writing pipe
Shallow patty tins, 2½ inches/6 cm in diameter, oiled
A 6-inch/15-cm plate
A selection of dried flowers e.g. heather
8 round pillars, each 3 inches/7·5 cm high

Lining a Round Tin
Brush the tin with melted fat. Cut out two rounds of greaseproof paper the size of the base of the tin, place one in position and brush with melted fat. Cut a doubled strip of greaseproof paper, 2 inches/5 cm deeper than the tin and long enough to go round the inside of the tin. Turn the folded edge up 1 inch/2·5 cm, then make slanting cuts to the crease at 1-inch/2·5-cm intervals. Fit this paper strip inside the tin so that the snipped edge fits neatly into the base. Place the other round of paper on top and brush the entire lining with melted fat.

Cake Mixture
Mix thoroughly together all the fruit, the chopped peel and walnuts, ground almonds and grated orange rind. Sift the flour with the salt and mixed spice and stir a third of this into the dried fruit mixture.

Beat the butter to a soft cream – you may find it easier to do this with your hand rather than a wooden spoon – add the sugar and continue beating until the mixture is light and fluffy. Beat the eggs together, then add them gradually to the creamed mixture, beating well between each addition. Finally, using a metal spoon, fold in the sifted dry ingredients alternately with the fruit mixture and rum. Turn the mixture into the prepared tins – they should each be about two-thirds full – smooth over the surface and hollow out the centres quite deeply so that the cakes rise evenly.

Cooking Times

Follow the baking times given in the chart. If you cannot cook all three cakes at the same time, bake the large cake first and then the two smaller ones together later. No harm will come to the cake mixture if it is left for 24 hours, covered, in a cool, dry atmosphere.

Test the cake by pushing a warmed skewer into the centre – if it comes out clean the cake is ready, but if any mixture adheres to it, bake the cake for a little longer, then test again. Allow the cakes to stand in the tins for about 30 minutes then turn them out and leave to cool completely on a wire rack. Wrap the cakes first in greaseproof paper then in foil and store them for up to 3 months so the flavours mature.

Almond Paste

It is best to make the almond paste separately for each cake as handling the mixture too much makes it oily. Mix together the ground almonds, icing sugar and caster sugar. Beat the egg yolks and add them to the mixture with enough lemon juice to make a fairly stiff dough. Keep the almond paste in a polythene bag if it is not to be used immediately.

Covering a Round Cake

Trim the top of the cake level if necessary, then turn the cake upside down so that the base becomes the top.

Cut the almond paste in half. On a lightly cornfloured work surface, roll half the paste to the size of the cake and using the tin as a guide, trim it to fit.

Brush the top of the cake with warmed, sieved apricot jam, then turn the cake on to the almond paste, jam side down, and when you are sure it has stuck, turn the cake back up the right way. Measure the circumference of the cake by encircling it with a piece of string. Roll the remaining almond paste into a long sausage shape the length of the string. Flatten the roll evenly with a rolling pin, and trim the strip to the exact depth of the cake. Brush the sides of the cake with warmed, sieved apricot jam, then turn the cake on its side and roll it along the strip of almond paste so that it adheres. Press firmly to the cake, especially at the joins.

Cover the cake with a clean tea towel and leave it in a cool, dry, airy place for about a week so that the almond paste dries.

Round Three-Tiered Cake

Ingredients	*12-inch/30-cm*	*9-inch/23-cm*	*6-inch/15-cm*
Currants, cleaned	1½ lb/675 g	12 oz/350 g	6 oz/175 g
Raisins, cleaned	8 oz/225 g	4 oz/100 g	2 oz/50 g
Sultanas, cleaned	1 lb/450 g	8 oz/225 g	4 oz/100 g
Glacé cherries, washed, dried and quartered	1¼ lb/575 g	10 oz/275 g	5 oz/150 g
Mixed chopped peel	8 oz/225 g	4 oz/100 g	2 oz/50 g
Walnuts, chopped	6 oz/175 g	3 oz/75 g	1½ oz/40 g
Ground almonds	6 oz/175 g	3 oz/75 g	1½ oz/40 g
Oranges (grated rind)	4	2	1
Plain flour	1¾ lb/800 g	14 oz/400 g	7 oz/200 g
Salt	1½ teaspoons	¾ teaspoon	¼ teaspoon
Mixed spice	4½ teaspoons	2¼ teaspoons	1¼ teaspoons
Butter	1½ lb/675 g	12 oz/350 g	6 oz/175 g
Dark soft brown sugar	1½ lb/675 g	12 oz/350 g	6 oz/175 g
Large eggs (size 2)	9	4	2
Rum	9 tablespoons	5 tablespoons	3 tablespoons
Baking times	Gas mark 4 or 350°F/180°C for 30 minutes, then gas mark 2 or 300°F/150°C for 4¼ hours.	Gas mark 4 or 350°F/180°C for 30 minutes then gas mark 2 or 300°F/150°C for 3¼ hours.	Gas mark 4 or 350°F/180°C for 30 minutes then gas mark 2 or 300°F/150°C for 2 hours.
Approximate number of servings for each cake	**100**	**45**	**32**
Almond paste			
Ground almonds	1½ lb/675 g	1 lb/450 g	8 oz/225 g
Icing sugar, sifted	12 oz/350 g	8 oz/225 g	4 oz/100 g
Caster sugar	12 oz/350 g	8 oz/225 g	4 oz/100 g
Egg yolks (large, size 2)	5	3	2
Lemon juice (approximately)	2 tablespoons	1 tablespoon	1 dessertspoon
A dusting of cornflour			
Apricot jam (approximately)	8 oz/225 g	4 oz/100 g	4 tablespoons
Royal icing (for the base coat)			
Egg whites (large, size 2)	7	5	3
Glycerine	1 tablespoon	2 teaspoons	1 teaspoon
Lemon juice	1 tablespoon	2 teaspoons	1 teaspoon
Icing sugar, sifted	3 lb/1·5 kg	2¼ lb/1 kg	1½ lb/675 g
Brown and yellow food colouring	A few drops	A few drops	A few drops

Royal Icing
Make this icing the day before it is required to allow any air bubbles to rise to the surface.

Put the egg whites, glycerine and lemon juice into a bowl and break the mixture up lightly. Gradually add enough sifted icing sugar to make the icing the correct consistency – it should run slowly off the back of a wooden spoon, leaving it well coated. Colour the icing a delicate shade of cream by adding a few drops of brown with just a touch of yellow colouring, but do remember the icing dries a darker colour.

Cover the icing and leave overnight for the air bubbles to work to the surface.

Icing a Round Cake
Stand the cake on a wire rack over a clean work surface. Pour the icing on to the cake and guide it to the sides. Let the icing flow down the sides of the cake, guiding it with a palette knife. Using the point of a skewer, burst any of the larger bubbles on the surface, then leave the cake in a cool, dry place for the icing to set. Leave the cakes for about 3 days before decorating.

Decoration
Cover the boards with the gold paper then encircle the edge of each one with the ribbon, sticking it in place with glue.

Put the egg whites into a bowl and break them up lightly, then gradually add the sifted icing sugar beating it in well until the icing is fairly stiff and stands in peaks. To make the icing a pale cream colour, beat in some brown colouring with just a touch of yellow. Remember that icing dries to a slightly darker shade.

The shells can be made several weeks before they are required and, once dry, they store very well in an airtight tin.

Snip the end off a paper icing bag and drop in the No 8 star pipe. Half-fill the bag with icing and fold over the end. Pipe a line of icing across the centre of one of the oiled patty tins, then fill in either side with four more lines, decreasing gradually in size to give the effect of a shell. Complete the base with two small lines piped one from each side of the centre of the shells. Altogether the three cakes require 18 shells so I suggest you make 20 in case of accidents. Leave the patty tins in a cool, dry place for 48 hours so that the shells dry completely, then remove them from the patty tins and store them until required. If the shells tend to stick to the tins, just warm them slightly to soften the oil.

Wedding Cake

Smear a little icing on to each board and position the cakes in the centre.

First pipe the trellis on the top of the cakes. This is the same on all three cakes except that the base cake is divided into eight scallops, the middle cake into six and the small cake into four. Cut circles of greaseproof paper the size of the top of each cake, and fold the circles into four, six or eight segments. Open out the paper, lay it on top of the cake and mark the cake at each fold so the top is evenly divided into the number required. Position the 6-inch/15-cm plate between the marks and using a skewer, draw around the edge of the plate so that the cake is marked into scallops. Cut the tip off an icing bag, drop in the No 2 writing pipe, then half-fill the bag with icing and seal the ends. Pipe around the outline of the scallops, then fill in the scallops with two layers of trellis. Outline the edge of the trellis and the top edge of the cake with little leaf shapes. To make the leaves, half-fill a piping bag with icing and seal the end. Cut a small arrowhead in the tip of the bag, squeeze out a little icing and pull the bag sharply away, making a small leaf. Practise on the work surface before starting on the cake.

Cut the tip off an icing bag, drop in the No 8 star pipe and half-fill the bag with icing then pipe a shell edging around the base of the cakes.

Fill each shell with a small selection of dried flowers sticking them into the shell with a little icing. Place the shells carefully around the sides of the cake, sticking them in position with icing. Each shell should come beneath the junction of 2 scallops.

To assemble the cake, position four pillars on the base and middle cake. Lift the middle tier on top of the base pillars then carefully lift the smallest cake on top of that. Complete the wedding cake with an arrangement of dried flowers on top.

Simnel Cake

For the Cake
Half quantity Christmas Cake mixture (see page 154), using 2 medium eggs (size 3)
For the Almond Paste
8 oz/225 g ground almonds
4 oz/100 g icing sugar, sifted
4 oz/100 g caster sugar
1 medium egg (size 3)
1 dessertspoon lemon juice
For the Icing
4 oz/100 g icing sugar, sifted
Beaten egg for glaze
A 6-inch/15-cm round cake tin
A 3-inch/7·5-cm plain cutter
90 cm of 5-cm wide yellow ribbon
90 cm of 4-cm wide green ribbon

First line the cake tin as instructed in the recipe for Wedding Cake (see page 157), then make up the cake mixture as for Christmas Cake (see page 154).

Next make the almond paste. Mix together the ground almonds, sifted icing sugar and caster sugar, then beat the egg and add it with enough lemon juice to form a stiff dough.

Turn half the cake mixture into the prepared tin and spread it level. Roll one-third of the almond paste into a 6-inch/15-cm round. Lay this in the tin on top of the mixture, then turn the remaining cake mixture on top and slightly hollow out the centre.

Bake the cake on the centre shelf of a moderately cool oven, gas mark 3 or 325°F/160°C, for 2 hours, or until a warmed skewer pushed into the centre comes out clean. Cool the cake on a wire rack then remove the paper.

Roll another third of almond paste into a 6-inch/15-cm round, using the cake tin as a guide, then cut out the centre with the cutter. Turn the cake over so the base becomes the top and brush with beaten egg. Lay the almond paste ring in place.

Gather together the trimmings and add them to the remaining almond paste. Cut off 2 oz/50 g then divide the rest into 12 and form them into balls. Brush each one with beaten egg and arrange them around the border.

Stand the cake on the grill pan and put it under a fairly low grill until the marzipan balls are tinged golden brown. Use the rest of the marzipan to make up a chick and some eggs.

Mix the icing sugar with enough cold water to make a thick pouring consistency. Turn the icing into the centre of the cake and leave it to set slightly before positioning the chick and egg. Encircle the cake with the ribbons.

Simnel Cake

Tunis Cake

For the Cake
6 oz/175 g butter or margarine
6 oz/175 g caster sugar
Grated rind of 1 lemon
3 standard eggs (size 3)
3 oz/75 g ground almonds
8 oz/225 g plain flour
1½ teaspoons baking powder
2 tablespoons milk
For the Topping and Decoration
8 oz/225 g plain chocolate
2 oz/50 g butter
4 oz/100 g icing sugar, sifted
7 pieces of walnut
An 8-inch/20-cm cake tin
A piping bag with No 8 star pipe attached

Brush the tin with melted fat and line the base with a circle of greaseproof paper cut to fit; grease the paper lining also.

Beat the butter until it is soft, add the caster sugar and lemon rind and cream them together until they are light and fluffy in colour and texture. Beat the eggs together, then add them gradually to the creamed mixture, beating in well.

Using a metal spoon, fold in the ground almonds with the sifted flour and baking powder, and enough milk to make a soft dropping consistency. Turn the cake into the tin and spread it to the sides, leaving the centre slightly hollow so the cake rises evenly when cooked.

Bake the cake on the centre shelf of a moderately cool oven, gas mark 3 or 325°F/160°C, for about 1¼ hours, or until the cake is golden brown and a skewer inserted into the centre comes out clean. Turn on to a wire rack to cool before decorating.

Break the chocolate into pieces and put into a bowl; add 1 tablespoon water and place the bowl over a pan of hot water until the chocolate is melted. Wrap a band of foil around the side of the cake so it extends above the edge of the cake by about ½ inch/1 cm.

When the chocolate is melted, carefully pour it on to the top of the cake and ease it to the sides; tap the cake gently to smooth the surface then leave the chocolate to set.

Meanwhile, make the buttercream. Beat the butter until soft then gradually beat in the sifted icing sugar to make a smooth creamy consistency. When the chocolate has set, peel off the foil, put the buttercream into the piping bag and pipe a shell edge around the top. Complete the cake with a whirl of buttercream in the centre and the walnuts as a flower on top.

Freezing Note *Store the basic cake for up to 6 months. Thaw overnight then decorate as in the recipe.*

Toyland Express

For the Cake
6 oz/175 g soft margarine
6 oz/175 g caster sugar
6 oz/175 g self-raising flour
3 large eggs (size 2)
2 tablespoons milk
For the Decoration
8 oz/225 g butter
1 lb/450 g icing sugar, sifted
1 dessertspoon cocoa powder
3 oz/75 g desiccated coconut
A few drops of green and red food colouring
1 large chocolate Swiss roll
1 mini jam Swiss roll
Smarties
6 chocolate flakes
Chocolate Matchmakers
18 chocolate-coated ring biscuits
Liquorice cuts, bootlaces, strips and Allsorts
An 8-inch/20-cm square cake tin
A 16-inch/40-cm round cake board

Brush the tin with melted fat and line the base with a piece of greaseproof paper cut to fit; brush the paper lining also.

Put the margarine into a bowl with the sugar, flour, eggs and milk and mix them together, then beat them for a minute to incorporate some air. Turn the mixture into the tin and spread it to the sides, hollowing out the centre slightly. Bake the cake on the centre shelf of a moderate oven, gas mark 4 or 350°F/180°C, for about 45 minutes, or until it feels springy to the touch. Turn the cake on to a wire rack and leave to cool.

Beat the butter for the icing until it is soft, then gradually beat in the icing sugar. Place 4 rounded tablespoons of buttercream in a bowl, mix in the sifted cocoa powder and spread this over the surface of the round cake board. Put the coconut into a bowl and work in some green food colouring, then scatter this over the board to resemble grass. Cut a 2-inch/5-cm strip from the square cake, then cut this in half to make two pieces, each 2 × 4 inches/5 × 10 cm – these are for the engine cabin. The Rest of the cake is cut into three trucks, each 2½ × 6 inches/6·5 × 15 cm. Cover the trucks with plain buttercream. Colour the rest of the buttercream red.

Cut a 2½-inch/6·5-cm wide slice from the large chocolate Swiss roll – this is for the tanker truck. Cover it with red buttercream and place it on one of the trucks. Stand the two pieces of cake for the engine cabin upright and stick them together with a little buttercream, then stick the remaining piece of Swiss roll in front for the engine. Cut a third off the mini Swiss roll and, with the larger piece in front, stand them on the engine for the funnels. Cover the engine with red buttercream, place it on the board and give the smaller funnel a domed top with the buttercream. Complete the train with the sweets, chocolate biscuits and liquorice.

The first truck is for coal, using the liquorice cuts. Then comes a truck with logs, which are the chocolate flakes, and the train is rounded off with a tanker truck. Make the track from two strips of liquorice

Toyland Express

with Matchmakers for the sleepers. Attach each truck by a strip of liquorice with buffers made from liquorice cuts with a Smartie on the end.

All aboard, the Toyland Express is ready for service.

Freezing Note *Store the basic cake for up to 3 months. Thaw for 4 hours then complete as in the recipe.*

Peter the Panda

For the Cake
12 oz/340 g soft margarine
6 large eggs (size 2)
12 oz/340 g caster sugar
11 oz/310 g self-raising flour
1 oz/30 g cocoa powder
2 tablespoons milk
For the Decoration
8 oz/225 g butter
1 lb/450 g icing sugar, sifted
6 oz/175 g desiccated coconut
2 tablespoons cocoa powder
A few drops of dark brown food colouring
2 light brown, 1 dark brown and 1 red Smartie
A small strip of liquorice
An 8½-inch/21-cm sandwich tin
A 6½-inch/16-cm sandwich tin
2 empty 15-oz/425-g cans
A 16½ × 14-inch/41 × 35-cm board covered with red plastic
A 1½-inch/3·5 cm plain cutter
A red bow

Brush all the tins with melted fat and line the base of each with a circle of greaseproof paper cut to fit; brush the paper lining also.

Put the margarine, eggs, sugar, sifted flour and cocoa into a bowl with the milk. Mix them all together and, using a wooden spoon, beat them until the mixture is light and fluffy. Fill the two cans just over half full and divide the rest of the mixture between the two sandwich tins. Spread the mixture to the sides of the tins so that the centres are slightly hollow. Bake the cakes on the centre shelf of a moderate oven, gas mark 4 or 350°F/180°C, for about 1 hour, or until they are slightly shrinking away from the sides of the tin and feel springy to the touch. Turn them on to a wire rack to cool.

Beat the butter to a soft consistency, then gradually beat in the icing sugar. To shape the cakes, first trim a little off the large and small rounds so that the head and body join together. Slice the two tiny cakes into three, and use the four flatter pieces for paws. Take one of the small cans and press out half-circles – two at the top and two at the bottom – in the larger cake. The paws are inserted here later.

Peter the Panda

The remaining pieces of cake are used for the nose and ears. Use the most dome-shaped piece for the nose – you may have to trim it into shape a little. Cut the other round of cake in half and place it in position for the ears, again trimming away a little of the sponge at the top of the head if required.

Stick the head and body of the panda to the board with some of the plain buttercream, then stick the nose in position. Cover the entire surface with more buttercream, keeping it fairly smooth. Scatter over some desiccated coconut for fur. Sift the cocoa powder into the remaining buttercream. Put the rest of the coconut in a bowl and, using a fork, work in enough brown colouring to give the effect of dark fur. Holding the paws one at a time on a fork, cover them carefully with chocolate buttercream then, using a palette knife, press the dark coconut all over the surface. Place the paws in position and repeat the process for the ears. For the eyes, take the plain cutter and place it lightly half on the head and half on the nose, then scatter the dark coconut inside the cutter and very carefully lift it off. If any dark coconut should stray on to the white, use a pair of tweezers to remove it. Put the lighter brown Smarties in the centre of each dark circle for eyes. The darker brown Smartie and the liquorice are for the mouth and the red Smartie for the tongue. Complete Peter the Panda with a red bow under the chin.

Freezing Note *Store the basic cakes for up to 3 months. Thaw for 4 hours then complete as in the recipe.*

Vanilla Gâteau

For the Cake
6 oz/175 g butter or margarine
6 oz/175 g caster sugar
3 large eggs (size 2)
A few drops of vanilla essence
6 oz/185 g self-raising flour
1 tablespoon warm water
For the Filling and Decoration
2 egg whites
4 oz/100 g icing sugar, sifted
4 oz/100 g butter
A few drops of vanilla essence
2 oz/50 g finger biscuits (Langues de Chat)
A few crystallised violets
A piping bag with No 8 star pipe attached
Two 7½-inch/19-cm sandwich tins

Brush the tins with melted fat and line the base of each with a circle of greaseproof paper cut to fit; brush the paper linings also.

Beat the butter to a soft cream with a wooden spoon, then add the sugar and continue beating until the mixture is light and fluffy in both colour and texture. Beat the eggs together, then gradually add them to the creamed mixture, beating well between each addition. Mix in the vanilla essence. Fold the flour into the creamed mixture lightly and quickly, using a metal spoon, adding the warm water at the same time.

Divide the mixture between the two tins and spread it to the sides, leaving the centres slightly hollow so that the cakes rise evenly.

Bake the cakes on the centre shelf of a moderately hot oven, gas mark 5 or 375°F/190°C, for 25 to 30 minutes until well risen and golden brown. The cakes should be slightly shrinking away from the sides of the tins and feel springy to the touch. Loosen them from the sides of the tins and turn on to a wire rack to cool. Remove the greaseproof paper just before you are going to decorate the gâteau.

Put the egg whites and icing sugar into a bowl suspended over a pan of hot water and whisk them together until they are white, thick and fluffy – this will take about 5 to 10 minutes. Remove the bowl from the heat and continue whisking until the mixture cools. In a separate bowl, beat the butter until it is soft and creamy, then gradually beat in the egg white mixture. Leave the buttercream in a cool place for several hours so that it thickens and becomes firm enough to pipe, then flavour it with vanilla essence.

Sandwich the two sponge cakes together with a thin layer of buttercream, then evenly spread some more over the top and sides of the cake. Spoon the rest into the piping bag and pipe a zigzag line about 1 inch/2·5 cm wide around the top edge of the cake.

Arrange the biscuits, slightly overlapping, around the sides and on top of the cake, then place small pieces of crystallised violet on the buttercream, between each biscuit on top.

Freezing Note *Freeze the gâteau unwrapped. The next day wrap and seal well and store for up to a month. Thaw uncovered overnight.*

Vanilla Gâteau

Gâteau Diane

Serves 6–8

For the Meringue
4 large egg whites (size 2)
8 oz/225 g caster sugar
For the Filling
8 oz/225 g granulated sugar
½ pint/300 ml water
4 large egg yolks (size 2), beaten
8 oz/225 g butter, softened
4 tablespoons cocoa powder
1 tablespoon instant coffee powder
2 oz/50 g toasted flaked almonds
Icing sugar for sprinkling

Make the meringue. Whisk the egg whites until they are very stiff and stand in straight peaks. Add 1 level tablespoon caster sugar from the measured amount for every egg white used and whisk again until the mixture regains its original stiffness. Using a metal spoon fold in the rest of the sugar lightly and quickly. The meringue is then ready for immediate use.

Spread the mixture evenly over four 7-inch/18-cm circles drawn on to a baking tray lined with Bakewell paper. Bake in a very cool oven, gas mark ¼ or 225°F/110°F, for about 3 hours, until quite dry.

Dissolve the sugar in the water then bring to the boil and boil rapidly until it forms a short thread between the thumb and first finger when some is carefully taken off a wooden spoon.

Whisk the syrup into the beaten egg yolks until they are thick and creamy. Beat this mixture into the softened butter then add the sifted cocoa and coffee powder.

Use some of this buttercream to sandwich the four meringue rounds together then spread the rest over the top and sides, so that all the surfaces are fairly smooth.

Stand the cake in a circle of toasted flaked almonds and, using a palette knife, run them up the sides of the cake.

Cut three 1-inch/2·5-cm strips of greaseproof paper. Lay the paper strips evenly spaced on top of the cake, dust the surface thickly with sifted icing sugar, then carefully remove the strips to leave the plain spaces.

Serve Gâteau Diane the following day.

Note The cooked meringue rounds will store in an airtight tin for up to a month.

Gâteau Diane

Black Forest Gâteau

For the Sponge
4 large eggs (size 2)
5 oz/150 g caster sugar
¼ teaspoon vanilla essence
1½ oz/40 g plain flour
1 oz/25 g cocoa powder
1 oz/25 g butter
For the Syrup
8 oz/225 g caster sugar
½ pint/300 ml water
1 miniature bottle or 2 tablespoons kirsch liqueur
For the Filling and Decoration
1 lb/450 g ripe cherries (preferably black)
½ pint/300 ml double cream
2 tablespoons icing sugar, sifted
4 oz/100 g plain chocolate
Three 7½-inch/19-cm sandwich tins

Brush the tins with melted fat and line the base of each with a circle of greased greaseproof paper, cut to fit.

Break the eggs into a bowl, add the

sugar and vanilla essence, then suspend the bowl over a pan of hot water, making sure it does not touch the water. Whisk the eggs and sugar together using a wire or rotary whisk, until the mixture is very thick and creamy. (The whisk, when lifted out of the mixture, should leave a definite trail, enabling you to write a figure 8 without the beginning disappearing before you have finished.) Remove the bowl from the heat and whisk the mixture for a few more minutes. Alternatively, the eggs and sugar can be whisked in an electric mixer, in which case the bowl need not be suspended over hot water.

When the mixture has reached the required consistency, sift over the flour and cocoa powder and, using a metal spoon, very carefully fold them into the mixture. Melt the butter over a low heat and add it to the mixture by pouring it down the side of the bowl then, again using a metal spoon, fold in the butter very lightly and carefully. Do not overmix at this stage, or this could result in very shallow and disappointing sponges.

Divide the mixture evenly between the tins and spread them level before baking all three cakes at once – two on the top shelf and one on the shelf below – in a moderate oven, gas mark 4 or 350°F/180°C, for about 30 minutes, or until they feel springy to the touch. When the top two are cooked, remove them from the oven and put the third sponge on to the top shelf for a further 5 minutes to finish cooking.

Leave the cakes to cool slightly in the tins before running a knife around the inside edge and turning them on to a wire rack to cool completely.

Wash the cherries and keep about 20 aside for decoration – pick out all the pairs or trebles for this purpose. Remove the stalks from the rest, then take out the stones – the end of a potato peeler is the ideal tool for this job.

Put the sugar and water into a pan over a very low heat and dissolve the sugar. When it has completely dissolved, add the kirsch and bring the syrup to the boil. Boil it rapidly for about 5 minutes, then reduce the heat, add the stoned cherries and poach them for 5 to 7 minutes until they are just tender. Drain them through a sieve and leave both the cherries and syrup to cool.

Remove the greaseproof paper from the base of the sponges then prick them with a skewer. Stand the wire rack over a tray (to catch all the drips), then spoon the syrup over the sponges. Leave for 2 hours to soak.

Whip the cream until it is stiff and holds its shape then stir in the sifted icing sugar. Spread a thin layer of whipped cream over the top of two of the sponges and divide the poached cherries betwen them. Layer the sponges with the plain one on top. Spread more cream around the sides and over the top of the cake, levelling it with a palette knife.

Grate the chocolate coarsely, letting it fall on to a piece of greaseproof paper. Form the chocolate into a ring and place the cake in the centre, lifting it carefully on a fish slice. Using a palette knife, coat the sides of the cake with grated chocolate by lifting some with the knife and running it up the sides of the cake to adhere to the cream. Transfer the cake – again on the fish slice – to a cake stand and decorate it as follows.

Start with a pair of cherries, pressing one into the cream on top and let the other hang down the side. Repeat this with another pair and go on building up the pile until the centre of the cake is reached and all the cherries are used. Serve the cake as a dessert or for a special teatime treat.

Black Forest Gâteau

Note The cake can also be made when fresh cherries are out of season. Use two 15-oz/425-g cans of cherries, drain them, remove the stones, then stir the kirsch into the juice to make the syrup and follow the rest of the recipe as usual.

Freezing Note *Store the unfilled sponges for up to 3 months. Thaw for 2 to 3 hours then continue as in the recipe.*

Breads and Scones

I don't think there is
a more welcome smell than that of home-baked bread.
Rich and warm it wafts from the kitchen like a summons to all the family.
But if time is short for bread-baking, it is very
quick and easy to make scones, and fresh
from the oven they really
are irresistible.

Traditional Bread

Makes 2 large or 4 small loaves

1 dessertspoon caster sugar
1½ pints/900 ml tepid water
1 oz/25 g dried yeast (see Note)
3 lb/1·4 kg strong plain white flour or wholewheat flour
1 tablespoon salt
2 oz/50 g butter
Beaten egg for glaze

Note Use twice the quantity of fresh yeast to dried – so 2 oz/50 g is required for 3 lb/1·4 kg flour. Mix it into half the amount of tepid water at the first stage, then add it to the flour with the other ingredients and mix to a dough.

Dissolve the sugar in ¾ pint/450 ml tepid water, sprinkle over the dried yeast, then leave the jug in a warm place for about 10 minutes for the yeast to dissolve – it is ready when there is a good froth on top.

Meanwhile, tip the flour on to a work surface, mix in the salt, then rub in the butter until evenly distributed. Form the flour into a ring and tip the dissolved yeast into the centre with the remaining tepid water. Flick the flour from around the edge of the ring into the centre, working it into the liquid with the other hand. When the liquid has absorbed enough flour to make a soft dough, work in the rest of the flour using both hands. Knead the dough, using the heel of one hand to bring the outside of the dough into the centre and turning the dough round continually with the other hand. (There should be no need for any extra flour on the work surface.) After 5 to 10 minutes' kneading, when the dough should have an even smooth surface, form it into a round. Oil a polythene bag by pouring a few drops into the bag and then rubbing the insides together so that the oil covers them. Put the dough into the bag, tie it loosely and leave in a warm place to rise for about 45 minutes, or until it has doubled in size. Turn the dough on to a lightly floured surface and knead it gently so that it returns to its original size – the dough is now ready to shape.

Shaping and Cooking the Bread

Tin Grease the loaf tin with a little melted fat. Take a quarter of the dough for a 1-lb/0·5-kg tin, or half the dough for a 2-lb/1-kg tin, and punch it into a rectangle the length of the tin and three times the width. Fold the dough into three. Pick the dough up, turn it over, then drop it into the tin with the folds underneath, turning the ends under to give the loaf a good rounded top. Beat an egg with some salt and brush a little over the surface for gloss. Prove the loaf again in a warm place for about 20 minutes or until it stands ½ inch/1 cm above the sides of the tin. Bake the loaf in a very hot oven, gas mark 8 or 450°F/230°C. The 2-lb/1-kg loaf will take 35 minutes, the 1 lb/0·5 kg loaf 25 to 30 minutes. To test if the loaves are cooked, remove them from the tin and tap the base – if the loaf sounds hollow it is ready. Leave on a wire rack to cool.

Cottage Using half the total dough, cut from it a quarter. Knead both pieces into rounds then stick the smaller round on top of the larger with a little water. Flour a wooden spoon handle and plunge it through both loaves. Put the bread on to a greased baking tray; glaze, prove and bake as for the 2-lb/1-kg tin loaf.

Plait Divide a quarter of the total dough into three, roll each piece into a 14-inch/35-cm length with a bulge in the middle. Join the three rolls together at one end, plait the strands and join the other end. Lift the plait on to a greased baking tray

Traditional Breads

and tuck under the ends; glaze, sprinkle with poppy seeds if liked, prove and bake as for the 1-lb/0·5 kg tin loaf.

Crown Grease a 6½-inch/16-cm sandwich tin. Cut a quarter of the total dough into six even pieces, then knead each one into a ball and arrange them in the tin – five round the outside and one in the middle. Brush the dough with egg glaze and sprinkle it with porridge oats. Prove and bake as for 1-lb/0·5-kg tin loaf.

Caterpillar Divide a quarter of the total dough into four and roll each piece into a barrel, the length of each being the width of the tin. Lay the pieces in a greased 1-lb/0·5-kg loaf tin, brush the tops with egg glaze and leave to prove before baking it as for the 1-lb/0·5-kg tin loaf.

Large Bap Taking a quarter of the total dough, knead it into a round, put on to a greased baking tray and flatten it slightly. Sprinkle the bread liberally with flour, then leave it to prove in a warm place for about 15 minutes before baking it as for the 1-lb/0·5-kg tin loaf.

Coburg Knead a quarter of the total dough into a round. Lift it on to a greased baking tray and cut a fairly deep cross in the centre of the loaf. Brush the top, but not the cross, with egg glaze. Leave the dough to prove for 10 minutes, then bake as for the 1-lb/0·5-kg tin loaf.

Individual Rolls Grease a baking tray. Cut a quarter of the dough into six even pieces and knead each one into a round roll. Place on the baking tray, brush with egg glaze and prove for 10 to 15 minutes. Bake them in a very hot oven, gas mark 8 or 450°F/230°C, for 15 to 20 minutes.

Freezing Note

Uncooked *Make the dough to the stage where it is shaped into loaves for the final proving then place it straight into the freezer and freeze it for 12 hours. Remove it from the tin or baking tray, wrap it in foil or a polythene bag, label it and store until required; it will keep for up to 3 weeks.*

To cook the bread, remove it from the freezer, unwrap, brush with beaten egg glaze and leave in a warm place to thaw and prove. A 1-lb/0·5-kg loaf will take about 4 hours and a 2-lb/1-kg loaf about 5 hours. Bake the bread as normal.

Cooked *Bread can be frozen very successfully after it has been cooked and cooled. Wrap it in foil or polythene, label then freeze. The bread will keep for up to 2 months, after which time the crust starts to come away.*

Thaw at room temperature for about 2 hours then, if liked, warm through in a moderate oven for 10 to 15 minutes.

Currant Loaf

½ oz/15 g dried yeast
1 oz/25 g caster sugar
¼ pint/150 ml milk
¼ pint/150 ml water
1 lb/450 g strong plain white flour
A pinch of salt
1½ oz/40 g margarine
2 oz/50 g currants, cleaned

For the Glaze

2 tablespoons granulated sugar
2 tablespoons water
A 2-lb/1-kg loaf tin

Put the yeast into a jug with 1 teaspoon of the measured sugar. Warm the milk and water to blood heat and whisk into the yeast. Leave this mixture in a warm place to dissolve the yeast; it will take 10 to 15 minutes.

Sift the flour and salt into a bowl, rub in the margarine and stir in the currants with the rest of the sugar. Pour the dissolved yeast into the centre of the flour and, using a fork, mix the ingredients together to form a dough.

Turn the dough on to a lightly floured work surface and knead it, using the heel of one hand to bring the outside of the dough into the centre and turning it continually with the other hand until the surface is smooth.

The kneading may take up to 5 minutes. When the dough is ready put it into a greased bowl, cover it with a damp tea towel or sheet of greased polythene and leave in a warm place for 45 minutes to rise – it should double in bulk.

Grease the loaf tin with melted fat. Knock the risen dough back to its original size, then shape it into a rectangle the length of the tin and three times the width. Fold the dough into three and drop it into the tin, tucking under the ends.

Prove the loaf again for 20 minutes. When it has risen to the top of the tin, bake it in a very hot oven, gas mark 8 or 450°F/230°C, for 20 minutes then reduce to gas mark 6 or 400°F/200°C for a further 25 minutes, or until the loaf, removed from the tin, sounds hollow when it is gently tapped on the base.

While the loaf is cooking, make the glaze. Dissolve the sugar in the water over a low heat. When every grain has dissolved, bring the syrup to the boil then turn off the heat and the glaze is ready.

Put the cooked loaf on to a wire rack, brush the top with glaze then leave to cool.

Serve cold, sliced and buttered.

Chelsea Buns

Makes 12

For the Dough
$7\frac{1}{2}$ fl oz/225 ml milk
$\frac{1}{2}$ oz/15 g dried yeast
2 oz/50 g caster sugar
1 lb/450 g strong plain white flour
A generous pinch of salt
4 oz/100 g margarine
1 large egg (size 2), beaten
For the Filling and Glaze
1 oz/25 g butter, melted
4 oz/100 g currants, cleaned
2 oz/50 g chopped mixed peel
1 teaspoon ground cinnamon
2 oz/50 g caster sugar
2 tablespoons milk
A 9-inch/23-cm square cake tin

1 Warm the milk to blood heat and whisk in the yeast with a teaspoon of sugar. Leave in a warm place for 10 to 15 minutes until a good froth appears. Sift the flour and salt into a mixing bowl, rub in the margarine, then stir in the remaining sugar with the egg and yeast liquid.

2 Bind all the ingredients together to form a dough; turn it on to a floured surface and knead for about 5 minutes, until smooth and elastic. Put the dough in a greased bowl and cover with greased polythene. Leave in a warm place to rise until doubled.

3 Turn the risen dough on to a floured surface and gently knock it back to its original size. Roll into an oblong about 18 × 9 inches/45 × 23 cm and brush with the melted butter. Sprinkle over the currants, mixed peel and cinnamon, then roll up to make an 18-inch/45-cm length.

4 Now make the glaze. Heat the caster sugar and milk slowly in a saucepan to dissolve the sugar completely. Bring to the boil, then put the glaze on one side to use later. Mark the roll of dough into 12 and cut it into even-sized pieces. Brush the cake tin with melted fat.

5 Space the buns evenly in the tin, fairly close together with the cut side uppermost. Cover the surface of the tin with a piece of greased polythene and leave in a warm place for 15 to 20 minutes for the buns to prove, until they are just touching each other.

6 When the buns have risen sufficiently, bake them on the centre shelf of a hot oven, gas mark 7 or 425°F/220°C, for 20 to 25 minutes, until golden brown. While the buns are still hot, brush them over with the glaze then cool on a wire rack.

Freezing Note *Store the buns for up to a month, then thaw overnight.*

Bun Round, Orange Flower Bread, Apple Plait

Orange Flower Bread

2 teaspoons dried yeast
2 oz/50 g caster sugar
4 tablespoons milk
2 tablespoons water
2 oz/50 g butter
Grated rind and juice of 1 orange
½ teaspoon ground mixed spice
1 large egg (size 2), beaten
12 oz/350 g strong plain white flour
¼ teaspoon salt
Beaten egg for glaze
For the Icing
2 oz/50 g icing sugar, sifted
Grated rind of 1 orange
1 tablespoon orange juice
A plain 8-inch/20-cm flan ring
A plain 3-inch/7·5-cm cutter

Put the dried yeast and 1 teaspoon of the sugar into a jug. Warm the milk and water to blood heat (that is when it feels neither hot nor cold to the touch), then whisk it into the yeast. Leave the jug in a warm place for the yeast to dissolve; it will take about 10 to 15 minutes and is ready when the liquid has a good froth on top.

Meanwhile, cream together the butter and remaining sugar until soft and fluffy. Beat in the orange rind and mixed spice, then gradually add the beaten egg, mixing it in well with each addition. Finally, stir in the dissolved yeast, orange juice, sifted flour and salt. When the mixture forms a dough, turn it on to a lightly floured work surface. Knead the dough, using one hand to keep the dough turning and the other hand to bring the dough from the outside to the centre, for about 10 minutes, until smooth. Lightly grease a mixing bowl and put the dough in it. Cover the bowl with a damp tea towel or sheet of greased polythene and leave in a warm place for about 1 hour, or until it has doubled in size.

When the dough is ready, gently knock it back to its original size.

Grease a baking tray and the flan ring, and stand it in the centre of the tray. Turn the dough into the flan ring and press it to the sides. Take off the flan ring, place the cutter in the centre of the dough and, using a sharp knife, cut through the dough from the edge of the cutter to the outside edge of the dough at about 1-inch/2·5-cm intervals. Replace the flan ring then, taking each strip of dough separately, twist it twice and put it back into the ring. Brush the dough with egg glaze and leave in a warm place to prove for 15 minutes, or until it just rises above the top of the flan ring.

Bake the bread on the centre shelf of a moderately cool oven, gas mark 3 or 325°F/160°C, for 50 to 55 minutes, until it is golden brown and sounds hollow when gently tapped on the base. Cool the loaf on a wire rack.

Mix the icing sugar with the orange rind and juice, then pour it on to the centre of the bread and leave the icing to run down the sides. Serve the loaf sliced and buttered.

Freezing Note *Store the bread uniced for up to 1 month. Thaw for 4 hours then ice as in the recipe.*

Bun Round

1 lb/450 g strong plain white flour
A pinch of salt
¼ pint/150 ml milk
¼ pint/150 ml water
½ oz/15 g dried yeast
1 oz/25 g caster sugar
1½ oz/40 g margarine
4 oz/100 g sultanas, cleaned
1 oz/25 g chopped mixed peel
Beaten egg for glaze

Sift the flour and salt into a large bowl and leave in a warm place. Warm the milk and water to blood heat, pour into a jug and whisk in the yeast and half the caster sugar. Leave in a warm place to dissolve the yeast – it will take about 10 minutes and is ready when the liquid has a good froth on top.

Rub the margarine into the flour. Add the rest of the sugar and the yeast liquid. Mix together to form a dough, then turn on to a lightly floured work surface and knead for about 10 minutes, or until smooth. Put the dough into a greased bowl and cover with a sheet of greased polythene or a damp tea towel. Leave in a warm place for about 45 minutes, or until it has doubled in size. Knead the dough again lightly and work in the sultanas and mixed peel. Form into a 9-inch/23-cm round. Lift the round on to a greased baking tray, brush the surface with egg glaze and mark it into eight pieces. Leave the baking tray in a warm place for about 15 minutes for the round to prove.

Bake on the centre shelf of a hot oven, gas mark 7 or 425°F/220°C, for 10 minutes, then reduce to gas mark 6 or 400°F/200°C, and cook the round for a further 10 to 15 minutes, until the bun round is golden brown and well risen.

Leave the bun to cool, then serve it sliced and buttered.

Freezing Note *Store for up to 6 weeks, thaw for 4 hours then serve slightly warm, if liked.*

Apple Plait

6 tablespoons milk
1½ teaspoons dried yeast
2 oz/50 g caster sugar
8 oz/225 g strong plain white flour
A generous pinch of salt
2 oz/50 g butter
1 large egg (size 2), beaten
For the Filling
½ lb/225 g cooking apples
2 oz/50 g light soft brown sugar
2 oz/50 g seedless raisins
½ teaspoon ground cinnamon
For the Glaze
2 oz/50 g caster sugar
2 tablespoons milk

Warm the milk to blood heat, then pour it into a jug and whisk in the yeast with 1 tablespoon of sugar from the measured amount. Leave the jug in a warm place for the yeast to dissolve; it will take about 10 minutes and is ready when the liquid has a good froth on top.

Meanwhile, sift the flour and salt into a mixing bowl and rub in the butter using the fingertips only. Make a well in the centre of the dry ingredients and stir in the remaining sugar with the beaten egg and yeast liquid. Mix the ingredients together with a wooden spoon, then beat them with your hand until the dough starts to leave the sides of the bowl clean. Turn it on to a floured work surface and keep kneading the dough until it is smooth and elastic. Put it into a greased mixing bowl, cover with a sheet of greased polythene or a damp tea towel, and leave in a warm place for 45 to 50 minutes, or until the dough has doubled in size.

Meanwhile, prepare the filling. Peel, core and chop the apples and put them into a pan with the sugar, raisins and cinnamon. Cook over a low heat for about 10 to 15 minutes, until the apple is soft then turn into a bowl and leave to cool.

When the dough is ready, turn it on to a floured work surface and knock it back to its original size. Put on to a greased baking tray and roll it into an oblong 12 × 8 inches/30 × 20 cm. Spread the filling down the centre of the dough, then using a sharp knife make 2-inch/5-cm cuts at a slight angle towards the filling – the cuts should be about 1 inch/2·5 cm apart. Taking a strip at a time, cross them over the filling to give the top a plaited effect. Put the plait in a warm place for about 30 minutes so that it starts to rise, then bake on the centre shelf of a fairly hot oven, gas mark 6 or 400°F/200°C, for 25 to 30 minutes, until golden brown.

Leave the plait on a wire rack to cool, then make up the glaze.

Put the sugar and milk into a small pan and dissolve the sugar over a low heat, then bring to the boil and boil rapidly for 2 minutes. Brush the glaze over the Apple Plait then serve for a dessert or for tea.

Freezing Note *Store before glazing for up to 2 months. Thaw overnight then reheat at gas mark 4 or 350°F/180°C for 15 minutes. Glaze as in the recipe and serve slightly warm.*

Doughnuts

Makes 12

¼ pint/150 ml milk
½ oz/15 g dried yeast
1 oz/25 g caster sugar
1 lb/450 g strong plain white flour
A pinch of salt
1½ oz/40 g butter
2 large eggs (size 2), beaten
Cooking oil or fat for deep frying
To Coat the Doughnuts
4 oz/100 g caster sugar
1 teaspoon ground cinnamon

Heat the milk to blood heat – that is when it feels neither hot nor cold to the touch. Pour it into a jug and mix in the yeast and 1 teaspoon from the measured sugar. Leave in a warm place to dissolve the yeast; it will take about 10 minutes and is ready when a froth has formed on top.

Meanwhile, mix the flour and salt together, rub in the butter until it is evenly distributed, then mix in the rest of the sugar. Form a well in the centre of the flour and pour in the dissolved yeast with the well beaten eggs. Mix the flour into the liquid, beating the ingredients together well to form a soft and very elastic dough. Turn the dough on to a well floured work surface and knead it as for breadmaking until the dough is smooth. Oil a polythene bag by pouring a few drops into the bag and then rubbing the sides together so that the oil covers the inside of the bag. Put the dough in the bag, tie it loosely then leave in a warm place for about 45 minutes to 1 hour, until doubled in bulk.

When the dough is ready, turn it on to a lightly floured surface and knock back gently to its original size. Divide the dough into 12 pieces, knead each one into a round and make a large hole in the centre of each doughnut by pushing your finger through. Lay the doughnuts on to greased baking trays and leave them for about 15 minutes or until they double in size.

Half-fill a deep fat fryer with cooking oil, and heat it to about 350°F/180°C, that is when a cube of white bread dropped into the fat browns in under a minute. Put the caster sugar on to a piece of kitchen paper and mix in the cinnamon.

When the oil is at the right temperature, lower four doughnuts into it and fry them for about 2 minutes on each side until golden brown. Lift the doughnuts out with a draining spoon, place them on the sugar and sprinkle it all over.

Freezing Note *Store for up to a month then thaw for 4 hours.*

Stollen

For the Dough
1 lb/450 g strong plain white flour
A generous pinch of salt
½ oz/15 g dried yeast
4 oz/100 g caster sugar
7½ fl oz/225 ml milk
4 oz/100 g butter
1 large egg (size 2), beaten
Icing sugar for sprinkling
For the Filling
2 oz/50 g currants, cleaned
4 oz/100 g seedless raisins
2 oz/50 g glacé cherries, chopped
2 oz/50 g chopped mixed peel
1 oz/25 g angelica, chopped
3 tablespoons sherry or orange juice
1 oz/25 g butter, melted

Mix together the currants, raisins, cherries, mixed peel and angelica, then stir in the sherry or orange juice and leave the mixture on one side to soak while making the yeast dough.

Sift the flour and salt into a mixing bowl and leave in a warm place. Put the yeast and 1 teaspoon of sugar from the measured amount into a jug. Heat the milk to blood heat – that is when it feels neither hot nor cold to the touch – and whisk it into the yeast with a fork. Leave in a warm place to dissolve the yeast; it will take about 15 minutes and is ready when the liquid has a good froth on top.

Rub the butter into the flour and, when it is evenly distributed, stir in the remaining sugar with the beaten egg and dissolved yeast. Bind the ingredients together to form a dough, then turn the mixture on to a floured work surface and knead for 5 minutes until smooth.

Brush the mixing bowl with a little melted fat and return the dough to it. Cover the dough with a damp cloth or piece of greased polythene and leave in a warm place to rise – it will take about 50 minutes and is ready when the dough has doubled in size.

Turn the dough on to a lightly floured work surface and knock it back gently to its original size. Turn the soaked fruit into the centre of the dough and knead it in so that it is evenly distributed. Roll the dough into a 12 × 8-inch/30 × 20-cm rectangle. Pour over the melted butter and spread it to the edges, then brush one long side with water. Fold the dough into three lengthways, so that the dampened edge seals down the centre of the loaf. Lay the loaf on a greased baking tray and taper the ends slightly, pushing the centre of the loaf together so that it is well rounded. Leave the Stollen in a warm place to prove for about 30 minutes – it is ready when the dough has nearly doubled in size again.

Bake the loaf on the centre shelf of a fairly hot oven, gas mark 6 or 400°F/200°C, for 20 minutes, then reduce to gas mark 5 or 375°F/190°C for a further 20 minutes.

When the loaf is cooked, place it on a wire rack, dust the surface thickly with sifted icing sugar, and leave to cool. Serve the Stollen sliced and buttered. It keeps well in a cool dry place.

Freezing Note *Store for up to a month, thaw overnight then dust with more icing sugar before serving.*

Stollen and Speculaas (see recipe page 152)

Mixed Fruit Loaf

14 oz/400 g self-raising flour
2 oz/50 g margarine
2 oz/50 g lard
8 oz/225 g caster sugar
12 oz/350 g mixed dried fruit cleaned
½ pint/300 ml sour milk, or fresh milk with a dessertspoon of vinegar added
A 2-lb/1-kg loaf tin

Brush the tin with melted fat and line the base with a piece of greaseproof paper cut to fit; grease the paper lining also.

Sift the flour into a mixing bowl and add the margarine and lard cut into small pieces. Rub in the fats until they are evenly distributed and the mixture resembles fine breadcrumbs. Stir in the sugar and the dried fruit so they are thoroughly mixed.

Stir the milk into the dry ingredients to form a soft dropping consistency, then turn the mixture into the prepared loaf tin and spread the surface level. Bake the loaf on the centre shelf of a moderate oven, gas mark 4 or 350°F/180°C, for 1 hour then reduce the heat to gas mark 3 or 325°F/160°C for a further hour, or until a warmed skewer pushed into the centre of the loaf comes out clean.

It is best to keep this loaf in a polythene bag or an airtight tin for 2 days before cutting it, as it is then more easily sliced. Serve the loaf cut into thick slices and spread with butter for tea.

Note Lemon juice can also be used to sour the milk.

Freezing Note *Store for up to 2 months. Thaw for at least 4 hours before serving.*

Orange and Walnut Tea Bread

8 oz/225 g self-raising flour
3 oz/75 g butter
3 oz/75 g caster sugar
2 oz/50 g walnuts, chopped
2 oranges
1 large egg (size 2)
2 tablespoons caster sugar for sprinkling
A 2-lb/1-kg loaf tin

Sift the flour into a bowl and add the butter cut into small pieces. Using the fingertips only, rub the butter into the flour until the mixture resembles fine breadcrumbs and the fat is evenly distributed.

Add the 3 oz/75 g caster sugar and the chopped walnuts then grate in the rind of both oranges, being careful not to include the pith. Remove any rind left on the grater and add it to the bowl.

Squeeze the juice from one of the oranges and pour it into the dry ingredients. Break in the egg then, using a wooden spoon, mix well to form a soft mixture that drops from the spoon when shaken lightly.

Turn the mixture into the tin and spread it level. Using a sharp knife, cut all the peel off the remaining orange by working spirally round the fruit, cutting just below the pith and above the flesh.

Divide the orange into segments by cutting the flesh from either side of the membranes, working in towards the centre of the orange. The segments should come out whole.

Overlap the orange segments diagonally across the loaf. Sprinkle with the sugar then bake in a moderate oven, gas mark 4 or 350°F/180°C, for 1¼ to 1½ hours, until a warmed skewer inserted into the loaf comes out clean.

Freezing Note *Store for up to 2 months. Thaw for 4 hours then serve cut into slices with butter.*

Orange and Walnut Tea Bread

Hurrell Loaf

This delicious loaf is best made about a week before serving as it improves with keeping.

6 oz/175 g wholemeal flour
4 oz/100 g self-raising flour
½ teaspoon baking powder
A pinch of grated nutmeg
6 oz/175 g sultanas, cleaned
2 oz/50 g walnuts, chopped
4 oz/100 g demerara sugar
8 oz/225 g black treacle
¼ pint/150 ml plus 3 tablespoons milk
A 2-lb/1-kg loaf tin, greased

Put the wholemeal flour into a bowl and sift in the white flour with the baking powder and nutmeg. Stir in the sultanas, chopped walnuts and demerara sugar.

Measure out the treacle – the best way to do this is to weigh a saucepan, then spoon the required amount of treacle into it, taking into account the weight of the pan. Add the milk to the treacle and, with the pan over a low heat, mix the two ingredients together until they combine. Stir this liquid into the dry ingredients and mix them all together, then pour the mixture into the tin.

Bake the loaf on the centre shelf of a moderate oven, gas mark 4 or 350°F/180°C, for 1 to 1¼ hours, until a warmed skewer inserted into the centre comes out clean. Cool the loaf in the tin for 15 minutes, then turn it on to a wire rack to cool completely.

Serve the loaf sliced and buttered.

Freezing Note *Store for up to 3 months. Thaw overnight before serving sliced and buttered.*

Malt Loaf

Although this recipe has a delicious malty taste it is quite different to the malt loaves bought at bakers. They usually contain yeast whereas our recipe has been specially created to be quick to make.

12 oz/350 g self-raising flour
6 oz/175 g sultanas, cleaned
2 oz/50 g margarine
2 tablespoons black treacle
2 tablespoons golden syrup
4 tablespoons malt extract
¼ pint/150 ml milk
2 large eggs (size 2), beaten
A 2-lb/1-kg loaf tin

Lightly grease the tin with a little melted fat.

Sift the flour into a mixing bowl and stir in the sultanas. Put the margarine, treacle, syrup, malt extract and milk into a pan and melt them together over a low heat, but do not allow to boil. Stir the melted mixture into the flour with the well beaten eggs. When the mixture is smooth, turn it into the tin and, using a palette knife, ease it to the sides, hollowing out the centre slightly.

Bake the Malt Loaf on the centre shelf of a moderate oven, gas mark 4 or 350°F/180°C, for 20 minutes, then reduce to gas mark 3 or 325°F/160°C, for a further 40 minutes, or until a warmed skewer inserted into the loaf comes out clean.

Leave the loaf to cool in the tin for 10 minutes then turn it on to a wire rack to cool completely. Leave overnight, then serve the Malt Loaf sliced and buttered.

Freezing Note *Store for up to 2 months. Thaw for at least 4 hours before serving.*

Lemon Bread

8 oz/225 g caster sugar
3 oz/75 g margarine
Grated rind of 1 lemon
Grated rind of ½ orange
1 large egg (size 2)
8 oz/225 g plain flour
1 teaspoon baking powder
¼ pint/150 ml milk
For the Topping
Juice of 1 lemon
1 tablespoon caster sugar
A 2-lb/1-kg loaf tin

Brush the tin with melted fat and line the base with a piece of greaseproof paper cut to fit; brush the paper lining also.

Beat the caster sugar and margarine together until they are combined – the mixture will look rather like desiccated coconut when it is ready. Beat in the lemon and orange rind with the egg, then sift in the flour and baking powder and stir them into the mixture together with the milk.

Pour the cake mixture into the prepared tin and bake the Lemon Bread on the centre shelf of a moderate oven, gas mark 4 or 350°F/180°C, for 1¼ to 1½ hours. The cake is cooked when it is shrinking away from the sides of the tin and a warmed skewer inserted into the centre comes out clean. If any mixture adheres to the skewer, cook the cake for a little longer.

While the Lemon Bread is cooking, mix the lemon juice and sugar together for the topping. Remove the cake from the oven as soon as it is ready, take it out of the tin and peel off the paper. Stand the tea bread on a wire rack, prick it with a fork then pour over the lemon juice and sugar so that it soaks into the bread.

Leave the Lemon Bread to cool completely before serving it sliced for tea. It has a quite delicious flavour.

Freezing Note *Store for up to 2 months then thaw for at least 4 hours before serving.*

Plain Scones

Makes 8–9

8 oz/225 g self-raising flour
A pinch of salt
1½ oz/40 g margarine
About ¼ pint/150 ml milk
Beaten egg for glaze
A 2½-inch/6-cm plain cutter

Sift the flour and salt into a mixing bowl. Add the margarine and rub it in until it is evenly distributed. Bind the ingredients together with the milk to make a soft dough.

Turn the dough on to a lightly floured work surface and roll it out to ½ inch/1 cm thick. Cut out as many rounds as possible, then gather up the scraps and cut out more rounds. Put the scones on to a baking tray and brush the top of each with a little egg glaze.

Bake the scones on the centre shelf of a hot oven, gas mark 7 or 425°F/220°C, for about 15 minutes, until golden brown and cooked.

Fruit Scones Stir into the dry ingredients 2 oz/50 g sultanas and 1 oz/25 g caster sugar. Continue as for Plain Scones.

Cheese Scones Stir 2 oz/50 g grated cheese into the dry ingredients before adding the milk. Sprinkle the cut out scones with a little extra cheese before baking as for Plain Scones.

Freezing Note *Store baked scones for up to 3 months, thaw for 1 hour then reheat in a moderate oven for 10 minutes.*

Ginger Griddle Scones, Fruit Scones, Lemon Bread, Honey Scone Ring

Ginger Griddle Scones

Makes 8

- 8 oz/225 g plain flour
- A pinch of salt
- 1 teaspoon bicarbonate of soda
- 1 tablespoon ground ginger
- 2 oz/50 g margarine
- 2 oz/50 g caster sugar
- 2 teaspoons cream of tartar
- ¼ pint/150 ml milk

Sift the flour, salt, bicarbonate of soda and ginger into a mixing bowl. Rub in the margarine and, when it is evenly distributed, stir in the sugar. Dissolve the cream of tartar in the milk and bind the dry ingredients together with the liquid to make a soft dough.

Turn the dough on to a floured work surface and divide it into two portions. Knead each portion lightly, and form into a round about ½ inch/1 cm thick. Divide each round into quarters.

Heat a griddle pan or heavy-based frying pan and cook the scones in two batches for 10 minutes, turning them halfway through the cooking time.

Serve the Ginger Griddle Scones still warm with plenty of butter and jam if liked.

Honey Scone Ring

Makes 10

- 8 oz/225 g self-raising flour
- 1½ oz/40 g margarine
- 1½ oz/40 g caster sugar
- 1 tablespoon clear honey
- 6 tablespoons milk
- Milk for glaze
- *A 2¾-inch/6·5-cm fluted cutter*

Sift the flour into a mixing bowl, add the margarine and rub it in until evenly distributed. Stir in the sugar. Stir the honey into the milk, then mix into the dry ingredients to make a soft dough.

Turn the dough on to a lightly floured work surface and knead it gently until smooth. Using a floured rolling pin, roll it out to about ¼–½ inch/5 mm–1 cm thick. Cut out as many rounds as possible, then gather up the scraps and cut out more rounds, making 10 in all. Stand a jam jar in the centre of a baking tray and arrange the scones around it, overlapping as you work. Remove the jar, brush the tops of the scones with milk and bake immediately on the centre shelf of a hot oven, gas mark 7 or 425°F/220°C, for 10 to 15 minutes, until golden brown.

Freezing Note *Store for up to 3 months in a rigid container so the ring does not break. Thaw for 2 hours then reheat in a moderate oven for 10 minutes.*

Drop Scones

Makes about 20

These are a marvellous standby to serve to the unexpected visitor as they are so easy to make, quick to cook and scrumptious served still warm with butter and jam. Normally Drop Scones are cooked on a griddle but a heavy-based frying pan can be used just as effectively.

- 8 oz/225 g self-raising flour
- A pinch of salt
- 1 tablespoon caster sugar
- 1 large egg (size 2)
- Just over ¼ pint/150 ml milk

Sift the flour and salt into a mixing bowl and stir in the sugar. Make a well in the centre of the dry ingredients, break in the egg and add the milk gradually, stirring from the centre to incorporate the liquid and make a fairly thick batter.

Heat the griddle or frying pan, moving it occasionally over the heat so that it is an even temperature. Grease the surface carefully with a little lard held in a piece of paper, then increase the heat and drop tablespoonfuls of the mixture on to the pan. As each scone cooks, bubbles will rise to the surface. Turn the scones over and cook the other side, then place them in a tea towel to keep warm while cooking the rest of the batter.

Quickie Bread Rolls

Makes 8

- 8 oz/225 g plain flour
- ½ teaspoon salt
- ½ teaspoon bicarbonate of soda
- 1 teaspoon cream of tartar
- ½ oz/15 g margarine
- ¼ pint/150 ml milk
- Beaten egg for glaze
- Poppy seeds

Sift the flour, salt, bicarbonate of soda and cream of tartar into a mixing bowl and rub in the fat. Bind the ingredients together with the milk to make a soft dough, then turn it on to a lightly floured work surface and knead until smooth. Divide the dough into eight equal pieces. Roll each piece into an 8-inch/20-cm length and tie it in a knot.

Arrange the rolls on a greased baking tray, brush them with egg glaze and sprinkle with poppy seeds. Bake the rolls on the centre shelf of a moderately hot oven, gas mark 5 or 375°F/190°C, for about 15 minutes until golden brown.

Freezing Note *Store for up to a month. Thaw for 2 hours and serve slightly warm if liked.*

Preserves

There is nothing quite so rewarding as to preserve surplus fruits and vegetables in jams, jellies, pickles or chutneys for future use. An important point to remember is always to ensure the produce is in peak condition and as fresh as possible, preferably picked or purchased on the day of use.

Strawberry Jam

Makes 7 lb/3·25 kg

4 lb/1·75 kg strawberries
Juice of 1 lemon
4 lb/1·75 kg preserving or granulated sugar
1 oz/25 g butter

1 Select fresh and slightly under-ripe strawberries, remove the stalks and put the fruit into a large pan. Pour in the lemon juice and put the pan over a low heat.

2 Gently simmer the fruit, covered, for about 15 minutes until the strawberries are really soft, pressing them against the sides of the pan to extract the juice. Add the preserving or granulated sugar.

3 When every grain of sugar has dissolved, bring the jam to a rapid rolling boil and boil it steadily for about 10 minutes until the setting point is reached.

4 To test if the jam has set, remove the pan from the heat. Spoon a little jam on to a plate and leave it to cool. Then, using a finger, gently push the surface; if the jam wrinkles it is ready.

5 Stir in the butter – this helps to reduce the scum – then leave the jam to stand for about 10 minutes so that the fruit is evenly distributed. Ladle or pour into warmed jars.

6 Either cover the jam immediately or when it is cold with a waxed paper disc, wax side down; then stretch over a transparent cover, damp side up. Secure with a rubber band, label and store.

Strawberry Jam

Dried Apricot Jam

Makes about 12 lb/5·5 kg

2 lb/1 kg dried apricots
3 large lemons
5½ pints/3·5 litres water
7 lb/3·25 kg granulated sugar
2 oz/50 g blanched almonds, shredded

Wash the apricots and, if they are large, cut in half. Put in a very large bowl. Grate the rind of the lemons finely and add it to the apricots.

Squeeze the juice from the lemons. Tie the pips in a piece of muslin and add both the bag of pips and the lemon juice to the apricots. Pour the water over the fruit and leave to soak for 24 hours.

Put the soaked apricots and the liquid into a preserving pan, together with the lemon pips, and bring to the boil. Boil rapidly for about 5 to 10 minutes, or until the apricots are tender.

Take the bag of pips out of the jam, add all the sugar and dissolve it gradually. Bring the jam to the boil again, stirring frequently, then allow to boil rapidly for about 30 minutes, or until the setting stage is reached. (To test if the jam has set, see the Strawberry Jam recipe.)

Skim and stir in the almonds. Cool for 5 to 10 minutes, then pour into jars. Seal, label and store.

Strawberry and Orange Jam

Makes about 6 lb/2·75 kg

4 lb/1·75 kg strawberries
Grated rind and juice of 3 oranges
4 lb/1·75 kg preserving or granulated sugar
1 oz/25 g butter

Select fresh and slightly under-ripe strawberries. Remove the stalks and put the fruit into a preserving pan, then pour in the orange juice and add the rind. Put any pips into a small piece of muslin, tie it into a bag, then fasten the bag to the side of the pan so that it sits in the jam. Put the pan over a low heat and gently simmer the fruit, covered, for about 15 minutes, until the strawberries are really soft, pressing them against the sides of the pan to extract the juice. Remove the bag of pips and squeeze out all the juice. Add the sugar and stir the mixture until every grain has dissolved, then bring the jam to a rolling boil and boil rapidly for about 10 minutes, until the setting point is reached. (To test if the jam has set, see the Strawberry Jam recipe.) Stir in the butter – this helps to remove any scum.

Leave the jam to stand for about 10 minutes, then pour into warmed jars. Seal, label and store.

Gooseberry and Lime Jam

Makes about 6 lb/2·75 kg

2 lb/1 kg gooseberries
2 limes
2½ pints/1·4 litres water
4 lb/1·75 kg preserving or granulated sugar
1 oz/25 g butter

Top and tail the gooseberries, using a pair of scissors, and wash them thoroughly. Coarsely mince the limes, or chop them finely, removing the pips. Put the pips into a piece of muslin, tie it into a bag and fasten the bag to the side of the preserving pan so that it will sit in the jam. Put the limes into the pan with the gooseberries and water, then bring the mixture slowly to the boil and simmer gently. Using a wooden spoon, crush the gooseberries against the sides of the pan as the mixture is simmering to extract as much of the juice as possible. Cook the fruit for about 15 to 20 minutes, until it is tender. Remove the bag of pips and squeeze out all the liquid that has been absorbed.

Stir in the sugar and, when every grain has dissolved, bring the jam to a rolling boil and continue to boil for about 20 to 25 minutes, until the setting point is reached. (To test if the jam has set, see the Strawberry Jam recipe.) Stir in the butter.

Leave the jam for about 10 minutes, then pour into warmed jars. Seal, label and store.

Rhubarb and Rose Petal Jam

Makes about 2 lb/1 kg

1 lb/450 g rhubarb
1 lb/450 g granulated sugar
½ pint/300 ml water
Juice of 1 lemon
2 large handfuls of rose petals (preferably red for most flavour)
A knob of butter

Wipe the rhubarb, trim off the base and the leaves and cut the sticks into 1-inch/2·5-cm lengths. Put the rhubarb pieces into a bowl and mix in the sugar, water and lemon juice. Cover the bowl and leave the mixture in a cool place overnight so the sugar starts to dissolve.

Next day, turn the rhubarb mixture into a preserving pan. Wash the rose petals, then chop them roughly and add to the rhubarb in the pan. Stir the mixture over a gentle heat until every grain of sugar has dissolved, then bring the jam to a rolling boil and boil rapidly for 5 to 7 minutes, until setting point is reached. (To test if the jam has set, see the Strawberry Jam recipe.)

Stir in the butter. Leave the jam to stand for about 10 minutes then pour into warmed jars. Seal, label and store.

Cherry and Blackcurrant Jam

Makes about 7 lb/3·25 kg

2 lb/1 kg blackcurrants
1 lb/450 g black cherries, stoned
2 pints/1·15 litres water
4 lb/1·75 kg preserving or granulated sugar
1 oz/25 g butter

Strip the blackcurrants from their stems by running a fork along them. Wash the blackcurrants and cherries and place them in a preserving pan. Add the water and simmer the fruit, covered, for 30 minutes, until tender. Add the sugar and stir the mixture until every grain has dissolved. Bring the jam to a rolling boil and boil steadily for about 25 to 30 minutes, until the setting point is reached. (To test if the jam has set, see the Strawberry Jam recipe.) Stir in the butter – this helps to reduce the scum.

Leave the jam for about 10 minutes so that the fruit is evenly dispersed, then pour into warmed jars, filling them to the neck. Seal, label and store.

Peach and Raspberry Jam

Makes about 5 lb/2·25 kg

2 lb/1 kg peaches
2 lb/1 kg raspberries
¼ pint/150 ml water
3 lb/1·5 kg preserving or granulated sugar
A knob of butter

To peel peaches, drop them into a pan of boiling water and count to 10. Remove them with a spoon – the skins should now be easily removed with a sharp knife. Halve the peaches and remove the stones. Using nut crackers or a rolling pin, carefully crack the stones and remove the kernels. Slice the peaches and put them into a preserving pan with the kernels. Hull the raspberries and add them to the pan with the water, then cover the pan. Cook the fruit mixture gently for about 15 to 20 minutes, until the fruit is tender. Add the sugar and stir until every grain has dissolved, then bring the jam to a rolling boil and boil rapidly for 15 to 20 minutes, until the setting point is reached. (To test if the jam has set, see the Strawberry Jam recipe.) Stir in the butter.

Leave the jam for about 10 minutes so that the fruit is evenly dispersed, then pour into warmed jars. Seal, label and store.

Assorted Jams and Jellies

Favourite Jam Chart

Follow the method for Look and Learn to Strawberry Jam on page 178, preparing the fruit as follows.

Blackcurrant Strip the fruit off the stalks by running a fork down each stem.

Gooseberry Top and tail the fruit using a pair of scissors.

Plum Halve and stone, or cook whole and take out the stones just before the jam is to be potted.

Raspberry Remove the stalks and wash the fruit.

Flavour	Fruit	Water	Extras	Sugar	Cooking to tender	Boiling to set	Yield
Blackcurrant	3 lb/1·5 kg blackcurrants	2¼ pints/1·25 litres		4½ lb/2 kg	15–30 mins.	10 mins.	8 lb/3·5 kg
Gooseberry	3 lb/1·5 kg gooseberries	1 pint/600 ml	1 teaspoon ground ginger	3 lb/1·5 kg	30 mins.	10 mins.	5 lb/2·25 kg
Plum	3 lb/1·5 kg plums	10 tablespoons		3 lb/1·5 kg	15–20 mins.	12–15 mins.	6 lb/2·75 kg
Raspberry	4 lb/1·75 kg raspberries			4 lb/1·75 kg	10–15 mins.	5 mins.	6 lb/2·75 kg

Apricot and Grape Jelly

Makes about 4 lb/1·75 kg

- 2 lb/1 kg apricots, halved and stoned
- 2 lemons
- 1 lb/450 g black grapes, washed
- 1 lb/450 g preserving or granulated sugar to every 1 pint/600 ml of juice
- *A jelly bag or large square of doubled muslin*

Chop the apricots and the lemons roughly and put into a preserving pan with the grapes. Almost cover the fruit with water and bring to the boil; reduce the heat, cover the pan and simmer the fruit for about 20 minutes, until tender. As the fruit is cooking, crush it against the sides of the pan to extract as much juice as possible.

Pour some boiling water through a jelly bag to sterilise it, then suspend the bag over a bowl. Pour the fruit mixture into the bag and leave it to drip for about 4 hours or overnight – avoid squeezing the bag as this could make the finished jelly cloudy. (If you do not have a jelly bag, use a doubled piece of muslin. Put the muslin over a bowl and ask someone to hold it over the side of the bowl as you ladle the fruit into the centre. Gather up the edges and tie with string, then suspend the bag over a bowl.)

When all the juice has dripped through, measure the juice. Weigh out 1 lb/450 g of sugar for every 1 pint/600 ml of juice and put the juice and sugar into a preserving pan. Over a low heat dissolve the sugar, stirring the juice occasionally. When every grain of sugar has dissolved, bring the liquid to the boil and boil rapidly for about 30 to 35 minutes, until setting point is reached. (To test if the jelly has set, see the Strawberry jam recipe.) Pour into warmed jars. Seal, label and store.

Sage Jelly

Makes about 1 lb/450 g

- 2 lb/1 kg cooking apples
- 2 small bunches sage
- 1½ pints/900 ml water
- ¼ pint/150 ml white vinegar
- 1 lb/450 g preserving or granulated sugar to every 1 pint/600 ml of juice
- *A jelly bag or large square of doubled muslin*

Wash the apples and chop them roughly – there is no need to peel or core them – then put them into a preserving pan. Wash one of the bunches of sage and add it to the pan with the water and vinegar. Cover the pan, bring the mixture to the boil and simmer gently for about 15 to 20 minutes, or until the fruit is reduced to a pulp. Strain the fruit through a sterilised jelly bag as described in the Apricot and Grape Jelly recipe. Leave the fruit to drip overnight but do not squeeze the bag as this will make the jelly cloudy.

When all the juice has dripped through the bag, measure it. Weigh out 1 lb/450 g of sugar for every 1 pint/600 ml of juice and put the juice and sugar into a preserving pan. Place over a low heat and, stirring occasionally, dissolve the sugar. When every grain has dissolved, bring the liquid to the boil and boil rapidly for about 30 minutes until the setting point is reached.

Strip the leaves from the remaining bunch of sage, chop finely and stir into the jelly. Bring back to the boil, remove from the heat and leave for about 10 minutes before pouring it into a warmed jar. Seal, label and store.

Chunky Grapefruit Marmalade, Lemon Shred Marmalade

Chunky Grapefruit Marmalade
Lemon Shred

Traditional Marmalade

Makes about 11 lb/5 kg

- 3 lb/1·5 kg Seville oranges
- 2 sweet oranges
- 8½ pints/4·75 litres water
- A knob of butter
- About 7 lb/3·25 kg preserving or granulated sugar

Wipe the oranges and remove the dark, outer stalk ends. Place the Seville and sweet oranges in a preserving pan with 8 pints/4·5 litres of the water and bring to the boil. Cover the pan and cook the oranges for about 1½ to 2 hours, until they are really soft and tender. Drain the oranges, reserving the liquid, and leave the fruit to cool.

Cut each orange into four and put the pips into a small bowl. Scrape out the flesh and add it to the liquid in which the oranges were cooked; add any excess pith to the pips. Using a sharp knife, shred the peel to the desired thickness, then add it to the large bowl of liquid. When all the fruit has been prepared, turn the pips and pith into a small saucepan, add the remaining ½ pint/300 ml of water and simmer for 15 minutes, covered, then strain the liquid into the orange pulp mixture.

Rub the inside of the preserving pan with a little butter to prevent a scum forming. Measure the orange pulp mixture and put it into the pan, adding 1 lb/450 g of sugar for every 1 pint/600 ml of pulp. Place the pan over a low heat and, stirring occasionally, dissolve the sugar. When all the sugar has dissolved, but not before, bring the marmalade to a rapid boil – it should 'roll' all over the surface. Stir the marmalade occasionally and move the pan slightly so that a different part of the base comes in direct contact with the heat. After the marmalade has boiled for about 40 minutes, test for set. (To test if the marmalade has set, see the Strawberry Jam recipe.)

Leave for 10 to 15 minutes to prevent the peel rising in the jars.

Have ready enough dry, clean, warm jars and stand them on a wooden board or thick newspaper, but not on metal, enamel or marble as the coldness may crack the jars.

Using a jug, fill the jars with marmalade right to the top. Wipe each jar carefully with a damp cloth to remove any stickiness, then cover the tops with a disc of waxed paper, wax side down.

Leave the jars to cool completely (as the marmalade cools it will thicken), then cover them with cellophane discs. To do this, wet one side of the cover and stretch it over the jars, wet side uppermost, and secure it with string or an elastic band. Label each jar with the variety and date. Store the jars in a cool, dry place.

Lemon Shred Marmalade

Makes about 5 lb/2·25 kg

- 5 lemons
- 1 large grapefruit
- 5½ pints/3·25 litres water
- About 3 lb/1·5 kg granulated sugar

Wipe the lemons and grapefruit with a damp cloth and remove the dark, outer stalk ends. Using a potato peeler, remove just the rind from the lemons and cut it into small strips. Put these pieces into a pan with ½ pint/300 ml of the water. Cover and simmer for about 35 to 55 minutes, or until the rind is really tender.

Meanwhile, chop the grapefruit and lemons into small pieces, about ½ inch/1 cm square, and put them into the preserving pan with the remaining water. Bring to the boil, reduce the heat, then cover the pan and simmer the fruit for about 1½ hours, or until the fruit is soft and pulpy.

Suspend a sterilised jelly bag (see the Apricot and Grape Jelly recipe) over a bowl and pour the fruit and liquid through it. Strain the liquid from the strips of rind into the jelly bag, keeping the strips on one side.

When the pulp has finished dripping – it can be left overnight – add the strips of lemon rind to the liquid and measure it back into the pan, adding 1 lb/450 g of sugar for every 1 pint/600 ml of pulp. Dissolve the sugar in the liquid over a low heat, stirring occasionally. When every grain has dissolved and not before, bring the marmalade to the boil and boil it rapidly for 20 to 30 minutes, until setting point is reached. (To test if the marmalade has set, see the Strawberry Jam recipe.)

Leave the marmalade for about 1 hour so the peel will not rise to the surface when potted. Pour the marmalade into warm jars. Leave to cool completely then seal, label and store.

Chunky Grapefruit Marmalade

Makes about 8 lb/3·5 kg

- 3 medium grapefruit
- 3 lemons
- 4½ pints/2·5 litres water
- A knob of butter
- About 6 lb/2·75 kg granulated sugar

Follow the method used for Traditional Marmalade, but boil the fruit in only 4 pints/2·25 litres of water. Cut the cooked peel coarsely, then continue with the method and sugar proportion as for Traditional Marmalade.

Boil the marmalade for about 30 minutes, until the setting point is reached. (To test if the marmalade has set, see the Strawberry Jam recipe.) Pour into warmed jars. Seal, label and store.

Pretty Pickle

Makes about 4 lb/1·75 kg

1 pint/600 ml white vinegar
10 peppercorns
1 teaspoon coriander seeds
6 allspice berries
1 teaspoon salt
2 oz/50 g granulated sugar
1 lb/450 g new carrots
3 tablespoons oil
3 green tomatoes
1 red pepper
1 medium onion

Put the vinegar into a pan with the peppercorns, coriander seeds, allspice, salt and granulated sugar. Bring slowly to the boil and simmer for 3 minutes. Leave the spiced vinegar until it is cold.

Meanwhile, scrape the carrots and cut into rings. Heat the oil in a large frying pan, add the carrots and cook gently, without colouring them, for a few minutes, turning to cook them on both sides – they should still be firm but not hard.

Slice the tomatoes and red pepper; peel and slice the onion. Pack the vegetables into jars using a wooden spoon. Fill the jars with spiced vinegar, completely covering the vegetables. Divide the spices evenly between the jars.

Cover the jars with a polythene cover or plastic-lined lid and leave for 2 weeks before using.

Marrow Chutney

Makes about 5 lb/2·25 kg

2 small marrows (weighing about $2\frac{1}{2}$ lb/1·25 kg after skin and seeds have been removed)
3 oz/75 g cooking salt
$1\frac{1}{2}$ lb/675 g red tomatoes
4 oz/100 g cooking dates
1 lb/450 g cooking apples
$\frac{1}{2}$ lb/225 g onions
5 oz/150 g sultanas, cleaned
$\frac{3}{4}$ oz/20 g mustard seeds
2 teaspoons ground allspice
2 teaspoons ground ginger
1 teaspoon ground cinnamon
1 teaspoon ground mace
1 pint/600 ml vinegar
1 lb/450 g demerara sugar

Chop the marrow into fairly small cubes and layer it in a basin with the salt, finishing with a good sprinkling of salt. Cover the basin and leave overnight.

The next stage can either be done the same day or the following morning. Peel the tomatoes, chop the dates and peel, core and chop the apples. Peel and chop the onions. Put these into a pan with the sultanas, mustard seeds, ground allspice, ginger, cinnamon and mace. Add the vinegar and simmer the mixture gently for about 1 hour. At this stage the chutney can be left overnight.

Add the sugar and dissolve it slowly. Drain the marrow from the liquid which has appeared round it, add it to the rest of the chutney and simmer for a further 1 hour, or until the chutney has a jam-like consistency and is free of a watery appearance on the surface.

Pot the chutney in warmed jars and cover the jars with a polythene cover or plastic-lined lid.

Store the chutney for 6 weeks before use so the flavours mellow.

Pretty Pickle

Tomato Chutney

Makes about 4½ lb/2 kg

2½ lb/1·25 kg red or green tomatoes
3 medium onions, peeled and chopped
1 lb/450 g cooking apples, peeled, cored and chopped
4 oz/100 g sultanas, cleaned
4 oz/100 g raisins, cleaned
2 sticks celery
1 teaspoon black peppercorns
1 teaspoon allspice berries
1½ teaspoons mustard seeds
2 cloves
½ oz/15 g salt
1 pint/600 ml distilled white or cider vinegar
8 oz/225 g demerara sugar

First peel the tomatoes: put them into a large bowl and cover with boiling water, count to 20, then if the skin peels easily off one tomato, pour off the hot water and replace it with cold. (Give them a further few seconds in the hot water if necessary so that they peel easily.)

Mince the onions, tomatoes, apples, sultanas, raisins and celery. Tie the peppercorns, allspice berries, mustard seed and cloves into a square of muslin then put them into a fairly large pan with the minced ingredients. Add the salt and vinegar and simmer the ingredients for about 1 hour, until the ingredients are all well combined.

Add the sugar and stir until it has dissolved. Cook the chutney for a further 30 to 45 minutes until the chutney is free from the watery appearance on the surface. (Gentle cooking is best to bring out all the flavours.)

Take out the bag of spices then pot the chutney into warmed jars. Cover with a polythene cover or plastic-lined lid. Label and store for about a month before using.

Eastern Chutney

Makes about 4 lb/1·75 kg

1 lb/450 g oranges
1 lb/450 g onions, peeled and roughly chopped
1 lb/450 g cooking dates
8 oz/225 g sultanas, cleaned
1½ lb/675 g demerara sugar
2 oz/50 g salt
¼ teaspoon cayenne pepper
1 pint/600 ml malt vinegar

Remove the rind thinly from one of the oranges, using a potato peeler, and leave it on one side. Peel all the oranges – including the one without the rind – removing as much of the pith as possible. Chop the fruit roughly, and discard the pips. Using the coarse disc on a mincer, shred the onions, dates, oranges and orange rind on to a plate. Put the sultanas, sugar, salt and pepper into a preserving pan or large saucepan and add the vinegar. Bring the mixture to the boil, then add the minced ingredients. When the chutney has returned to the boil, reduce the heat and simmer, uncovered, for about 30 minutes, or until it is thick and leaves a clear line when the spoon is drawn across the base of the pan.

Pour the chutney into warmed jars. Leave to cool, then cover with a polythene cover or plastic-lined lid. Label and leave to mature for 8 to 12 weeks.

Note This chutney can also be made substituting lemons for oranges.

Piccalilli

Makes about 6 lb/2·75 kg

2 small cauliflowers
2 medium cucumbers
1 small marrow (weighing 1½ lb/675 g)
1 lb/450 g French beans
1 lb/450 g onions
Salt
4 oz/100 g demerara sugar
½ oz/15 g ground ginger
1 oz/25 g dry mustard
½ oz/15 g turmeric powder
1 tablespoon plain flour
2 pints/1·15 litres white vinegar
1 oz/25 g allspice berries

Break the cauliflowers into small sprigs; peel and dice the cucumbers and marrow; string the French beans and cut them into diamonds. Peel and slice the onions. Mix the vegetables in a large bowl, sprinkle with 3 tablespoons salt, cover with a plate and leave to soak overnight.

Put the demerara sugar, ground ginger, mustard, turmeric and flour into a basin and blend to a smooth paste with a little of the vinegar. Put the rest of the vinegar into a pan with the allspice berries and bring slowly to the boil. Strain the boiling vinegar on to the blended ingredients, stirring all the time. Return the mixture to the pan and bring it slowly to the boil, stirring all the time.

Drain the vegetables thoroughly, add them to the vinegar mixture and bring to the boil. Simmer for 20 minutes.

Pot into warmed jars. Cover with a polythene cover or plastic-lined lid. Label and store for about a month before using.

Index